THE GIFT OF DRAGONS

THE GIFT OF DRAGONS

A NOVEL

RACHEL A. GRECO

atmosphere press

Published by Atmosphere Press

Cover design by Matthew Fielder

atmospherepress.com

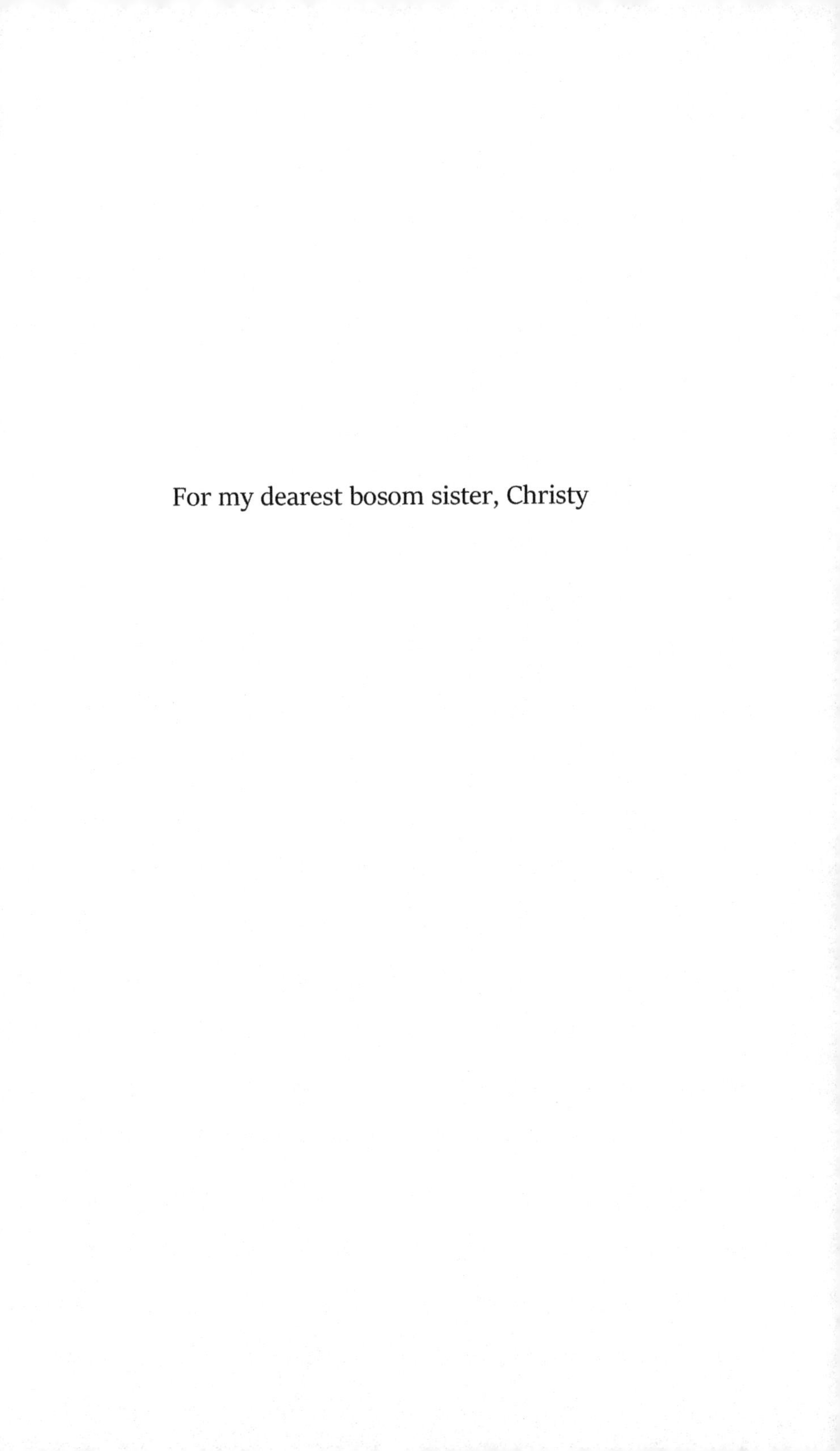

For my dearest bosom sister, Christy

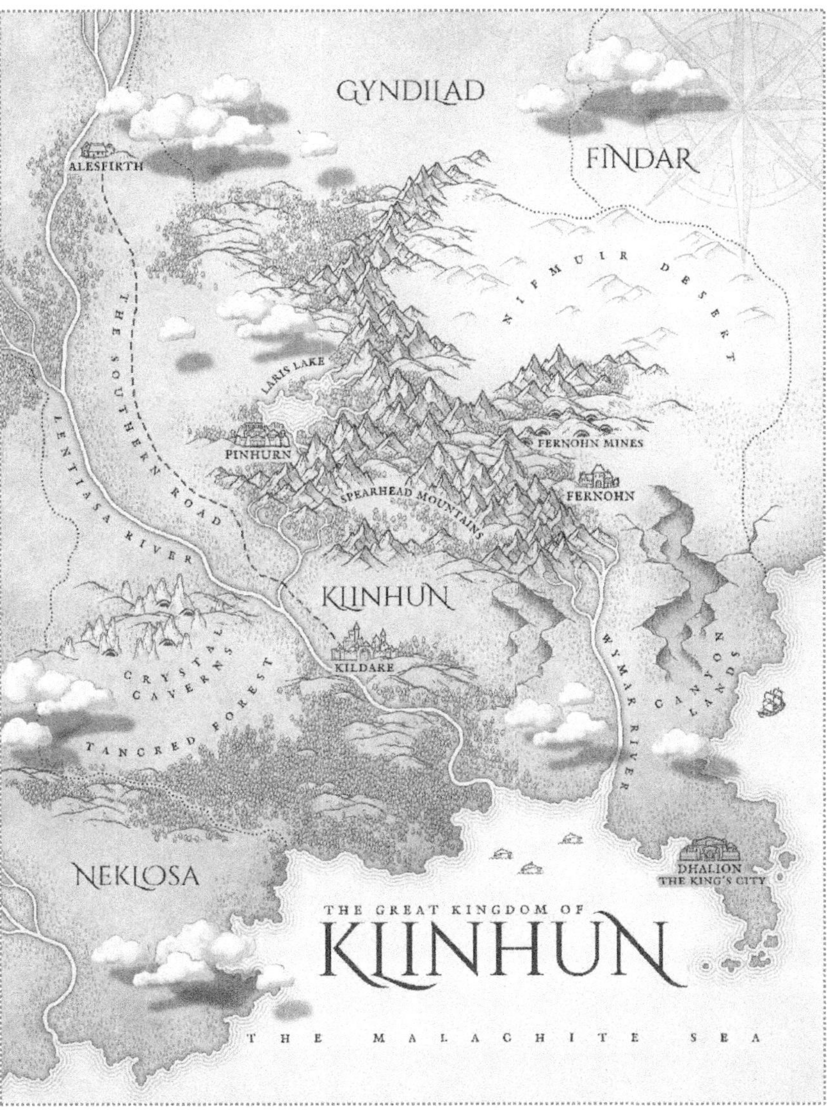
GYNDILAD
FINDAR
ALESFIRTH
NIFMUIR DESERT
THE SOUTHERN ROAD
LARIS LAKE
PINHURN
FERNOHN MINES
FERNOHN
LENTIASA RIVER
SPEARHEAD MOUNTAINS
KLINHUN
KILDARE
CRYSTAL CAVERNS
TANCRED FOREST
WYMAR RIVER
CANYON LANDS
NEKLOSA
DHALION
THE KING'S CITY
THE GREAT KINGDOM OF
KLINHUN
THE MALACHITE SEA

Prologue

Before Adelaide loved her sister, she resented her. It wasn't Emma's fault. She was as sweet as the apple pie their mother would scrape together for festivals. But that only made being around her more difficult. Adelaide felt she could never measure up to her kind, gentle older sister, and shame pierced her whenever Emma helped someone before she could. Or before she even thought of helping.

One day, when Adelaide was thirteen winters old, her sister fourteen, in frustration she had asked Emma, "How are you not exhausted all the time?"

"What do you mean?" Emma's golden braid dangled over her shoulder as she pulled up wild onions growing alongside the burbling Lentiasa River. "Ooh." Her eyes landed on a patch of velvety violet irises. "Mom will love these. Help me pick some."

"That's what I mean," Adelaide said as she pulled up an iris. "Thinking of others all the time."

"I don't think of others all the time."

"Well, you do more than me."

Emma looked up at Adelaide, her eyes the same color as the spring sky above them. "It's not a competition, Ade. You're good at other things."

"Like what?"

"Like thinking of ways to use ingredients creatively." She held up her basket of onions. "And you wish to help everyone in a more lasting way than just giving them food or feeding their chickens."

Adelaide remembered the day before, when one of Lord Lambert's knights from the nearby town of Alesfirth had thrown their neighbor, Giles, onto the ground. Giles hadn't bowed fast enough at the knight's arrival to collect his money for the spring tax.

Only Emma's arm had kept Adelaide from trying to drag the knight off, saving her from a lashing or worse.

And then there had been reports that some knights from the country to the north of Klinhun—Gyndilad—had been spotted riding near Alesfirth. Gyndilad was a country of thieves, greed, and darkness. Or so the stories went.

Gyndilians had fought skirmishes at the northern borders of Klinhun before, but not in Adelaide's lifetime. When they invaded, they were ruthless and hardly ever left survivors. Alesfirth was now the closest town to the Gyndilian border, so if the country decided to invade, their town would be the first and hardest hit.

Her parents hoped King Ganelon would send more knights to protect them, but there was no sign of them yet. Adelaide doubted it would happen. King Ganelon and his son only showed interest in them when they didn't pay their taxes fast enough.

She ripped up another iris, taking the roots with it. "Not that I can do anything for our people."

Emma placed a hand on her arm. "Not yet. But mayhap when you're older. Look." She pointed at a white lily surrounded by a patch of mud. "It's lovely."

Adelaide knew her sister wouldn't venture through the mud, even for such a beautiful flower, so Adelaide slopped her way through, trying to hold her dress out of the muck. She plucked the lily out. Pretending to be a nobleman, she bowed to her sister and offered her the flower. "For you, fair lady," she said in a deep voice.

Emma laughed, curtsied almost as gracefully as a noblewoman, and inhaled the flower's honey-sweet scent. "And you said you didn't do things for others."

"Not often." Adelaide surveyed the muddy ground, thinking of their younger brother. "Let's get something for Odo too." She dug a hand into the cool, sticky mud.

"Gross. What are you going to do with that?"

"Put it in Odo's boots."

To her surprise, instead of trying to dissuade her, Emma laughed and grabbed her clean hand. "Come on."

The next morning, when Odo shrieked and sputtered, his ears turning red at the icky gloop in his boot, Adelaide and Emma's eyes met over his head. A friendship, an alliance, had formed between them.

From then on, Adelaide saw Emma more as a sister than a rival. Thinking of ways to prank Odo turned into walks by the river, chatting and teasing about boys, and searching for fireflies.

The day Adelaide found an injured hawk in the woods deepened the sisters' friendship even further.

Adelaide had walked into the summer-cloaked trees looking for a missing chicken. It had probably been eaten by a coyote or taken by a starving neighbor—which could have been anyone since they were all starving. But Emma loved the chickens as if they were her children, so Adelaide wandered through the woods, hoping Lord Lambert's knights weren't out hunting with his hounds. If they saw her, they'd accuse her of hunting on his lands and mark her with the brand of a thief.

While passing the base of an oak that she'd snuck out to climb a few times with Emma and their friends, Gunter and

Conrad, Adelaide heard some rustling in a bush peppered with red berries. She stalked toward it.

Peering in, Adelaide made out a flapping shape. Instead of dirty-white plumage, the bird had soft, downy feathers—just a fledgling. Adelaide recognized it as a small version of the hawks that often soared overhead or those Lord Lambert used to hunt when tired of his hounds.

The hawk squeaked feebly, melting Adelaide's heart. Its amber eyes, when turned on her, seemed to see inside her soul. Did it belong to Lord Lambert? If so, what was it doing out here all by itself?

As Adelaide leaned toward the bird, she noticed one of its wings was bent at an awkward angle. Carefully, she scooped the fledgling up and cradled it in her dress. The bird tried to flutter away, its wings beating weakly against her chest.

"Shh. It's okay," Adelaide murmured, walking back to the cottage.

When she entered the house's smoky room, Emma glanced up from pounding dough beside their mother. "Did you find Snow?"

"No, but I found this." Adelaide gently placed the bird on the straw bed they all shared.

Emma gasped. "He's beautiful."

"I think his wing's broken." Part of Adelaide, the part that still sometimes resented her sister, didn't want to ask Emma for help. But she couldn't heal the bird without her sister's knowledge of healing. "Can you fix his wing?"

Emma frowned at the bird which stared back. "I'll try."

"Use oak saplings for the splint and powdered Glorph's wort for the pain," their mother advised as Emma left the cottage.

That night, after everyone had fallen asleep but Emma and Adelaide, they watched the hawk's white-feathered chest rise and fall as it slept in Adelaide's lap. Emma had crafted a splint for its wing and received several cuts on her hand from its beak in gratitude.

Adelaide squeezed her sister's uninjured hand. "Thanks, Em."

"I hope it works. What are you going to name him?"

Adelaide glanced up at her sister, surprised. Emma was the one who loved animals, and she'd healed his wing after all.

Emma must have noticed Adelaide's puzzlement, for she said, "You're the one who found him. You should be the one to raise him. Besides, I've always thought of you like a hawk."

"Truly? Why?"

"You're fierce and brave, not afraid of anything."

Adelaide shook her head. "I'm scared of plenty of things."

"Like what?"

Adelaide's thoughts wandered to the fresh rumors of a Gyndilian garrison being built not far from their town. There was no news of extra knights on their way from the King's City of Dhalion to protect them, so if the Gyndilians struck, as they had struck northern towns before, Adelaide's family and the entire town could be destroyed. She shuddered. "I'm afraid of losing my family."

Emma squeezed her arm. "That's a worthy thing to fear. But I'm not going anywhere."

Adelaide released her breath. She gazed down at the hawk, which didn't look so brave and fierce now with his bedraggled feathers and splinted wing, but hopefully would one day. "I'll call him Cyr."

Chapter One

Two years later

Cyr screeched overhead, urging Adelaide and Emma faster over the dirt path leading to the bedraggled town of Alesfirth.

When they reached the top of the hill cluttered with stone houses and shops, Emma raised her arms. Her summer-sky eyes lit with victory. "I won! Now you must do my chores for a fortnight."

"A fortnight?" Adelaide tugged her sister's flaxen braid. "No way. That's too long for a simple race."

"Then..." Emma watched a bent-backed woman push a cart bulging with glossy red apples through the rickety wooden gate toward the covered food stalls. She faced Adelaide again. "You get to see how much the leather costs for father's shoes."

Adelaide's face fell at the thought of wading into the cloud of rancid stink surrounding the tanner's hides. The smell of the sharp animal urine he used for treating the leather always made her want to vomit. "That's unfair, Em."

"No, it's not. You lost, and one of us has to go there anyway. I'll go next time." Emma placed a few silver klins in

Adelaide's hand, then darted to the food booths which smelled of baked bread, fresh cheese, and golden harvests: much more tantalizing than the tanner's booth.

Muttering words she'd never let Odo hear, Adelaide swerved around threadbare dogs nosing for scraps, skeletal children scurrying about, and carts piled high with firewood. She passed the lord's cedar hall where buttery and azure flags embellished with a black buck—the symbol of Alesfirth—hung. Red-faced men, probably colored so from drinking too much wine, could be seen guffawing through the hall's open windows.

As she passed the raised stone dais in the middle of town, an orange-capped boy almost knocked her over.

"Sorry, Miss," he called back at her.

Adelaide waved at him then followed the ripe stench of urine past the dais toward the tanner's booth. She nodded to him and told him what she wanted.

As the tanner picked up hides and rattled off prices, screams sharp with fright pierced the normal chatter of the market.

Adelaide whirled around. Knights on horseback galloped down the road, their upheld swords flickering with cold sunlight. Black and silver tunics peeked from beneath their chain mail, marking them as Gyndilians. Adelaide shivered.

A Gyndilian's sword cut down into the orange-capped boy she'd seen earlier. He collapsed like hacked wheat, blood pouring from his chest.

Adelaide jerked back, her heart stuttering.

Another knight, this one cloaked in the blue and gold colors of Klinhun, stepped out of the tavern, a mug of ale in his hand. He stared at the mounted Gyndilian who was now attacking an older man, then darted away, his sword swaying uselessly from his girdle.

Adelaide longed to scream at the knight, beg him to return and help the boy, even if it was too late. There were plenty of others falling around her that he could protect—was bound to protect.

But Adelaide had to find Emma. She plunged under horses' legs, leapt over prone, wailing people, trying to block out their desperate cries, and wove past Gyndilians striking anyone in sight. Smoke now clogged the air, and Adelaide, coughing, squinted through the thick haze.

A horde of Klinian knights darted in the same direction as she toward the town's gate. As she hopped over a too-still young man, Adelaide slipped in a pool of blood and tumbled to her knees.

Something whooshed by her head. She rolled over just in time to dodge an arrow. It struck a bag of oats on the ground behind her. They cascaded to the ground in a tawny waterfall.

Not wanting to give the Gyndilian another clear shot, Adelaide dove under a table, knocking over a basket of turnips. She'd finally made it back to the food market at the front of town. Now she just had to find her sister.

"Emma? Emma, where are you?" Her voice was hoarse from smoke and heaving breaths. She crawled under tables through sticky blood and spilled fruits and vegetables.

From the sound of swords ringing out above, the Klinian knights must be fighting back. But too few and too late to save those already dead.

Adelaide coughed. "Emma?"

Nothing but the clashing of swords and frantic shouts. She called out louder, "Emma! Answer me."

Panic clung to her skin, stickier than the blood covering her hands. Where was her sister?

She continued crawling until she saw a familiar golden braid. Emma lay in a pool of crimson—*it's not hers, it can't be hers*, she told herself fiercely—next to the motionless form of the bent-backed woman she'd seen pushing the apple cart.

"Em," Adelaide murmured, reaching for her sister. She pulled her into her lap and gave her a slight shake. "Come on,

Em. We have to go."

Emma's cloudless blue eyes fixed somewhere above Adelaide. She didn't move, didn't laugh, didn't turn and tell Adelaide she was only teasing her.

The horrifying truth dropped into Adelaide's heart, panic exploding into grief and rage that tore her apart.

The grief and rage never let go over the next few months. The only thing that kept the emotions from ripping Adelaide apart completely was the resolve hardening into iron that she must do something, *anything,* to stop this from happening again. Not just for Emma, but also for the orange-capped boy, the bent-backed woman, and the dozen others who had died because King Ganelon and his son had failed to protect them.

Well, Adelaide would protect them—one way or another. The time to help her people had come.

Chapter Two

Adelaide held onto that resolve now—more than a year after Emma's death—as she climbed up the steps of Alesfirth's stone dais. Two troubadours in black cloaks over matching purple and orange tunics stood at the top, entertaining those who had come in from the outlying farms for the Fire Festival.

The taller man sang a ditty about the dragons' destructive end while the other played a wooden recorder. But Adelaide passed them by; she wasn't here for the festivities. Not yet.

The idea of protecting her people had grown into a small, secret rebellion to overthrow the king and prince. Apparently, she wasn't the only one afraid of what the Gyndilians would do next without anyone to stand in their way. Nor was she the only one weary of feeding the already-sumptuous lords and having hardly any food leftover for themselves.

Thanks to an elderly knight who had found it amusing to teach Adelaide how to throw daggers at trees, she could now hit one dead-center from forty paces away. Some of the men in her rebellion were almost as good, and though that didn't mean they could take on skilled knights, at least it gave them all a glimmer of hope. For what other options did they have?

No one else was fighting for them.

At her rebellion's meeting last night, ten-winters-old Hubert had mentioned that a few knights had arrived in Alesfirth. They would have weapons Adelaide and her band of men desperately needed to defeat the king's knights, especially now that Adelaide would be leaving soon with her friend Gunter for Dhalion. They would rally more people to their cause along the way, then finally put their plan into action in the King's City.

The usual anxiety reared its head when she considered what that plan might look like, but she pushed it down into the cave where her sorrow and rage over her sister's death lived. The emotions would only incapacitate her if she let them, and then she wouldn't be able to protect anyone.

Behind the troubadours, several less-brashly dressed men erected a wooden stand for the nobles to sit on that night during the Fire Festival. In the middle of the dais, other men hauled and stacked hefty pieces of wood into a pile. Adelaide recognized the spiky brown hair of one and walked toward him.

"Good day, Gunter," she said when she reached him.

He threw a chunk of wood onto the pile that already stood as large as a house. He came over, sweat dripping down his face and staining his white tunic. "Good day, Ade." He wiped his face with his arm. "Is everything ready for the Festival?"

"All except for one thing." She gave him a knowing look, not willing to say more so close to the others. He had been at the meeting last night and knew her real reason for coming to town today.

Gunter stepped closer and gazed past her. "It appears little Hubert was right about the king's knights. They arrived not long ago and went into the tavern for a drink. They left their wagon outside."

"Are there weapons in the wagon?" Adelaide whispered, her eyes following Gunter's to a cart filled with sacks of goods in front of the squat tavern.

"I don't know. I haven't had a chance to take a look, and I wanted to wait for you to arrive."

"Come on, then. The knights could come out any moment."

Gunter told an older man he was taking a break. Then he and Adelaide dashed down the steps, dodged town-folk and darting children, squeezed past merchant stalls, and stopped a few paces from the wagon and horses tied outside the tavern.

"Keep watch while I look through the goods," Adelaide said.

"Be careful and quick."

She nodded and strode to the wagon, a thrill of excitement whispering through her.

"Elias, a maiden is looking through our wagon," Berold announced.

Elias watched with fascination as a slim woman about his age—seventeen-winters—explored the sacks with lithe fingers, glancing up every so often. She withdrew two daggers and slid them into the black girdle around her waist, concealed from behind by her wool cloak.

"Sir, our daggers." Berold stepped forward, but Elias stuck out his arm to stop him. He didn't want to create a scene or use force, as was Berold's inclination.

"I'll take care of this. Hold my drink." He took a last swig of ale, handed it to his friend, and walked out of the tavern toward the woman.

He reached her as she stepped away from the cart. Before she could dart away, he said, "Good day, fair lass."

She spun toward him. Noticing his green cloak and richly embroidered blue tunic, she dipped her head, her eyes wary. "Why do you call me fair, sire, when there are so many lovely maidens strolling about today?"

"All maidens are fair in one way or another," Elias replied. Although, some caught his eye more than others, including this one with her swinging black braid and flashing hazel eyes.

The woman raised an eyebrow. "That's an interesting opinion. Now, if you don't mind, I'm needed to help prepare for the Festival."

She walked away, her ebony braid swinging like a horse's mane.

Elias followed, intrigued. Why would a peasant woman need a dagger? And what kind of person would attempt to steal one in the light of day with people everywhere? "Are you attending the Festival tonight, then?"

The woman continued walking. Her voice contained a slight mocking undertone when she answered. "Of course, sire. We're all required to attend the burning of the wood. Surely you know this."

"Of course," he said, taken aback by her bold speech. "What do you think of the festivity?"

The maiden stopped and met his gaze. "Since you asked, I think it's a waste of time to listen to a story our ancestors made up to entertain their children and liven up their demanding lives." Her eyes glowed with the heat of her words, and Elias guessed something horrible had happened to scorch her so.

"Everyone is entitled to their opinion, I suppose. Personally, I don't much care for the Fire Festival either."

She inclined her head. "Farewell, sire."

The woman disappeared into the crowd. Elias realized he had forgotten to confront her about the daggers. It didn't matter now, though. Something much more important was at stake than thievery.

This woman was the person Elias would try to persuade that the dragons everyone believed to be destructive and dead were actually good, still alive, and in need of help. If he could convince such a disbelieving, harsh person of this secret he and his father guarded, then they might actually have a chance of convincing all of Klinhun.

Chapter Three

Adelaide climbed the worn steps of the dais once more, this time alongside her family under the vigilant eye of darkness.

"I hope the flames are higher than last winter's." Odo's gaze darted to the pile of wood then to the buzzing crowd.

"They might be, though if they grow much higher, we won't be able to stand close to the fire." Adelaide's father regarded the enormous stack of wood that could keep her family warm for a week.

"There's Gunter." Adelaide nodded to him and his brother, Conrad, chatting near the pile. "I'll see you at the feasting."

Her father and brother told her farewell, and her mother gave her a concerned look that Adelaide pretended not to see. Ignoring with difficulty the silence and emptiness that Emma had once filled with laughs and teasing, Adelaide slipped through the crowd to Gunter.

Upon reaching him, she placed the bucket of water she had carried from home on the ground and shivered when some sloshed onto her arm. She didn't understand why they had to celebrate the Fire Festival at the darkest hour on the coldest day of the year.

Beyond the jumble of wood reaching to the sky in a silent plea, the nobles nattered like a flock of birds in the stands made specially for them.

"Good evening," Gunter said, and Conrad nodded at her before turning to speak to a friend.

Gunter glanced around, then lowered his voice. "Why didn't you come back this afternoon after you retrieved the daggers? And who was that man you were speaking with? Did he own the wagon?"

"I went home to hide the weapons and help my mother finish the apple pie."

"And the man?" Gunter prodded.

"He didn't own the wagon." Adelaide tried to banish the image of the admittedly fine-looking, yet odd man out of her mind. "He was only a talkative noble who didn't know how to amuse himself other than conversing with peasant maidens."

Gunter quirked an eyebrow but didn't say anything more.

Adelaide scanned the crowd; no one was looking in their direction. "Here," she whispered. She reached down to her boot and drew out the larger of the two daggers she'd stolen. She passed it to him beneath her cloak.

She would keep the other dagger—now hidden under the straw bed at home—for herself. Compared to the one she had nicked from a careless blacksmith shortly after Emma's death, the new dagger was almost too elegant to practice hurling at trees. Yet it possessed a sharper blade and no doubt soared straighter. She tried not to think about where, besides a tree, that sharp point would eventually hit.

She'd take the new dagger on her travels and perhaps give the chipped and warped one to Odo when he was older, although he'd probably accidentally stab himself with it before he hit anything useful.

"Thanks." Gunter slipped the steel weapon into the pouch hanging from his belt that usually held gloves or tools. "Now you just have to teach me how to use it."

Adelaide snorted. "I've been trying to do that for months." And had failed miserably. Gunter preferred to toss words more than a dagger. When he did throw it, he almost always ended up dropping it or sticking it in the ground. She didn't know who would be worse with the weapon—Gunter or Odo.

"Now that I have my own, I'll practice more." He lowered his voice and shuffled closer. "So, when do you want to leave for the King's City?"

"Gunter, you don't need to come with me. I can travel across Klinhun on my own."

"You've never even stepped foot outside the fields of Alesfirth before."

"Neither have you," Adelaide pointed out.

"True, but since I'm a male, I'll be able to enlist more people to our cause, which we desperately need."

It was true, however much she hated to admit it, and his company would be welcome, but Adelaide didn't want to take him away from his family longer than she had to.

"What's more, I *want* to go with you." Gunter rubbed the scruff on his cheeks. He never grew it out because, as he had told her more than once, it made him look dangerous and rough—something the females loved. But Adelaide didn't find him tough with his easy demeanor and short stature and had yet to spot a swarm of maidens flocking him.

"It'll be daring and exciting," he said. "And more meaningful than working the lord's land all day. So when do you want to leave?"

Adelaide abandoned her attempt to reason with him. "Probably four or five days. We still need to gather supplies, and I have to think of a reason for my absence."

Gunter nodded. "It's a good thing my family has Conrad, or I wouldn't be able to go with you." Even then, his family would be short one set of hands for planting. If Adelaide didn't believe the rebellion could fish them all out of their depths of misery, she never would have begun it.

"Good evening, fair maiden. A fire will be most welcome this frosty night, will it not?" The green-cloaked nobleman Adelaide had met earlier said, striding out of the crowd.

His presence sent Adelaide's heart galloping. Why was he speaking to her as if she wasn't a commoner? And why wasn't he conversing with the other nobles?

A smile softened the man's well-molded face. "I'm afraid I was too distracted to ask your name earlier."

"Why would you like to know?"

He shrugged. "I'm just curious."

"She's Adelaide, and I'm Gunter, sire," her friend said while gazing at the golden embroidery decorating the man's cloak.

Adelaide hurled an irritated look at Gunter, wishing Cyr was on her shoulder and not off hunting. Perhaps he could nip some sense into her friend or frighten the haughty nobleman away.

"It's a delight to meet you both," the noble stated. "Now I must depart, for the Festival's about to begin." The man strode away, his green cloak swirling around him like a leaf in the wind.

Adelaide whirled on her friend. "Why did you tell him who I was? We don't know anything about him except that he's a noble, which is more than enough reason not to tell him anything."

"Calm down, Ade." Gunter placed a hand on her arm. "As you said, he's merely a wealthy man who likes to talk. He didn't treat us with disdain like the others, so I didn't think it would hurt to tell him our names."

Adelaide shook off Gunter's arm and drew her cloak tighter. For all they knew, the man's politeness was a pretense to lure her into his bedchamber to warm him until morning; such things had happened to unwary peasant girls before.

Lord Lambert waddled up to the woodpile, his wide girth threatening to burst through the glittering girdle encircling his orange tunic.

Adelaide swallowed her bile at the sight of the lord's extravagance next to that of her brother's thin face and tattered tunic. She listened as he chanted the *Tale of Dragons* from memory in a dull voice. The candle he held aloft flickered feebly against the night's hungry maw.

"When time first breathed and woke
men and dragons walked side-by-side.
The dragons' might sheltered humans like a cloak,
and the humans' love was the dragons' guide.

But the proud beasts desired power
more than the gaiety of their two-legged allies.
The dragon king, Aloysius, filled with anger,
convinced his friends to act unwise.

They came in the innocence of night,
ripping and tearing and destroying.
Unquenchable fires flashed like a new sunlight,
and the people's wounded hearts never stopped bleeding.

Children, women, and men the dragons had smote.
The valiant Theodoric gathered every fighting man
to cut Aloysius' giant scaled throat
and quiet the beasts' roars and lofty plan.

Theodoric and his rage-roaring band
struck the beasts as they gloated on blood and gore.
Surprised and slow from their feast, the beasts fled inland.
The men followed, haunted by the dead's cry for war.

Many mighty beasts died that night,
and the humans piled up their foes.
Promising to never return, the dragons took flight,
and the cliffs rang with men's triumphant echoes.

Never has a dragon soared in Klinhun since,
And the future of men with glorious hope glints."

Adelaide had heard the tale since she'd been a babe, enough that she could recite it with Lord Lambert. But this year the battle scenes made her flinch. The attack last year was still a branding iron on her mind.

Lord Lambert stepped closer to the pile of wood and glanced back at the stand filled with the wealthy. The peculiar noble who had spoken to her twice strode over, his expression as serious as fire.

The lord turned back to the solemn crowd. Raising the flickering candle high, he proclaimed, "The fire the dragons spread throughout our land!" He lowered the candle to the young nobleman, but the man shook his head. Why did he refuse to light the fire? She couldn't recall anyone doing that before.

Lord Lambert turned from the man to the huge pile of wood and thrust the flame at the kindling near the base.

As the flames quickened the dead lumber into a pulsing heartbeat, both crowds—peasant and noble—sang a song of mourning for their ancestors who had died from the terrible beasts' blaze.

The fire spoke a crackling language to the stars as it filled the night with heat and vitality. Those closest to it stepped back, and Adelaide had to tilt her head to see the flames racing up to the top of the pile.

When their voices intensified as bright as the flames' hungry hues, the crowd picked up their buckets and hurled water onto the fire. Several people jumped when drops of the cold liquid splashed them, and most of the water in Adelaide's bucket sloshed onto the stony ground. The majority of the others' reached the flames, however, and they sputtered out at the same instant as the voices.

The sudden silence and coldness reached down with empty and bleak fingers into Adelaide. She shuddered beneath her cloak.

Into the quiet, Lord Lambert announced, "And the dragons'

fires lit up Klinhun no more."

After the fire's death came Adelaide's favorite part: the feasting.

People lit candles throughout the square, which glimmered with more warmth than those staring down from above. The merchants had put away their wares and the lord's servants had covered the stalls with food ranging from simple loaves of dense brown bread to whole-roasted pigs garnished with sugary baked apples.

This was the only time of year the peasants could eat food baked by the lord's cooks, so they squeezed past the nobles to cram their wooden plates with flaky pastries oozing sweet red juices, airy white bread, and rare haunches of juicy meat that one barely had to chew, they were so tender.

Adelaide sat with both her family and Gunter's on one of the benches below the dais, enjoying a chunk of venison flavored with orange and basil.

"One thing is certain," Gunter said between bites of a golden chicken leg, "Lord Lambert and his new cooks make the best food. His father's chicken was never seasoned as well as this."

Adelaide nodded as she took another bite of venison.

"I wish the Fire Festival occurred more often so we could eat this kind of food all the time," Odo said.

Adelaide smiled at the honeyed sauce smeared all over his face from the bread and nut pudding he was devouring.

Cyr landed on her shoulder, and she gave him a piece of venison. "You always know when food's nearby, don't you?"

The hawk gazed at her with a clever amber eye, and she offered him another piece. He snapped it up.

"That bird is larger every time I see him," Gunter's mother said, eyeing Cyr with a mixture of fascination and wariness.

"I still don't believe you've trained him to bring you meat and that he doesn't just eat it all himself," Conrad said.

"It's true," Adelaide protested. "I—"

"Good evening, or good night, I should say," the nobleman who was becoming too familiar too quickly strode up to them. A man robed in orange hovered behind him, shifting on his feet and looking anywhere but at their faces.

"How's the fare?" The nobleman gestured at their plates.

Why was this man so interested in them? Adelaide fiddled with her braid as she attempted to puzzle it out.

"It's quite good, sire. You'll have to give Lord Lambert our appreciation and compliments," Adelaide's father said as he appraised the noble.

"Indeed, it is some of the finest food I've tasted." The man's smile glinted from the glow of the candle in his hand. "Lord Lambert is certainly a connoisseur of every kind of food."

Cyr nudged Adelaide's hand with his beak, and she gave him another piece of meat.

The nobleman turned his attention to the hawk. "That's a magnificent bird. What's he called?"

"Cyr," she replied, stroking his feathers. She couldn't help feel proud; hardly any peasants owned birds, especially hawks.

The man gazed at Cyr, and the bird turned his attention to him and cocked his head. The man reached out and rubbed his wing. The hawk stretched his neck in pleasure.

Adelaide watched the exchange with surprise and annoyance. Cyr never let anyone else ruffle his feathers. The first and only time Gunter and Odo had attempted to, the hawk had screeched and snapped at them. So why was he acting pleasant to a stranger—and a noble—of all people?

"It's impolite to touch another's bird without asking." She shifted away, and Cyr stretched out his russet wings for balance.

The nobleman withdrew his hand. "Forgive me. I haven't seen a hawk as majestic as yours in all my years in Klinhun. Where, might I ask, did you procure him?"

"She found it by an oak tree two years ago. It was just a

chick, so she's basically raised the bird," Gunter said before gulping down some ale and adding, "It's stayed with her ever since."

"Cyr's a 'he,' not an 'it,'" Adelaide told him with a clenched jaw. Gunter should know better than to spout off personal details to a noble, especially after their talk earlier. The man could shape Gunter's words for his own ends. He could tell Lord Lambert that Adelaide had stolen the hawk from *him,* who had found and raised him. And Lord Lambert would believe him because he's a noble.

Gunter just raised his eyebrows at Adelaide before lifting a bowl of frothy pink-tinted soup to his lips.

"Why didn't you light the fire tonight, sire?" Odo asked, his cheeks red.

"Odo, it's impolite to ask this young man such a personal question," Adelaide's mother, Galiena, berated him.

Not that he *had been asking* them *personal questions*, Adelaide thought in irritation.

"I don't mind." The man turned to her brother. "I've never enjoyed the Fire Festival for reasons that will remain my own, so taking part in it tonight would have gone against some of my deeply held beliefs. I couldn't do such a thing."

Adelaide scrutinized the man, pondering what beliefs could have prohibited him from lighting the fire.

"Sire, we should make our way back to Lord Lambert and the others. They will soon wonder where we've gone," the man's companion said.

The nobleman glanced back at his friend and sighed. "You're right, as usual, Berold."

He glanced back at them, his gaze lingering on Adelaide. "Farewell, good folk. Perhaps I will see you again sometime."

When he walked away with his friend, Adelaide breathed a sigh of relief, and the tension in their gathering unwound.

◆◆◆

After Adelaide finished dressing the next mid-afternoon, someone rapped on their door. She went and opened it.

The nobleman from the night before stood in front of her, wearing what must be clothes, though they hardly seemed to fit her idea of the word: a blue tunic embellished with swirling silver patterns, soft leather trousers, and a gleaming red cloak trimmed in gold thread. A silky horse as black as a sunflower seed cropped the grass behind him.

Adelaide stared at the man, stupefaction and terror scaring any words out of her mouth. Did he somehow know about her rebellious plans? Was he here to haul her to Lord Lambert so the lord could burn the mark of a traitor onto her skin?

"Good day, fair Adelaide. I don't believe I had a chance to introduce myself yesterday." He rubbed a hand through his wavy, acorn-colored hair. "I'm Prince Elias, son of Ganelon, King of Klinhun."

He swallowed. "I was wondering if you would consider acquiring my friendship so that one day I might ask for your hand?"

Adelaide's mouth flew open. Why hadn't he told her he was the prince? And why in all the fields of Alesfirth would he ask for her—a peasant's—hand in marriage? Perhaps he did know about her plans to overthrow the king and his son—who was apparently this man in front of her—and his words about marriage was just a ruse to take her quietly, to kill her. He certainly would if he knew what she was planning.

Or...the daggers! What if it had been his wagon she'd taken them from? Then she would have stolen not from just a noble, but the *prince*. Dread kicked her in the gut, and she had to clutch the door to keep herself upright. Even if Prince Elias didn't know about her plans to overthrow him, he could just as easily kill her for stealing a dagger.

Without thinking, Adelaide slammed the door shut.

Chapter Four

"Adelaide!" Lightning flickered in her father's eyes. "Did you just shut the door on the Prince of Klinhun?"

"Yes." Her voice sounded as squeaky as the mice Cyr sometimes brought back alive.

"The prince is here? Where?" Odo sat up on the bed, causing the chicken lying beside him to squawk and half-flap, half-fall to the ground.

Ferand strode to the door while Galiena said, "Truly, Adelaide, we didn't raise you to treat a prince so disgracefully. He could punish us for that if he chose." Adelaide's mother was right, but it was hard to imagine a pain deeper than the loss of her sister.

Her father opened the door and welcomed the prince inside. Adelaide wished for Cyr's presence on her shoulder, but he was off hunting, and she didn't want to whistle for him and end his flight.

Prince Elias sat at the table and ate the coarse brown bread and hard cheese—after her mother had cut the mold off—as if he always dined with them. The food had been put aside for their evening meal, but of course, no one told him this.

Adelaide's parents stood across from the prince, talking about the Festival as Odo watched from a spot on the floor.

Adelaide remained by the fire, mulling over the prince's presence and desire for her hand. If he wanted to take her away for stealing the daggers from his wagon, if it was his, then why was he sitting at their table discussing the sweets from the previous evening so cordially with her parents? He must not know she took the daggers. But then why? His suggestion of betrothing her was as ridiculous as the image of Gunter surrounded by a flock of women.

"I'm sorry, again, your highness, for my daughter's rude behavior." Ferand shot her a flaming look. "We weren't expecting such highly-regarded company today."

The prince waved his apology away. "I should have let you know last night that I intended to come by, but I didn't know myself until earlier today."

"So, your highness, to what do we owe the pleasure of your royal presence in our humble home?" At the honey oozing from her mother's voice, nausea roiled in Adelaide's stomach. How could they treat the prince as if the last year of heart-tearing anguish hadn't happened? As if it wasn't his and his father's fault that her sister and many others now lay silent and still in the earth's uncaring soil?

It was true the Gyndilians were the ones to swing the blades and burn down half the town, but it was the king's men who had run, who had failed to protect them. King Ganelon and Prince Elias had known something like the attack could happen, and they had done nothing.

"I know it's unusual, but I'm interested in marrying your lovely daughter someday." He looked at Adelaide as if trying to peek into her thoughts. She glanced away.

Ferand's eyes widened. "Ah. Well, that is—that is a mighty honor." He gazed at his wife and Adelaide, then back at the prince. "Please, your highness, let us think about this for several days. It came a bit unexpectedly."

"Certainly. I don't have any immediate action planned regarding your daughter's future. I just wanted to let you know my desire to become acquainted with her and receive your permission to do so."

"Of course you may visit any time and speak with her. It would be a pleasure and honor for our family." Ferand dipped his head.

"Good. I'll be in Alesfirth a few more days and will come by when I have time." The prince stood and straightened his tunic. "Thank you for your kindness."

He turned toward Adelaide, a smile pulling up one side of his mouth. "Farewell, fair maiden."

Once the prince left, Galiena clasped her hands together, grinning. "This is wonderful. Adelaide, you could possibly live in the palace at Dhalion very soon. Emma would have been so happy for you."

"Don't speak of Emma," Adelaide growled. "The prince and his father are the reason she's dead." She clenched her hands in an attempt to keep her wail of sorrow inside.

After a long, tight moment, Ferand said, "It's odd that the prince would want to marry a peasant. In all my long winters in Klinhun I've never heard of such a thing."

"It's because Adelaide is beautiful and intelligent," Galiena said as she strode to the fire, "even if she is discourteous."

"If Adelaide moves to the castle, can I live there too?" Odo asked.

Pushing down a rising panic at the future they planned for her, Adelaide escaped outside to find Cyr. She would need to leave for Dhalion sooner than she had expected. The thought caused her palms to sweat and her heart to ache. She had never left her family before, not even for a night.

Would her mother be able to manage all the baking and fire-tending without her younger, stronger hands? Would her father be able to sleep through the night without her nightly back kneading? Who would smack Odo's shoulder when he was being annoying? And Emma... perhaps it would be easier, less painful to live without the absence of her sister shouting at her from every piece of straw in the home they had grown up in.

That night, when everyone slept and the coals' orange glow of life slumbered, Adelaide prepared to leave.

After putting on her dusty-brown dress and grey cloak, she filled a cloth bag with her other dress and Emma's cloak. She threw in a few apples, a chunk of cheese, half a loaf of bread her mother had baked for the next day, and an animal skin full of water. The provisions wouldn't last long, but Cyr could find fresh meat, and soon there would be wild onions and berries growing along the road.

She took a few precious coins from the jar and placed them in the sack. Finally, she retrieved perhaps her most important item—her new dagger—from beneath the straw and placed it in her girdle where it nestled against the small of her back out of sight.

Adelaide slung the satchel over her back and whistled softly. From his spot perched by the fire, Cyr flicked his dark eyes open and landed on her shoulder.

She bent over Odo and prodded him awake.

He groggily opened his eyes.

"I have to leave, Odo," she whispered into his ear. "Tell mother and father I should be back after planting season. Tell Gunter to meet me at the town I mentioned at the time that I said I'd be there." She couldn't trust Odo with more information, but couldn't leave without reaffirming the plan to meet the men in Dhalion by spring. Her parents would worry, and she would most likely not be back as soon as she said—if she came back at all—but perhaps the small lie would quell some of their fears.

Odo's eyes were now wide-open. "What? Why?"

She wished she didn't have to lay this burden on Odo, but there was no other way. "Just tell them, please."

Perhaps he saw something sharp as stone in her expression, because Odo didn't argue. He just nodded once.

Adelaide kissed him on the nose. "Farewell. I'll be back as soon as I can. Take care of yourself." She stepped away from him with great strength of will.

"Where are you going?"

"Shh." She turned and placed a finger on his mouth. "I'll be back. Be strong for our parents."

Adelaide was only able to turn her back on her brother by remembering the screams of her people and knowing the situation would only become worse if she remained with her family and did nothing.

Even so, her heart felt gnawed clean through when she walked out of her house into the lonely winter night.

Chapter Five

Elias finished adjusting Starflare's saddle, then rubbed the white stripe on her smooth black forehead. She snorted against his hand.

"I don't have any treats for you today, girl. Perhaps tomorrow."

Berold entered the stable that reeked of manure and oats and blinked in the dim light. "Where are you going?"

The prince hung the red leather bridle over Starflare's ears. "Just for a short ride. You know how much I dislike being indoors, especially when the sun's shining so brightly."

"Shall I join you?" Berold walked over and stroked his bay's nose while the horse munched its oats.

"Nay. I'd like some solitude, and I shan't be gone long."

"Good, because Lord Lambert mentioned he'd like to take us hunting this afternoon with his most 'highly regarded hounds', as he put it. If they are as portly and out of shape as he is, we'll be lucky to even make it to the forest."

Elias chuckled. "You better watch your mouth, my friend, before it gets you into trouble." He mounted Starflare. "I'll be back by the hunt. Until then, don't treat Lord Lambert's men too roughly, especially if you fight them on the sword field. I'm not ready to give up his fine cooking just yet."

Berold grinned. "Nor am I, especially the roasted deer. The fare in Dhalion is delicious, but the cooks don't season venison as well as they do here."

"You're right, though I do miss seafood." Starflare stamped a hoof. "I should leave if I'm to be back by the hunt."

Berold's forehead scrunched in worry. "Are you sure you don't want me to accompany you? We're much closer to Gyndilad here than anywhere in Klinhun, and if they knew the prince was here..."

"I'll be fine. I have my sword." Elias touched the bronze scabbard at his belt.

"You're not as skilled as I am."

"True, but even if you were the best swordsman in all of Klinhun—" Berold raised an eyebrow, "—which you essentially are, you couldn't defeat an entire army singlehandedly. No, I shall go alone. Save some food for me." He nudged Starflare toward the door.

"I'll eat all of it if you make me go on the hunt alone with Lord Lambert and his sheep-witted knights," Berold called after him.

Elias chuckled, wishing his friend could accompany him. But he wasn't merely riding for pleasure as he claimed, and his friend wouldn't understand the reason for his destination—Adelaide's house.

Elias had no intention of marrying Adelaide, and the lie bit at him. Too many lies surrounded him now. He had lied to Berold, the first friend he had made at the castle. Like most Klinians, Berold still believed dragons were as fierce as all the songs and stories claimed. Elias and his father had decided, before Elias left Dhalion, that Berold already had too many responsibilities as Captain of the Guard to burden him with the knowledge that the dragons weren't destructive. Revealing the truth of the dragons now, after so many years of friendship, could create a crack between them that would splinter their friendship for good.

And now he was lying to Adelaide. But it was the only way he could think of to spend time with her and earn her trust. Lives were worth a few lies.

Once outside the bustling town, Elias let Starflare run. As her hooves dug into the soil, sending her and Elias racing through the open fields, he leaned next to her whipping mane, glorying in the wind's stinging song and the flying landscape. In this moment, he was not Prince Elias weighed down with all of Klinhun. He was Elias, as light as the clouds, as strong as his horse's legs, as reckless as a diving falcon.

He slowed Starflare, much to her and his regret, before reaching Adelaide's house. It wouldn't ease her parents' or Adelaide's mind if he came galloping up like an uncontrolled child, especially after their last uncomfortable meeting.

Elias brushed a hand through his wind-whipped hair and left Starflare grazing beside an oak. He wasn't going to let Adelaide shut the door in his face again, even if she had a good reason to hate nobility. Thankfully her parents didn't share her hatred. Distrust, yes, but that was common among peasants throughout Klinhun.

The slim, black-haired girl didn't greet him at the door, but her mother, Galiena did. She dipped low. "Good day, your highness. My heart is full of joy that you would grace us with your presence again so soon." She appeared anything but joyful as she stepped aside to let him in, her eyes red and her hands fluttering about her dress.

"Good day, Galiena. I hope I'm not disturbing your work." Once he entered the smoky cottage, she closed the door behind him.

"Of course not, your highness." She rubbed her hands on her stained ash-grey dress. "If you were wondering, Adelaide isn't here."

"Where is she?" Elias glanced around the small room, but it held no answers. Just a goat nibbling the straw littering the floor.

"She left sometime last night. This morning Odo told us that she had told him she had to leave but would be back after the planting. She also wanted him to tell Gunter to meet her somewhere. That's all she said.

"Odo left a while ago to give Gunter the message and ask if he knew anything. Odo should be back anytime now." She stared at the door as if it would disgorge her son or daughter any moment.

Confusion clouded Elias' thoughts; why would Adelaide leave a message for a friend then disappear? What reason could she have to leave her family?

His musings didn't help him arrive at any conclusions, and Galiena appeared as puzzled, if not more so, than him as she drooped toward the door, her eyes bleeding sorrow. Her bewilderment might also be from how he had singled her family out and now stood in her home genuinely wondering where her daughter had gone.

He spoke into the taut silence. "Is there anything I can do for you?"

Galiena gazed at him blankly, then blinked. "Forgive me, your highness. I've been exceptionally rude. Wouldn't you like to sit down?"

He wouldn't, but Galiena pulled out a bench for him, so he sat. She offered him some ale and bread, and he forced himself to chew, though he felt far from hungry and knew this bread might very well be their only food for the day.

He attempted to discuss lighter matters with the woman, but she kept glancing toward the door, not listening to him.

During their rather one-sided conversation about the weather, Adelaide's brother flung the cottage door open.

"Odo!" Galiena sprang toward him. "Did you give Gunter the message? Did he know anything about where he was supposed to meet Adelaide?"

The lanky boy who hadn't yet grown into his ears bowed

to Elias before ambling to the rickety cupboard and pulling out a hunk of cheese. "I gave him the message." Elias watched in amazement as Odo stuffed the entire hunk into his mouth.

"That was for dinner, Odo! You'll only be able to have bread, then." She glanced at Elias and flushed.

The boy frowned, but couldn't retort with all the food in his mouth. When he swallowed the last bite, he said, "Gunter didn't know why Adelaide told him to meet her somewhere, but she had said she wanted to go to Fernohn to get some medicine for Father. Gunter didn't think she would be leaving for a while, if at all, and not by herself."

Galiena contemplated this, then slowly nodded. "That makes some sense, I suppose. Your father's back pains have grown worse this winter, but surely she wouldn't have left without telling us or Gunter."

Elias stood. "I'm sorry for your trouble." He glanced at Galiena. "I will find Adelaide and try to convince her to return home."

Galiena gaped at him. "Why would you do that, your highness?"

"Your daughter is of special concern to me." This, at least, was not a lie.

The woman kneeled at his feet. "Thank you so much, your highness. If there's anything we can ever do for you..."

"Nay." Elias helped her to her feet. "Only this: keep watching and hoping for your daughter's safe return."

Adelaide's mother nodded and clasped her hands.

Outside, as Elias untied Starflare, Odo sidled up to him. "Can you truly find my sister, your highness?"

The prince wished he could offer more hope. "I will do all I can."

"What if she doesn't want to be found?" Odo asked quietly.

Elias regarded the cloud-heavy sky. "That's a much different matter, and one I have no answer for."

Chapter Six

Screams sharp as a sword's edge pierce Adelaide's ears as men in shadowy black cloaks chase her and Emma. One of the men throws a sword at Emma. It pierces her chest, and she falls onto the ground, blood streaming from the wound. The sword turns into a snake, writhing around Emma. Adelaide grabs the snake and throws it at the men. Then, as she reaches out to wipe away the blood marring Emma's skin, her sister's body disintegrates into ash.

Adelaide jerked out of her nightmare and sat up. Snow drifted by, fat and lazy, and the tree above was just an outline of a deeper shade of night. Somewhere on its branches Cyr slept more peacefully than her. She slid her new dagger out of her girdle and hurled it at the tree trunk to dispel her terror from the too-vivid images.

She had been traveling down the Southern Road for three days, but it felt much longer. She missed the warmth of her cottage and her family sleeping beside her.

She closed her eyes and stretched. She had never walked so far so quickly, and it felt like her very bones had turned to stone. She could have brought her family's horse and arrived in Pinhurn in only a day or two more, but her family needed the horse for plowing. The old mare wouldn't survive long in the wilderness at the summit of winter anyway.

According to the merchant who had shown her the map of Klinhun, she should arrive in Pinhurn in another few days. If it continued to snow, though, it would take longer, and Adelaide didn't have longer. The men in the rebellion were counting on her to rally more help before they reunited in the spring.

An orange glow, as if from a fire, erupted in the darkness not far behind her. Who else would be traveling in the middle of winter? The few visitors from the Festival had passed her two days before, and traders rarely came to Alesfirth, especially since the Gyndilians' attack, and never during winter. The person or group must be skilled with flint and wood to start a fire in the wet, heavy snow.

Adelaide retrieved her dagger, which now felt more familiar—almost too familiar—with a few nicks in it from the tree. She whistled. Cyr landed on her shoulder as soundlessly as the snowflakes on the ground, but not as lightly. Grasping her satchel, she crept to the fire's glow.

A lone figure held a stick pierced with meat over the fire's heart. Adelaide snuck as close as she could while remaining in shadow.

The man had brown, wavy hair, a strong jaw, and a glimmering red cloak.

Adelaide's stomach plummeted. Prince Elias must be following her—why else would he risk freezing out here? But why? Perhaps he did know about the daggers. Or maybe he wanted to steal her virtue where no one would see, like some nobles did. He couldn't want to truly marry her—a peasant. The idea was as absurd as Cyr speaking.

It didn't matter what the man's motives were; he was the prince, and she must escape him somehow.

His gaze shifted to where she hid in the fire's silhouette.

"Good evening, fair Adelaide and proud Cyr. Would you like some rabbit? I caught it not long ago."

"Why are you following me?" Adelaide's voice trembled, much to her embarrassment.

Prince Elias rotated the stick, and juice fell and sizzled in the flames. "It's far more agreeable than going on Lord Lambert's unending hunts, though Berold will detest me for abandoning him. He probably ate all the lord's food, which of course doesn't matter now." Wrinkles smudged his forehead as he gazed at the charred meat.

Adelaide had no idea what he was talking about and turned to leave. Before she could, he said, "I'm mostly following you because I told your parents I would find you and take you home."

She faced him. "Gunter received the message from Odo then?"

"Yes. However, your friend didn't understand what you meant by meeting him in Fernohn to trade for medicine. And your parents are confused why you left without telling anyone." He peered at her as if attempting to pull her secrets out with his gaze.

She could never let him, of course; they were too dangerous, not only for herself, but for those she loved.

She was grateful, though, that Gunter had thought of an excuse for her quick flight, however paltry. Her father did experience back pain after falling off a roof he'd been mending four years ago. The pain increased each year, making his work in the fields miserable. Emma had always talked about saving up to trade for some special herbs or creating her own salve to ease his pain; Adelaide's rubs did only so much.

And Gunter had done well to mention Fernohn, since it was a mining town many leagues away, widely known for the wealthy traders who set up wares every summer for the silver-hoarding townsfolk. For the few who could afford them, rare and valuable things could be bought or traded, like healing balms and herbs that only grew in certain places in Klinhun.

After everything that had happened last year, Adelaide hadn't thought once about acquiring medicine for her father. Guilt niggled her, but the salve—if one even existed—would be costly, and more important matters begged for her attention.

She had become skilled in lying the last year to her parents about the rebellion and didn't falter now. "What Gunter said is true. I told him to meet me in Fernohn if I wasn't back by a certain time, which he's apparently forgotten. I wanted the purpose of my trip to be a surprise to my parents. I'm on my own because no one else could be spared, not even Gunter." It was easier lying to the prince than to her family; it hardly pricked.

"It sounds as if you and your friend need to work on your communication." The prince rotated his roasting rabbit. Its smoky smell taunted Adelaide's stomach. She'd only eaten an apple and a few bites of bread since she left home.

"Are you certain you don't want to sit by the fire?" The prince patted a damp log beside him. "The night feels like it'll be one of the colder ones we've had this year."

Fear and distrust wound through Adelaide, but this time her voice barely trembled. "I'd like for you to leave me alone. I shall return to my family when I have the salve my father needs."

She turned and stalked back to her tree.

Each night after her conversation with Prince Elias, orange light sprang up near the road behind her. He never made camp nearer to her than the first night, and his form was always a small figure on a black horse during the day. Although he never approached her, Adelaide's irritation and anxiety mounted each time she saw him.

The second night his fire spoke to the sky, she contemplated wounding him so she could go about her task more easily. She had never hurt anyone with her dagger before, and the thought sent tremors up her fingers.

No, she must keep to her original plan. The relief from this decision quickly dissolved, since sometime soon she would have to throw the dagger at more than bark to save her family and friends from their power-hoarding rulers.

Chapter Seven

Six days after leaving home, Adelaide arrived at the town of Pinhurn.

Sheer, jagged cliffs slathered in snow slammed up against the gray sky like their namesake: The Spearhead Mountains. They formed a formidable edge behind the haphazard town and farms of Pinhurn, then marched south and east through the middle of Klinhun.

Adelaide could just barely see Laris Lake peeking out from behind the town. From its faint dusting of snow, it looked like a cloud kidnapped by earth. Black shapes circled above—probably geese deciding if they should land on the frozen surface or seek warmer refuge.

Cyr launched off her shoulder and flew in their direction, presumably to hunt or display his superior speed. Adelaide wished to go to the lake as well. She had never seen a large body of water before, only the perpetual slithering of the Lentiasa River. But before she could quench her curiosity, she must try to persuade some people to join the rebellion. Maybe that way, *they* could harm the king and his knights, and she wouldn't have to.

What a horrible thought. Shame spread hot fingers across her face.

Adelaide glanced back, and when she didn't see the prince behind her, she melted in relief. Perhaps she could lose him in town.

As she neared the open stone gate looming much larger than the one encircling Alesfirth, a knight guarding it said to the one beside him, "Riding bareback is much more enjoyable. It requires more skill than riding with a saddle."

The other knight spat on the ground. "Riding bareback is for the poor or for children who don't know how to ride properly. It always gives me the worst leg pains, and what's more, you bobble about like a—"

"Speaking of the poor," the first knight nodded to her.

Adelaide stopped a few paces away. "Good-day. I'm from Alesfirth on my way to Fernohn. I wish to spend the night here, if you please."

The two men regarded her, then the knight who had spat said, "Go ahead."

As Adelaide walked past, the first knight addressed his friend, "We'll let the debate stand for now. Tell me, what do you think is the best way to attack an oncoming army when on lower ground?"

Adelaide shook her head. Knights had too much time to do nothing, whereas peasants had too little time to do everything.

The town of Pinhurn was constructed the same way as Alesfirth: craftsmen's homes and shops surrounded a raised stone dais that overlooked merchant stalls. The lord's hall—crafted from a glossy wood and the same dark gray stones as the wall—sat like a fat cat at the far end of town.

Unlike Alesfirth, the village didn't look as if a strong wind could blow it all the way to Gyndilad; the wooden buildings stood on firm rock foundations.

On the wall encircling the town, knights stood or paced, their chainmail glimmering in the winter sunlight. On their gold and blue painted shields, a kind of cat looked about to pounce. Adelaide wondered why no one in Alesfirth patrolled its outskirts like they did here. After all, the Gyndilians had attacked Alesfirth, not this village. Lord Lambert and King Ganelon apparently weren't worried about another imminent attack or the lives of its citizens.

Adelaide crossed the cobbled ground to a building with a sign of a tankard hanging over its door. Inside the stuffy, raucous room, she ordered a mug of ale from a thin woman with drooping skin. She gave the woman one of her precious coins and took the slopping drink to a table near the wall.

The tavern slowly filled with craftsmen resting from work, nobles gleaning the latest news or arranging for a woman for the night, and a few peasants stopping by on their way in or out of town to trade. She was glad to see that Prince Elias wasn't inside. Hopefully, he would finally leave her in peace.

After a few moments, she heard what she was listening for. A table away, two men, peasants by the look of their tanned skin and filthy hands, discussed in whispers the lord's new edict outlawing fishing in the lake.

Adelaide took a swig of her bitter drink, wished Gunter was with her, and sat at a table closer to them.

"What are you looking at, lass?" One of the men—the bald one—asked with narrowed eyes.

Adelaide shrugged, trying to act casual, though her palms poured sweat. "I overheard your conversation about not fishing in the lake, which made me curious."

"Why does it matter to you?"

"Eudo, she's just a girl." The second man said, plucking at his brown beard and measuring her with spring-green eyes.

Eudo scowled at the other man but didn't respond.

"I'm from Alesfirth, and we've had a rough time since the Gyndilians attacked." She lowered her voice and leaned forward. "I was wondering if other towns are weary of the nobility's endless appetites for everything we can give them."

She knew this kind of talk could get her killed if the men ratted on her, but she had counted the cost when she stole her first dagger. The risk of dying was worth a chance at a better life for her family and friends.

The second man nodded so hard, his beard flopping, that some ale sloshed out of the mug he held. He didn't appear to notice. "Oh, yes. We peasants used to be able to fish in Laris Lake any day except for feast days, as long as it didn't interfere with our work and as long as we gave a third of our catch to Lord Wymar. But just a few days before the Fire Festival, he announced that anyone caught fishing at the lake would have one of their hands cut off."

"We think his sudden change of mind," Eudo added, apparently finding Adelaide trustworthy since his friend did, "has something to do with Lady Hadwisa, whom he married last autumn." His face scrunched up in disgust. "She's horrible—always complaining about something or other."

"Do you remember when she made a large fuss when the wind blew her handkerchief across town?" The bearded man asked his friend. "She screeched as loud as a wailing animal and yelled for someone to fetch it. Now, every time I see her, I swear she's going on about how her best handkerchief is ruined, as if the wind can be tamed." He waved his arms for emphasis, and Adelaide smiled.

"And you can't even eat a handkerchief," Eudo grunted.

When he and the other man calmed down and Adelaide reassured herself that no one was paying them any attention, she asked, "So, have the people continued fishing? Is anyone guarding the lake?"

Eudo spun his empty mug on the table. "A friend of ours went up a few days ago early in the morning to try to catch some. He didn't see any knights. But on his way home, a knight at the back gate searched his satchel and found the fish. He brought him to Lord Wymar, who had his hand cut off." The mug fell over and Eudo stared at it, not bothering to right it.

Adelaide had seen plenty of people in Alesfirth without hands or legs as punishment for stealing food or not paying taxes. When she was ten she had even seen a woman stoned to death by some knights. According to their closest neighbors, she had been caught sleeping with one of them, and probably at their request. Adelaide hadn't known all that then, though. She'd just known the screams and nightmares that had chased her at nights into Emma's soothing arms.

Adelaide shoved the gloomy memories aside. "When it's dark, meet me outside the tavern, and bring anyone you trust," she whispered. "We'll discuss how some in Alesfirth are going to take action against the one who keeps these lords in power. Only by fighting him do we have a chance of getting rid of these arrogant lords.

"If anyone else finds out about what we've discussed, you might find me on the other end of a dagger pointed at your heart." Her voice was stone-steady, but her hands trembled as she set her cup down and grabbed her satchel.

The men gawked at her. She might have been too dramatic there at the end, but they needed to know how serious she was, even if the very thought of harming them made her hands sweat.

"You're a woman. Why do you speak of such things?" The bearded man asked, recovered from his shock.

Adelaide gazed at him as if her eyes were swords. "Do women not feel pain or hunger or thirst? Do women not feel loss and anger and sorrow as men do? Do they not have as much right to fight for those they love as others?" She stood. "Meet me outside the tavern with those who feel the same as we do and can keep their mouths closed."

Adelaide nearly fled the tavern, clutching her satchel with white hands.

She walked toward the back of town, hoping a visit to the lake could calm her. She bought a hunk of slightly-stale cheese from a woman selling them out of a cart since her traveling fare was nearly depleted.

She soon found her way to the back gate that matched the one in the front with its hefty stones and thick iron-embedded door. It would be a feat for anyone, even the Gyndilians and their army, to gain entry.

The knight guarding the door eyed her. “Where are you going, Miss?”

“Just to the lake. I’m a traveler and would like to see it before I leave.”

“We close the gates at nightfall, so make sure you’re back by then. And no fishing.”

Once she left the confining stone walls, Adelaide breathed the fresh, sap-scented cool air in deeply. Despite the protection of the fortifications, she didn’t enjoy being between them. She felt freer here, out where there was no ranking, just trees, dirt, and sky.

Laris Lake was only a short walk up the snow-sprinkled ground toward the base of the Spearhead Mountains. The expanse of snow covering most of the lake glimmered in the sun, and pine trees, guardians of its purity, encircled the lake.

Adelaide gazed at the serenity and stillness, letting it soak deep into her. Then she slushed through the snow to a lofty pine with crusty branches and hauled herself up. As she climbed, she remembered the first time she had learned to scramble up a tree, when she’d been about fourteen, after she and Emma had become friends.

“Must we climb *this* tree? It’s the tallest one on this part of the river.” Adelaide leaned back to take in the brown-skinned giant that appeared to be the king of the others lining the river’s bank.

Emma took her hand. “We don’t have to climb all the way to the top if you don’t want to. It’s the tallest tree I’ve ever seen.”

Her sister’s easy understanding calmed Adelaide. The older girl wouldn’t scurry up the tree and leave her behind, nor let the boys know how frightened she was.

"Are you maidens going to come up or just stand there staring all day?" Gunter's head poked through one of the branches laden with crisp apple-red leaves. A dead leaf clung to the nest of his hair.

Adelaide and her sister exchanged looks and laughed.

"What?" Gunter turned as red as the leaves partly obscuring his body.

"Gunter, be nice to them." Conrad neared them from the other side of the tree. "It's their first time to climb, and you could probably use some help as well." He grinned when he noticed his younger brother wobbling on the branch he perched on.

Gunter glared at his brother. "I was fine until they started laughing at me."

"Well, you do look a bit funny with that leaf stuck in your hair," Conrad said, then turned to Adelaide and Emma. "It's easier to get up on this side."

Adelaide glanced up at the sputtering Gunter. "Don't fall trying to get that leaf out. It wouldn't be fun carrying you home."

He frowned, and Emma elbowed her.

When they reached the place Conrad had chosen for them to ascend—a low, thick branch dropping like a jaw over the muddy earth near the swaying river—Adelaide's stomach clenched.

"This place is easy," Conrad said, standing beneath the limb. "Just grasp the branch with both hands and swing yourself up. Follow me and do what I do. I'll go slow so you can see." And with that, he was sitting on the branch above their heads.

So much for going slow. Adelaide didn't know what he'd done, and the branches looked far too high from down here. She wasn't a squirrel or a bird; she had no tail or wings to rescue her if she began to fall, and Conrad was already disappearing through the blushing leaves.

"Do you want to go first, or do you want me to?" Emma's hair fluttered like ripe wheat in the wind as she waited for Adelaide's answer.

"I will." Adelaide took a deep breath, grasped the branch with both hands, and hauled herself up.

With Conrad shouting instructions from above and Emma offering encouragement below, Adelaide made it to the top.

She sat shoulder to shoulder with Emma, gazing down at the gurgling river and the rug of red, orange, and yellow trees interspersed stretching past the water to the land of Gyndilad. It didn't look any different than their side of the river.

Adelaide couldn't enjoy the view for long because her world began to spin. She started to clumsily make her way back down and with a churning stomach.

Halfway down she stumbled and swayed backwards, flailing for the branch she had just been clinging to. Emma grabbed her arm and guided her back to the limb. Her sister stayed close the rest of the way down and offered a hand whenever Adelaide needed it.

At the base of the tree, they plopped down with their backs against the trunk.

"Thanks, Em," Adelaide said between heaving breaths, her hands shaky and her world still dizzy. "I could have died back there."

Emma hugged her. "Of course. I couldn't let you leave me stuck with Odo forever."

Adelaide pulled a strand of her sister's hair, and Emma chased her around the trees, their laughter sweeter than the birds' singing.

Chapter Eight

Adelaide hated climbing trees. Emma wasn't up here, and her head whirled as she looked out at the icy lake and snow-clad peaks that seemed to disdain her frail attempt to reach heights that only they could attain.

Adelaide swiftly descended. On the lake's bank, she closed her eyes against the dizziness and the familiar searing agony of loss. When she felt slightly less ripped up inside, she whistled for Cyr. He circled down onto her shoulder, blinking his voluminous golden eyes.

"Hi, handsome." She stroked his smooth head feathers. "Don't get too comfortable there, though. I need you to hunt." She thrust her arm up and whistled one sharp, clear note.

He flapped once again into the sky, and Adelaide wished he could take her with him.

He soon returned carrying a rabbit in his talons. She took the creature from him once he landed—always a dangerous feat, especially if he was hungry. Thankfully, he wasn't and let her take the prey without clawing or screeching at her. She cut the stomach—his favorite part—out with her dagger and tossed it to him.

After skinning the rabbit, she stuffed it into her satchel. She'd have to find a way to cook it that night wherever she slept. As she turned back to the village, Adelaide caught a glimpse of gold in the fading light near the far end of the lake that was free from the ice's grip. She gazed at the cobalt water for a moment longer but didn't see the glint again. The shy sun must have been playing with the water and withdrew once it realized she was watching.

"Come on, Cyr. It's getting dark, and we still need to find a place to stay tonight." She held her arm out, and he leapt on, his beak splashed with blood from his treat.

The knight guarding the gate gazed with suspicion at Cyr but said nothing. He searched her sack but thankfully let her keep the rabbit. They must be less valuable than fish here. Adelaide inquired where travelers could spend the night, and he suggested the inn next to the tavern.

The scents of fresh-baked bread and pea and onion pottage greeted Adelaide when she entered the inn, and her stomach rumbled. A fire blazed to her right, and she relaxed as its heat thawed her face and fingers.

Adelaide passed sturdy, circular oaken tables where guests chatted and ate and headed for the counter at the back.

"What can I do for you, miss?" A man with a bouncing belly and white facial whiskers asked as he wiped a mug.

"How much is it to stay here for the night?"

"Six klins per night, and two klins for supper."

Adelaide's stomach grumbled in disappointment. That was more than she was willing to pay; she needed to save her coins for food. "Is there anywhere else?"

The man set the mug down. "There's a stable nearby that's clean and dry. The nobles' horses aren't stabled there, so you don't have to worry about any of them bothering you."

"Thank you, sir. The stable's not far?"

The man gave Adelaide directions, then leaned forward, his crinkled eyes moving to Cyr who still sat on her shoulder.

"You might want to keep that bird of yours close. Lord Wymar enjoys falconry, and any hungry person wouldn't mind selling a hawk for a few coins to fill his belly." His eyes roved over the people in the inn. "There's more than enough hungry folk in this town, and that's a mighty nice-looking bird."

Adelaide nodded, glad for the reminder. The nobles in Alesfirth hunted more with hounds than birds, and she never took him into the village. "I will. Thank you again." She stroked Cyr and made her way to the stable.

The rabbit didn't taste as good as the smells that had wafted from the inn, but it was hot and filled her belly. She cooked it using wood near the wall that the pine trees on the other side had shed. Once she licked the grease off her fingers and Cyr picked the bones clean, she stalked through the darkness back to the tavern.

Eight people, including the two men she had spoken to earlier, stood in the shadows of the building's wall. In the darting light of the moon, she could tell all of them—except for one hunched woman toward the back of the group—were men between twenty to forty winters old.

"Good evening, folk of Pinhurn," Adelaide said when she drew close. She was glad for Cyr's presence on her shoulder as sixteen suspicious and curious eyes regarded her.

"You failed to mention that the person you spoke with in the tavern was a lass, Eudo," a short, stocky man hissed, turning to the bald man.

"Because I knew you wouldn't come if I had, and we could use your strength," Eudo returned, never taking his eyes off Cyr.

The stocky man turned back to Adelaide, his eyes narrowing. "Why should we trust you? You're just a maiden who probably hasn't even seen twenty winters. How can you lead a rebellion? If that's indeed what you have in mind?"

Adelaide sighed. This was one place where Gunter's presence would have helped. It was like starting with the men in Alesfirth all over again. But she knew she'd have to. "It *is* what I have in mind. And you don't have to trust me. You just have to want freedom from the nobility enough to join me and my friends."

She retrieved the dagger from her girdle, twirling it in her hand close to the man's face, who swallowed but didn't step away. "I've seen as much, probably more, horrors at the hands of our so-called protectors than anyone here and have as much right to lead an uprising as anyone in Klinhun." She stopped rotating the dagger so that it pointed at the man. She shifted her shoulder so Cyr squawked and ruffled his wings.

The short man glared at the dagger, but took a step back.

Adelaide glanced at the others, whose faces were masked in shadow.

"If any of you talks about our meeting and plans, or even that there was a stranger in town to anyone you don't trust with your life, I'll find out. Then that person will find himself at the end of my dagger." She flicked the weapon into the air, catching the handle. She wouldn't hurt any of these folk—just the thought sickened her—and probably wouldn't even know if they had told someone, but they didn't need to know that. They just needed to believe there could be repercussions for wagging tongues.

"I have a group of twelve men back in Alesfirth who are ready to fight any time," despite having enough weapons, but she didn't mention that. "They're planning to meet me in Dhalion when the first plants rise from their long sleep." She slid her dagger back into her girdle. "Now, how many of you are willing to do the same? If you're prepared to fight for a better life, then we need to discuss plans for meeting in Dhalion."

It took a while for the group to open up and commit to anything, but the two men from the tavern encouraged the others, and soon the assembly was discussing weapons, who they could recruit, how many of them could leave their farms, and what they would do in Dhalion once they arrived.

It was clear through their hesitation and brusque manner that they didn't trust Adelaide, which didn't surprise her. She didn't trust them either and didn't give them her name. The stocky man didn't confront her again but looked at her as little as possible, and when he did, he clenched his hands as if trying to control his anger. She wasn't worried about him as a threat to her safety since she could probably hurt him with her dagger before he could hit her. She worried more about him as a threat to the rebellion and those in it. She kept her gaze on him throughout the meeting.

They discussed plans far into the night, pulling their cloaks tight around them as they sat on the frosty ground. Adelaide mostly listened, but their desperation for the hope she offered filled her with warmth and sorrow.

Listening to them and seeing their frayed skin and shadowed eyes, she could clearly see their lives in her mind's eye: waking up with the sun, eating moldy cheese and tough bread, cutting up, smoothing, coaxing the land to offer them its abundance while fighting torrid dryness, pelting rain, insatiable weeds and bugs, and falling into bed with burning, dying bodies to give nearly everything they earned to the lords' hands.

Adelaide could see their daily lives so clearly because it was hers.

For these broken, desperate people, for her hope-filled family, for dear Emma, she would fight until their pride was restored, and they could stand tall once more.

Chapter Nine

The next morning, near a farm outside of Pinhurn, a brown and white-speckled dog barked at Adelaide. Cyr shrieked back, and the dog tilted its head at him. Behind the dog a thatched hut coughed out smoke into the blue sky. As Adelaide passed the dog, it turned back the way she had come and yapped, wagging its matted tail.

Adelaide followed the dog's gaze and swore. "Of all the apples on a summer tree!"

A short distance away, Prince Elias ambled down the road toward her, his red cloak vivid against the black of his horse, his stature tall and sure.

"Cyr, go pluck out his hair. I've had enough of that noble." The bird nibbled her ear instead, and she sighed.

She turned her back on the prince, her eyes skipping over the bare countryside. It was far too dangerous to let him follow her. If he found out about the people she had talked to last night, or what she intended to do... She shivered at the image of a noose hanging in front of those poor people and her friends—hungry for their breath.

A skinny red dun tied to a post near the hut snuffled the

dead grass. No sound came from inside the thatched house, and Adelaide couldn't see any movement through the cracks. She pushed down the guilt inside her and glanced at the dog gazing at her with plaintive bronze eyes. "You won't tattle on me, will you?" He responded by stepping over and licking her hand, which Adelaide took as assurance.

She crept to the horse and untied it. Her family used their horse mainly for farm work, so she wasn't as skilled at riding as the prince, but she had ridden bareback enough times to feel comfortable on the dun's bony back.

The dog stared at her, and Adelaide hoped he would remain mute. She didn't need the prince *and* the owners chasing her. She urged the horse into a run and glanced back.

Prince Elias had now nearly reached the house and gazed at her with a stunned look that mirrored the dog's. But he didn't remain shocked for long, because soon Adelaide heard his horse's hooves thudding nearer and nearer. Would he punish her for stealing the horse? He certainly had the authority and right to do so.

She squeezed her legs tighter against the horse's side, urging it to run faster over the sparse grass. As the neglected horse attempted to pick up its pace, it stumbled. Cyr—still on Adelaide's shoulder—screeched and whooshed over the horse's head.

The horse bolted. Caught off guard by the sudden burst of speed, Adelaide tumbled off, landing on her back.

"Ow," she groaned. "Cyr, you dirt-brained bird, I'm going to kill you."

She sat up, looking for the hunter that had become her prey, but saw only the hindquarters of the fleeing horse and Prince Elias dismounting his own unperturbed mount nearby.

"Are you hurt? That was quite a fall." He strode toward her and offered her his hand. "Let me help you."

"I'm fine." Adelaide stood, grimacing at the pain in her back, and shook the dirt off her dress. She felt like, and probably resembled, a sack of spilled potatoes. She could almost see her sister, who had always kept her cloak clean, shaking her head in dismay.

"Are you certain?" The genuine concern in the prince's eyes bothered her more than her fall. She hadn't noticed how tall he was before; she had to lift her head to meet his gaze instead of tilting it down, like when talking to Gunter. It was bothersome.

She flung her braid over her shoulder. "I'm quite well, thank you. Why are you here, your highness? I asked you to stop following me."

"I might if you stopped running."

She frowned at him. At least he hadn't mentioned the stolen horse yet. She glanced around for her satchel.

"Here." He handed her Emma's cloak from where it had fallen out of the sack during her fall.

She snatched it from him. "Thank you." She dusted it off and placed it carefully back into the satchel. Emma's cloak was stained and tattered, but it was the only part of her sister she had left. She would throw herself into a pit of dagger-sharp sticks to recover it if she had to.

"I suppose you still don't want me to accompany you to Fernohn?" Prince Elias asked.

"Nay." She picked up her satchel and scrutinized him. "Why do you wish to help me so much? Surely as prince you have other, more important duties to attend to."

"Not many. Besides, I promised your parents I would find you and return you home."

"Well, you'll have to break your promise then. I'm not going home yet." She began walking in the direction of the next town, Kildare, somewhere in the hilly distance.

"Wait, Adelaide. I'll make a deal with you."

The sound of her name dropping from the prince's lips yanked her to a stop like reins on a horse. She glanced up at him. "Excuse me?"

His eyes looked more blue than gray under the azure sky puffed with menacing clouds to the north. “I’ll teach you how to fish and won’t mention your attempted theft of that horse to anyone if you’ll let me take you to the Crystal Caverns.”

“What are the Crystal Caverns?” She wondered if they were a place the nobility stored their treasure, perhaps even poor peasant women whom they kept for their pleasure.

The prince glanced at the sky. “The Caverns are merely what they sound like—a cave system filled with crystals. It’s a beautiful sight. The dragons discovered them before they left this land, and many humans have forgotten about them. As for fishing,” his eyes took in her nearly-empty satchel, “it appears you could use more food, and it doesn’t look as if you know how to fish, which is a shame since you live by a—”

“Did you just say that dragons discovered these Caverns?”

He nodded.

“Well, good day then. And please stop following me.” Adelaide was proud of herself for throwing in the word, ‘please,’ when she’d rather curse him.

She turned away and continued south. She had never heard anyone speak of dragons without the words, ‘blood, death, killing, or beast’ following them. She wondered if the people of Klinhun knew their prince had a soft spot for the fire-breathing beasts that had destroyed their land, and if so, why they didn’t put up more of a commotion. They must not know.

“Need I remind you that you just stole a horse from a peasant family such as yours, and I am the son of the ruler of this land? That family would probably love to see the thief of their beloved horse lose a limb or two.”

Adelaide turned around and crossed her arms, though that did nothing to calm her fear at his words. “Are you threatening me now, your highness?”

His sudden grin took her by surprise. “I would never dare threaten a maiden who travels across Klinhun on her own, has a hawk finer than any kings', and steals horses. I was merely offering you a deal that would be foolish to refuse."

Adelaide gazed at the prince, mulling over his words. Could she trust him enough to go with him to these Caverns? Learning how to fish would be beneficial, and she definitely needed more food. If she suspected him of any treachery, she could always wound him or sneak away. He didn't appear to be the violent kind of nobility, and she would have a fair chance in overcoming him in a fight with her dagger since all he appeared to have was a sword.

"How far is it to these Crystal Caverns?" Adelaide asked.

"Three to four days, depending on the weather. The place at Lentiasa River where I'll teach you to fish is only a day or two away."

After another moment of contemplation, Adelaide said, "Very well. But I get to keep most of the fish and fishing equipment, and you shall leave me alone after I see these Caverns."

He shook his head. "I know it must seem odd and suspicious for me to keep following you, but I can't stop."

"Because you long for my hand in marriage so ardently?" She raised her eyebrows.

Prince Elias adjusted his horse's saddle and said in an undertone, "If only it was just that." He looked at her and raised his voice. "It's true that I desire your friendship. You're not like anyone I've ever met."

He *appeared* to be telling the truth. She would just have to leave him while he slept or hunted. "May we leave then, your highness?"

"Yes. You may ride with me. Starflare can be spirited around strangers, but I'll keep her controlled." He stroked the horse's neck as she cropped the brown grass.

Adelaide paced with nervous agitation toward Elias and Starflare. The sooner she went with him to visit this Cavern place, the sooner she could leave and continue rallying people to her cause. She might even learn useful tidbits about his father and the castle in Dhalion.

"Would you like some help?" The prince asked.

Adelaide mounted before he had finished asking.

"I guess not." The prince settled into the saddle in front of her, and the silver embroidered leather creaked. "Where's your hawk?"

"He's hunting. He'll come when I call."

With a squeeze of his legs, the prince urged the horse to a walk. Adelaide gripped the saddle.

"You can hold onto me if you need to," Prince Elias suggested.

"I'm fine, thank you."

Adelaide didn't respond to his questions about her family, since such private information could incriminate them if he found out about the rebellion or the dagger she had possibly stolen from him. So no doubt bored with her one-word responses, the prince erupted in song. He had a rich autumn-honey voice which coaxed Adelaide deep into the song.

"The grass is beaming,
the sky is calling
in my home Klinhun.

The dragons stomp,
the humans tromp
in my home Klinhun.

The wind whistles,
the water ripples
in my home Klinhun.

The birds soar,
the dragons roar,
in my home Klinhun.

Soon I will be there,
in that land fair,
in my home Klinhun.

The song made Adelaide's heart ache for she knew not what.

"That's an old traveling tune passed down through my family," the prince said.

"I've never heard it before." Most of the songs Adelaide knew involved romance between nobles, the ascension of kings and princes, or fights with dragons. She had never heard any other royalty singing such deeply yearning songs. And she couldn't fathom why he and whoever composed the ditty believed dragons weren't the vicious creatures everyone else in Klinhun believed them to be. The prince spoke before she could decide which question to toss at him.

"No." He sighed. "Very few remember this song or others like it, which is a tragedy, for there are so many significant songs in our country's history that have been forgotten."

"You must have a different history than I do then, for I've never heard such songs or tales."

"Perhaps that's because certain people pushed aside these songs to make way for others that hide or deny the truth," the prince suggested.

"Mayhap because they realized that dragons were horrible beasts that ate men and destroyed villages."

Prince Elias didn't reply, though his back straightened. Adelaide couldn't believe she just had a conversation about the decency of dragons. And with a prince, no less.

They stopped for the midday meal under a squat, thorny tree that stood alone in the barren grassland. The lack of trees made Adelaide feel vulnerable, as if the world watched her and knew what she planned on doing.

A cry pierced the quiet, then Cyr landed on her shoulder, his brown wings hitting her face.

"Well, good day." Adelaide watched with satisfaction as the prince gave a start at the hawk's sudden appearance.

"No wonder that horse bolted earlier. He has a way of dropping in, doesn't he?"

Adelaide scratched Cyr's head. "He enjoys being the center of attention and somehow always knows when I'm about to eat."

The prince rummaged around in a sack tied to his saddle. "Would you care to share some of my food? I have plenty."

His cheese *did* appear creamier and the bread nuttier, but Adelaide didn't want to owe him anything. "Nay. I have my own." She sat at the base of the tree and nibbled on the hard yellow cheese she'd bought in Pinhurn, ignoring Cyr's plaintive gaze.

Prince Elias sat across from her on a weatherworn boulder. "Why do you dislike nobility so much?"

She thought that was obvious, but mayhap just to peasants. "Many reasons."

"Such as?"

She decided to impart to him the least offensive reasons—those farthest from her heart and least deserving of a hanging. "They eat too much and play too often."

He chuckled—a hearty, light sound. "Do I eat too much?"

She glanced at his hunk of cheese and loaf of white, nut-filled bread that were only slightly larger than hers. "You're traveling."

"True, and I can't wait to eat some succulent sea bass from Dhalion swathed in a white wine sauce brought from Neklosa." He gazed up through the tree's branches, chewing slowly. "Nothing tastes better in all of Klinhun." He returned his blue-grey eyes to Adelaide. "You must see Dhalion sometime. The rhythmic waves lapping against the green cliffs and the boats with white sails glinting in the sun—it's a magnificent sight."

It did sound lovely, and she wished she could enjoy it while she was there instead of plotting to overthrow this man's father. Frustration at the place she'd ended up in bubbled out into her words. "Perhaps I would if I didn't have to work on Lord Lambert's land every day, sunup to sundown."

The prince's shoulders sagged, and he stared at his half-eaten piece of bread. "You're right. Most—if not all—of the lords are selfish, prideful pigs who care little for others. But my father and I are attempting to change that."

"Well, you're in no hurry to do so."

Prince Elias rubbed his forehead. His voice raised as he answered. "You cannot change a system that has existed for two centuries in eight years, even if you *are* the king."

"Perhaps, but surely more can be done. The king could act like he cares about his people, even if he doesn't."

"You don't know anything of the king," Prince Elias growled.

For the first time, Adelaide feared him. She leaned back, hoping she hadn't gone too far.

But the prince's grip on his bread relaxed, and he took a bite. Adelaide dared not say anything else on the subject.

Chapter Ten

That evening, as fat flakes fell onto them, they stopped to make camp in a hollow area between two boulders.

Adelaide sat on an icy rock and pulled her cloak tight around her. “How far is it from here to the Lentiasa River?”

“We should reach it sometime tomorrow.” The prince drew a wool blanket out of a saddlebag and handed it to her. “Here. It will only grow colder as the night passes.”

Adelaide took the gift because her teeth were chattering and she might not make it through the night without it. She finished the rest of her bread and cheese while watching Prince Elias groom his horse. Each of his movements whispered tenderness. He murmured to Starflare while brushing her mane and rubbing his large hands down her night-black skin.

Adelaide relaxed as the horse lowered her head and closed her eyes under his soothing touch. An ache bloomed in her heart and spread through her at the love he gave his mount and the unique bond between creature and human.

She spread the blanket over herself and laid out on the scratchy, snow-dusted ground. She cradled Emma’s coarse cloak close to her cheek and imagined it was her sister's hand wiping away her worries.

With a last stroke down Starflare's petal-soft cheek, Elias turned around. Adelaide slept with her back against a boulder, a few scattered snowflakes clinging to the woolen blue blanket. Her long black braid lay across her back. A few tendrils had come loose, hugging her sun-darkened face.

Her wary, preyed-upon look had eased away in the silence of sleep. Now she was an ordinary lovely woman—not a hard, closed fist of a person who had seen too much pain and injustice. Elias wondered what that pain was, but knew she wouldn't tell him unless he earned her trust. And that was proving more difficult than he had thought.

Cyr cried from where he perched on a boulder above Adelaide and took off into the snow-speckled sky. Elias watched the dark, ascending shape with yearning until the hawk's form merged into the dull grey sky, his own heart as heavy as the clouds. Hopefully, Adelaide would believe him soon so the dragons wouldn't have to hide anymore.

Elias wrapped himself in another wool blanket and watched the fierce maiden sleep. He remembered long talks he and his father would have in his father's room when the violent wind blew them inside. The fire crackled in its polished marble home while the sea thrashed in its cliff-bound lair. His favorite late-evening talks were those when his father told stories of the past.

Elias could clearly see his father's broad-shouldered form lounging in his favorite chair—a simple wooden piece with a plush purple cushion—the flames flickering in his father's iron-blue eyes.

"Those were peaceful, prosperous days," his father would begin, "when dragons lived alongside humans in this fair country. The fire-breathers soared freely through the sky, and the humans feared no attack from their scaled neighbors. The two species lived as friends for many long years, learning from each other and enjoying life together."

King Ganelon had leaned forward, staring into the fire. "Then one of the humans grew jealous of the dragons' power and afraid of their might. He stirred up the humans, and many sided with him. The dragons had no desire to hurt their human friends, as you know, son, and since too few listened to the fire-breathers' pleas, they decided to leave this land, their home."

The wind cried outside, forlorn and loud in the sudden silence. A log sparked in the fireplace.

"They tell it differently here," the younger Elias said.

His father turned crystalline blue eyes on him. "That's why we're here, son."

Elias wished for fire now and the wise counsel of his father. Instead, he merely possessed damp swirling snow and a woman as cold as winter itself.

Noticing Adelaide shivering, he realized he still had his cloak—the red, fur-lined cape his father had given him when he had completed his training at fifteen winters old. His father's words as he gave him the cloak resounded to him now in this frosty, somber place, "This is to remind you, son, wherever you are in this land's cold winters, of your family and heritage, and warm you with the memories and hope of who we are."

Elias took the red cloak and placed it gently over Adelaide's trembling form.

"Please trust me," he whispered. "More than one life depends on it."

Chapter Eleven

Adelaide wiped the sprinkling of snow off her face the next morning, thankful for the blanket that had protected her from the night's chill. But as she clutched the blanket tighter to ward off the morning's cold fingers, she noticed a familiar red cloak sitting atop her like an extravagant garnish on a raw, too-small chicken.

She stared at the cloak, taken aback by such finery laid across her filthy, bony body. She removed and folded it.

"Thank you, your highness." Adelaide offered the cloak and blanket to the prince who sat nearby, munching on a hard biscuit.

Prince Elias took the cloak and wrapped it around himself, but told her to keep the blanket. He looked much more regal and intimidating in the silky red cloak than just in his embroidered green tunic, though that was also finer than any she'd seen.

He motioned to the small ration of bread and cheese spread out on his lap. "Would you care to share some of my meal?"

"Nay. Cyr will hunt for me." She turned toward the barren,

snowy landscape and whistled long and high.

After a moment Cyr landed on her shoulder with a jolt. "Ow. Careful. I'm not a rock, Cyr."

The hawk dug his talons into the leather sewed to her dress, nearly piercing her skin, and she tried not to wince, aware of the prince's gaze on her. She whistled the short hunting note and thrust her arm into the still-sleepy sky.

Prince Elias stared at Cyr's fading shape with a look of longing. "To fly would be freedom itself."

Adelaide glanced at Cyr's dark speck. "Perhaps, but flying is only for those who have wings. Freedom is for anyone strong and brave enough to grab it." Adelaide shut her mouth; she'd been talking much too boldly in front of Klinhun's prince.

He turned to her. "What you say is true, but surely there are other ways to fly than just with wings."

Adelaide shrugged; such wonderings were best left to people with more time and education. She busied herself with stuffing the prince's blanket and Emma's cloak into her satchel.

Cyr soon returned with a blackbird in his talons, and Adelaide skinned it, then tossed him the stomach.

"How do you propose to cook that?" The prince asked. "There's not much wood in this area, and the little that's here is soaked from the snow."

Adelaide hadn't thought of this and mentally berated herself. She couldn't let her survival skills slide just because she was traveling with a prince.

She wrapped the chunks of dripping red meat with dead leaves and placed them in her sack. "I suppose I'll just have to wait until later, then." The meat would keep for a few days if the weather remained cool.

"Please take one of my biscuits. We have a long way to go, and it will hinder us if you fall off Starflare for lack of nourishment."

Adelaide gazed at the crusty bread, wishing her stomach would stop growling. She was used to going without food, but if the prince was offering... She took it from him. "Thank you, your highness."

"Please call me Elias. If I could have my way, everyone in Klinhun would call me that. But alas, my father would never let me be so informal." He watched Cyr gorging on his blackbird stomach. "Since you and I are traveling far from my father and other townsfolk, and I pulled you into this little adventure, I feel it's only fair."

Adelaide stared at him. All the lords she had seen or heard of relished their titles and lifted them high for all to gawk at. And this man was no mere lord, but the prince of their country. His words and gestures of kindness made her suspicious, but his honest face and laid-back attitude did not coincide with her misgivings. She didn't know what to make of him.

Adelaide finished her biscuit and slung her satchel over her shoulder. "May we leave now?"

"Once I finish grooming Starflare."

Adelaide watched the prince brush and saddle the horse, stopping to stroke and murmur into its swiveling ear every few moments. How could someone who cared so much for his horse not show the same care for the people he ruled?

"Starflare's ready," the prince said a while later. "I would help you mount, but I know you'd refuse." He held the reins while she climbed up, then alighted in front of her. Cyr sprang into the air.

As Adelaide and Prince Elias rode through the flatlands under a peeping sun, Adelaide supposed she should try to dig some information out of him to help the rebellion. She had no idea where to begin or what to ask without giving herself away, especially since he already knew she disliked nobility.

After braiding and re-braiding her hair twice, she interrupted the prince's soft humming. "What's your favorite thing about the castle, your highness?"

"You're not going to call me Elias, are you?"

She shook her head. "It's improper." And it would make him seem like an ordinary person and thus, harder to... overthrow. She couldn't think the word, "kill," even though Emma's blood screamed at her for his death.

Prince Elias chuckled. "I'm sure that's your primary reason."

"It's a good enough reason for me. And your favorite thing about the castle is....?" She prodded.

He squinted up at the overcast sky. "I'd have to say the view."

"The view? That doesn't have anything to do with the castle."

"Oh, but it does. The king who decided to build the castle high on a cliff for protection— King Alphonse, I believe it was— happened to construct it in the perfect spot to see the sun and sea merging into one at the end of each day."

"What does the sea look like?" Adelaide had heard from the rare trader who made it all the way from Dhalion to Klinhun say it was like a river stretching in all directions as far as the eye could see. She had a difficult time believing such a thing existed, and an even more difficult time imagining it.

"It's hard to describe. Water flows toward the cliffs and beach without end. It's like the water comes from the horizon itself, and on a day when there's not a cloud in the sky, the sea becomes a second sky, except for its never-ending babbling song."

To her dismay, Adelaide realized she'd been gaping at the prince's back as she tried putting his lovely words into images. She glanced away, remembering that she was supposed to be gaining information from him about the castle, not gawking at him like a child in front of a sweet shop. She couldn't think of another way to ask him without arousing his suspicions and hoped he might reveal something on his own.

"Does it sound like a place you'd like to visit sometime?" The prince asked, glancing back at her.

"The sea? Possibly, if I ever have the opportunity."

"I would gladly take you."

"Thank you, your highness, but I have more pressing matters to attend to, and I'm sure you have more important things to do than take me to the ocean." Fear popped inside Adelaide. What if she couldn't rout him and his father out? All those peasants in her revolt, both from Alesfirth and Pinhurn, as well as her family—though they didn't know it yet—depended on her to give them a better future. If she didn't, then who would? The weight of their hopes and her secrets bowed her shoulders.

"There's not much that my father needs help with at this time of year," Elias said. "Your plans are to go to Fernohn, yes? What kind of medicine are you trying to find again?"

Adelaide shifted under his penetrating gaze. "Pain medication for my father's back. It worsens every winter and makes it hard for him to work. They'll need me for the planting soon, which is why I'm in such a hurry."

Prince Elias scanned her face, and Adelaide hoped he didn't see her lie or anxiety. She nodded toward Starflare's head. "Shouldn't you watch where you're guiding your horse?"

"I suppose that would be good if one wanted to avoid hitting a tree, but there appears to be a shortage of them in this part of the country, or anything sticking out of the earth, for that matter." He patted the horse. "And Starflare's too intelligent to walk into anything."

But at Adelaide's continued coaxing, he faced the front once more, and she breathed more freely.

They reached the Southern Road at midday under a suddenly sociable sun. Adelaide stopped shivering and no longer had to wipe snowflakes off her face. Cyr's feathered white and brown body drifted above like a lost cloud against the brilliant blue.

"Our next stop will be at the river. Hopefully, we'll have fresh fish to eat soon," the prince said.

Adelaide's stomach rumbled, and he laughed. Although she had lived by the Lentiasa River her entire life, she rarely had the opportunity to eat fish. Her parents had never learned how and rarely possessed enough money to buy it at the market.

So, despite herself, Adelaide found herself looking forward to the lesson and food that didn't threaten to rip her teeth out when she took a bite.

Soon, cottonwoods stretching bare branches to the sky appeared across the flat horizon. The prince stopped at a free-flowing part of the river that reflected the trees' slender black branches. He tied Starflare to a cottonwood near the burbling stream. Adelaide filled her animal skin and took a drink; the coldness hurt her teeth but refreshed her body.

After splashing his face with water, which turned it a comic strawberry-red, Prince Elias stood. "Now, it's time to fish."

Chapter Twelve

Elias held up the slim branch he had just broken off one of the trees lining the bank. "Once you have a sturdy stick, you tie fishing line around one end like so." He secured the string he had retrieved from one of his saddlebags around the end of the branch. "You can easily find lines like these for good prices in Dhalion."

Adelaide carefully observed the movements of his fingers. "I've seen them in Alesfirth."

"Then you tie on the hook and weight. And find some bait. Worms can be found almost anywhere." He dug into the wet, soft soil near the river. When he glanced up, he noticed Adelaide ogling him. She probably had never seen a noble dirtying himself in such a way. Well, if she hadn't yet noticed that he wasn't a normal noble, then she would soon. At least she didn't run in fear or throw up when he stuck the worm onto the hook. If only she was as easy to hook into his plans for Klinhun.

"Once the worm is secure, then you're ready to fish." He showed her the finished makeshift pole. "It won't last as long as the ones crafted with stronger and more flexible wood, but it'll work for our purposes."

"Would you help me make one now?" Adelaide said it as a question, but from the resolve in her hazel eyes and the confidence in her stance, Elias felt she would punch him if he refused, prince or not. Her will always seemed to conquer his, probably because he let it. He had every right to insist on his way, but he had to surrender—however much it nettled him—if he desired her trust.

"Of course." He watched and proffered instructions as Adelaide made her fishing pole. She insisted on doing everything herself, even breaking the limb from a tree, which she accomplished on her first try with several grunts.

The maiden was a quick learner and soon had a pole to match Elias'. He led her upstream to a pool surrounded by pink and silver-flecked rocks standing against the river's current. After flinging his line into the rippling water, he ducked under a willow's branch and leaned against its bark. "And now we wait."

Adelaide frowned. "My least favorite part." She cast her line into the pool and sat on a stump.

"Who taught you how to fish?" She asked, gazing at the clear water swallowing and burping out rocks on the other side of the pool.

Elias smiled, remembering cool grass beneath his feet, a leathery, sun-spotted hand over his on a pole that felt awkward in his grip, and a creaky voice providing instruction and encouragement. "A man named Manfred. He taught both my father and me. He also taught us how to fish from a boat, which is a little trickier than sitting still on the side of a river. I prefer this way."

Adelaide turned to look at him, her long black braid swinging against her arm. "Why didn't your father teach you how to fish? Are you not originally from Dhalion?"

"Nay. My father and I moved to Dhalion from our home near the Wymar River when we heard that King Clerebold's—

my father's uncle's—health was failing."

"Why didn't you live at the castle if you were royalty?"

Elias tried not to squirm under her probing gaze. Lying to earn her trust seemed counter-productive, but if he told her the truth of who he was now, she'd run away screaming. Or, more likely, punch him first and *then* run away screaming. "My father wanted me to have a normal childhood, probably so I wouldn't end up a drunkard like King Clerebold's son. Remember, he spent so much of his father's coins on ale that Clerebold had to ask Findar for aid."

Adelaide nodded, no doubt recalling rumors of the intoxicated prince.

"Have you not heard my history before? I am the Prince of Klinhun."

"I knew that you and your father moved to the castle shortly after King Clerebold fell ill. But I never knew from where you hailed exactly. I don't concern myself with the details of the lives of nobility."

"Why do I not find that surprising?"

"Most peasants don't have time to learn the dramatic stories of our rulers. Those that do are wasting their time. It doesn't matter how the nobility came to power, just that they have and are abusing that power." Her hand tightened on her fishing pole.

Elias agreed with most of what she said, though he believed the history of a ruler did matter. Telling her so wouldn't elevate him in her eyes, though. Instead, he stared at the gushing water and wondered what the hermit Manfred was doing now. He came to the castle sometimes, but his last visit had been almost a year ago.

"Oh! I think I have a fish." Adelaide leapt to her feet, holding her now-wiggling pole with both hands.

"Pull in the line slowly so as not to scare it."

She did, never taking her eyes off the end of the spinning string. Soon a writhing, incandescent orange and green fish dangled over the water. Adelaide grinned as she held the gasping fish in her hand. "You'll be tasty tonight, won't you?"

The grin on Adelaide's face shone more brilliant and beautiful than the sun striking the fish's scales in a burst of rainbow light. Elias didn't think he had seen her smile before and stared at the way it transformed her face into a depiction of innocence and delight.

The smile disappeared as quickly as it had burst forth as Adelaide focused on freeing the fish from the hook. Elias decided to do whatever he could to sneak the smile out again; the way it changed her whole being, like a warm sunrise after days of chilly fog, was too beautiful to keep hidden.

"Excellent." He laid his pole on the ground and strode toward her. "That's a nice-sized fish. I'll teach you how to clean it tonight. You can put it in here for now." He dipped one of his satchels in the river and held it out to her.

Adelaide cocked an eyebrow. "How do I know I'll see it again once I put it in there?"

Elias sighed, though he couldn't blame her for mistrusting him with all the haughty rulers she'd lived under. Before his father reigned, King Clerebold had raised taxes to pay for an addition of the castle to hold all his wines. *His* father, King Barchune, had bribed Gyndilad not to attack after the country had destroyed a village on the northeastern edge of Klinhun. He'd also outlawed hunting and gathering in all the forests and fields of Klinhun, giving the land to the lords.

Elias had his work cut out for him in earning Adelaide's trust. "I'm going to catch my own fish, so why would I eat yours? Besides, you'll be within eyesight of me the entire time."

"I suppose those are fair reasons." Adelaide dropped her prize into the satchel, but placed the sack beside her as she sat back on the stump.

Elias picked up his pole and resumed waiting, wondering if all this effort to gain her friendship would be worth it in the end. Seeing that sunny smile again, though—that might make up for his frustration.

Late in the afternoon, after Elias had added two fish to the satchel and Adelaide had muttered about how much faster it would be if Cyr hunted for them, hoof-beats pounded on the road behind them.

Adelaide bolted up, fingering her fishing pole as if it had turned into a sword. The hoofbeats slowed, angling toward them.

Elias leaned his pole against a tree. "It sounds like a single horseman. I'll go meet them."

"I'll join you."

"Grab the fish. We don't want a creature stealing them after all our hard work."

She snagged the bag and followed him out of the trees still holding her fishing pole-turned weapon.

"Berold!" Elias regarded his brown-haired and flushed-faced friend with surprise. "What are you doing here?"

The knight dismounted and held his bay's reins in a clenched fist. He inclined his head, breathing hard. "I would like to ask you the same, Elias. I would also like to know why I had to hunt with Lord Lambert and his arrogant nobles all afternoon, only to return to find that you were still gone and your saddlebags missing.

"Then I had to search the entire town and surrounding farms for you. The only word I heard of you came in the middle of the night from a peasant family who said you went in search of their daughter who had mysteriously disappeared the day before, and whom you chose to pursue in marriage." Berold narrowed his blue-specked green eyes at Adelaide, who clashed his gaze with one of her own.

Elias stepped forward as if to shield the woman from his friend's sharp scrutiny—as if she needed shielding.

Berold returned his attention to Elias and gestured as if he could grasp an answer from the air. "What are you thinking?

The prince can't just disappear. What would your father say? Did you not think, Elias, that after all these years of training with you and accompanying you across Klinhun that I didn't deserve to at least know you were leaving Alesfirth?" His nostrils flared like his weary horse's.

Berold's just anger speared Elias. He held out his hands in a placating gesture. "Berold, you're my closest friend. If I could have told you I was leaving, I would have. But I didn't know when I went to Adelaide's cottage that she would be missing. I returned to get my traveling things and tell you I had to leave, but you'd already left on the hunt. I didn't have time to leave a message or I would have." He pleaded with his eyes for his friend to believe him.

"I still don't understand why you had to leave." Berold glanced at Adelaide, his shoulders tight. "This isn't the first time a peasant maiden has been lost, so why go after her? Unless it's true that you're seeking her hand? But why would you want to marry a peasant?" His nose wrinkled as if he could smell Adelaide and the scent disgusted him.

Elias stepped closer to her. "It's true, Berold." Elias loathed lying to his friend, but right now the truth would only cause a wider rift between them. "I'm seeking this fair maiden's hand in marriage, so be careful how you speak of her."

He turned toward the stiff young woman. "She has more personality than anyone I have ever met. She is strong and brave and full of deep loyalty and longing."

Adelaide blinked and glanced away, disbelieving his words. But this time, he had spoken the truth. He wished he could convince her of it somehow.

Berold gawked at Elias. "What will your father say?"

"He'll understand. Finding a woman to wed was part of the reason I came to Alesfirth." This wasn't true; gaining the trust of someone and convincing them of the true nature and plight of the dragons was the real reason. Elias still wished Berold could have been the one he told; it would have made so many things easier.

"Why would you want to marry someone from Alesfirth?" Berold asked.

"I've always heard the women there are more exciting." Elias grinned at Adelaide.

She swung the fishing pole around and loosened her hold on the wooden shaft. "This has been a delightful discourse, but I'm filthy and would like to bathe, if that's alright with you, your highness."

Elias balked at her sudden formality. "Of course." He turned to his friend. "And you and Tempest must be weary and hungry. Come with us to the river, and we can talk further."

Prince Elias followed Adelaide back to the water and watched her disappear behind a clump of trees before leading his friend to where Starflare nibbled the grass.

"You do like her," Berold said as he tied Tempest next to the black horse. The two nosed each other in greeting.

Elias rubbed a hand through his hair. "I'm just finding out who she is, which is rather more difficult than I thought it'd be." Besides, he couldn't romantically love this girl; it would hinder too many of his and his father's plans.

He held out some cheese to Berold. "Take this. I have plenty."

After a moment's hesitation, the knight took the food and sat on a log beside him. "Thank you."

"So how did you know where to find me?"

Berold watched the tumbling and bubbling of the river, his green tunic brightening his wearied eyes. "I didn't. I went to Pinhurn three days ago, and some people at the tavern said they saw you in town just the day before. After asking around a bit more, I realized you were no longer in town. So I left right away, hoping to overtake you. I was going to ride through the night, but the snow delayed me.

"The next day, I left at dawn and rode toward the river, for

I was low on ale. I also thought you might stop here for the same reason. I heard voices and rode toward the sound." He shook his head. "I didn't truly believe you were following a peasant until I saw her. Elias, what are you doing? You've never given a thought to women or marriage before."

The prince watched a squirrel scrambling from branch to branch on the opposite bank, wishing, again, that he could tell his friend everything. He settled on a portion of the truth. "Adelaide is different."

No matter how much Berold pried, Elias said nothing else. Berold finally gave up, and Elias wished he wasn't the cause of the hurt in his friend's eyes.

"Where are you and the fair maiden off to next? I hope we won't be traveling far. My body aches from chasing you across the country."

Elias fingered his cloak. "I wish you could come with us, but that's not possible. You must take a message to my father as soon as possible."

Berold straightened. "Pardon me?"

"You must tell my father I've chosen Adelaide and that I need to stay with her until I can earn her trust."

"Elias, you must be jesting." Berold fingered the scar on his hand that he'd received one afternoon when the two boys had played near the rocks at the beach back when life had been simpler. Elias' matching mark itched and made him think of warmth, salty skin, and the words they had exchanged after he grasped the boy's hand in his own—vows to always protect each other as brothers.

"We need you in Dhalion," Berold continued. "There could be a war against Gyndilad anytime. You need protection, and we know nothing of this maiden. Alesfirth doesn't produce the most obedient citizens, as you well know."

"I can protect myself, but I appreciate your concern." Elias grasped Berold's arm. "I must stay with Adelaide, and my father must know what I'm doing."

Berold stood, straightening his tunic and leather leggings. “I will leave now then, your highness.”

“Nay. Pass the night here with us. We have fresh fish, and you and Tempest must rest.”

“If your errand is as important as you suggest, I shall leave at once. And you apparently have no need of me here.” His eyes flicked downstream, then he went to his horse. “Thank you for the cheese, your highness. I will give your message to the king.” He bowed stiffly, untied and mounted Tempest. “Please be on your guard and remember that your country is more important than a woman, however pleasing to the eye she may be.”

“Berold...” Elias strode toward his friend, but the man kicked his horse and disappeared into the trees.

Starflare nickered after Tempest, and Elias sighed. “Berold, my brother in arms, what I’m doing *is* for the good of my country and people.”

Chapter Thirteen

Gunter glanced around at the brown dirt floor and brown straw walls of his home outside Alesfirth. He grew weary of looking at the same color all the time. He stuffed an extra cloak into his satchel.

Conrad entered, carrying a pile of wood. He eyed Gunter's satchel as he set the wood next to the smoking fire. "What are you planning?"

"I'm going to find Adelaide, and don't try to stop me." Gunter stuffed some dried apples into the satchel. "My mind's made up."

"I'm sure she's on her way to Dhalion since that's what she told us at our last meeting."

"I don't doubt it, but Prince Elias is following her." Gunter frowned at the thought of that colorfully-clad, conceited noble chasing Adelaide across the country. The man had seemed nice enough at the Festival, but when Gunter realized he had lied about his identity, only dislike remained. "I don't trust that man, and he could hurt our plans to overthrow his father, especially if he keeps close to Adelaide."

Galiena had told Gunter's mom about the prince's second

visit and quick departure three days ago. Gunter would have left right away, but his father had given him too many chores to slough off, and every time he saw his sister Elysande look at him with her spring-sky eyes, he quailed at leaving her. But Adelaide and the rebellion were more important than staying with his family.

Conrad contemplated him. “You fancy Adelaide.”

Gunter’s cheeks grew hot. “Of course not. She’s my closest friend, and she shouldn’t be traveling across Klinhun on her own, especially with a prince after her.”

Conrad grinned and crossed his arms over his chest. “You still care for her.”

“Yes, as a *friend*,” Gunter clarified.

“Are you going to tell Father you’re leaving?”

“Nay.” Gunter pulled the strings of his satchel taut. “That will be your duty.”

“Mine?” Conrad lifted a stick out of the pile and aimed its blunt end at him. “Why must it be mine, little brother?”

“Because,” Gunter grabbed his own limb and knocked it against Conrad’s, “it’s the least you can do for saying I fancy Adelaide.”

“It’s true, though.”

“It most certainly isn’t.”

They parried back and forth, their wood swords colliding with loud thwacks, their feet sending up puffs of dirt and scattering bits of straw.

As always, Gunter wished he was taller so he could wipe the smirk off his brother’s face with a well-aimed move. As always, he ended up on the ground, a stick poking into his stomach.

“You won.” Gunter shoved his brother’s stick aside and jumped up. “Now will you please tell Mother and Father I’m leaving? Just tell them the truth: that I’m going to find Adelaide because I’m worried about her.”

“Because you love her.”

Gunter punched his brother's arm, and Conrad's smile vanished. "I'll tell them, as long as you keep yourself safe."

"I will. Keep meeting with the rebels and gathering weapons. I'll see you in Dhalion before spring planting." He slung his satchel over his shoulder.

"You're leaving now?"

"Adelaide's already been gone three days."

His brother gripped both of his arms. "Be careful, and don't do anything foolish."

"Why would you even suggest such a thing? Say farewell to Elysande and Mother and Father for me." He swallowed hard at the shock his parents would feel when they realized he had left and at the image of his sister's big blue eyes filling with tears. Hopefully, he would see them all again soon.

"I will. Take care of yourself." Conrad squeezed Gunter's arms, then stepped back.

With a last look at his brother's freckled face and his quaint home, Gunter left to find his childhood friend.

◆ ◆ ◆

Gunter had just lain down to sleep beneath a sky smattered with stars when hands grabbed him from behind and hauled him up.

"What are you doing outside of town in the middle of the night?" A raspy voice with a guttural accent said from somewhere behind him.

"Ow. Let me go." He thrashed against the hands holding him, but they only squeezed tighter.

"I'll knock you out if you keep moving, little worm, then you'll have more than sore arms to deal with." The man holding him placed him on his feet. "Thurdoc, grab the cloth. We don't want this pig squealing the whole way."

Gunter's heart beat as fast as his thoughts. *What did they mean by 'the whole way'? Where were they going to take him?*

What could anyone possibly want with a poor peasant boy?

A piece of cloth tasting of dirt and sweat was stuffed into his mouth and tied at the back of his neck. Gunter caught a glimpse of a man with unnaturally long, greasy blonde hair smirk at him before his face and the stars were blotted out by another piece of fabric around his eyes. The men tied his hands behind his back with a rope that bit into them as if it had an appetite for flesh.

"Get his satchel," the raspy voice commanded.

The hands dragged him along, and after being punched in the face and stomach so hard that he couldn't breathe for several moments, Gunter stopped struggling. He shuffled bowed-over across the ground, his cheek and stomach stinging. Too late he remembered the dagger Adelaide had slipped to him the night of the Festival, now useless in his satchel.

Thinking of Adelaide sent a worse pain than the punches through him. He couldn't get to her now, and what good would he be in a rebellion if he could be captured so easily? If she had been here with him, she would have fought until her captors knocked her out or killed her. Gunter swallowed past his sudden shame; his best friend possessed more strength and courage than he did.

His captors yanked and pushed him onto a horse until he sat upright. They tied his legs to the stirrups so he wouldn't fall off. Other men—two or three—mounted their horses, and he felt someone settling in front of him.

"Follow me, lads," the raspy-voiced man commanded. "The sooner we're out of here, the better."

The horse beneath Gunter bolted, and if they hadn't tied him to the saddle, he would have toppled off. The other men's horses pounded behind him, and he swayed, his hands useless and aching. His stomach roiled with fear as he speculated about what purpose these men could have for kidnapping him.

They rode and rode, the only sound the hammering of

hooves. Gunter's jaw throbbed from clenching the rag, and his mouth burned for water.

When the edges of his blindfold brightened with the rising of the sun, the horse slowed to a walk.

"Welcome, filthy worm," the man in front of Gunter remarked, "to the lovely country of Gyndilad."

Chapter Fourteen

The icy water numbed Adelaide's skin and turned it bright red. No matter how hard she rubbed her skin, though, she couldn't rub what Prince Elias had said about her out of her thoughts. Had he meant what he'd said about her being strong, brave, and loyal? His face and voice had been earnest as he addressed Berold, but he always appeared that way. She squeezed water out of her loose tail of black hair. Why did she care if he had told the truth or not?

"I wonder what Emma would have thought of the prince," Adelaide said to Cyr, who preened his feathers atop a bare cherry tree nearby. "He's closer to her age than mine." She stumbled over slimy pebbles on the river's floor and sat on a rock to dry off before putting on her clothes again.

She rubbed her arms in an attempt to warm up. "Emma would think he's nicer than any other nobility. She'd tell me to stop being so rude to him since he's been so kind to me."

She could almost see her sister's face tilted to the side in exasperation as she said, "Ade, quit being a fool. Do you want to be imprisoned for your impoliteness? The prince only wants to be your friend. It wouldn't hurt to give him the opportunity."

But it will *hurt,* Adelaide argued with her sister's memory. *He and his father are the reason you're dead. If I become friends with him, it will hurt when I have to betray him for our people.*

She watched the rippling river, remembering how she and Emma used to sneak out on warm summer nights and play in the moon-mirror, sharing their hopes, dreams, and fears. The lack of protection from the king was the reason she would never do that again, nor devise new pranks to watch Odo's face flush or a hundred other things.

I must fight the royalty so we can live peacefully, Adelaide thought, though she wasn't sure if she was arguing with Emma's memory or herself now. Emma would want her to fight for their family and people. Wouldn't she?

Adelaide slipped on her undergarments, dress, and cloak, gathered her pole and sack of fish, and made her way back to the horses and prince with Cyr on her shoulder.

Prince Elias was blowing on a sparking pile of dead grass atop a mound of chopped wood.

"Your delightful guest has left?" Adelaide leaned her pole against a tree and set the satchel of fish by the woodpile.

"Yes, back to Dhalion." He glanced at her. "I'm sorry he treated you so disrespectfully. He had no—"

She held up her hand. "I've heard much worse."

"Perhaps, but Berold should have treated you differently. Since he travels with me, he's been around more peasants than most nobles. Growing up in the castle and being one of the best swordsmen in Klinhun is no excuse to behave in such a discourteous way." He scowled at the sibilant flames.

Adelaide wasn't worried about how the man had treated her; she had expected such a response. Instead, she was bothered about his knowledge of her existence. The more nobles who knew of her, the greater chance there was of one of them finding out about the rebellion. Traveling with the prince became more perilous every day.

"I'll show you how to clean the fish now." Prince Elias draped his red cloak on a boulder.

Gutting the fish wasn't much different than skinning the animals Cyr brought her. The hawk kept snapping his beak down, attempting to snatch up a tasty morsel. She finally gave him half of one to eat, which he carried to a nearby willow.

As the fading sun cast a bluish tint to the world and the first stars appeared, Adelaide and the prince stuck the cleaned fish and blackbird on makeshift spits over the now-roaring fire.

Adelaide sat on a boulder near the orange and red hues, enjoying the smell of fresh meat sizzling and the fire's warmth.

The prince sat beside her, gazing into the darkening sky. After a long moment he turned to her. "Would you care to hear a story?"

"No." She needed to contemplate how to escape from the prince and what she would do when she arrived in Dhalion.

"Well, a long, long time ago, when dragons lived in this land with humans, a maiden—"

"I said I didn't want to hear a story, your highness."

The prince turned a smile on Adelaide, irritating her. What was there to smile about?

"I know, but this one you'll want to hear."

"Why do you speak of dragons as if they didn't destroy hundreds of humans?" Adelaide asked the question that had gnawed on her since the prince had sung the song about Klinhun the day before.

He rotated one of the sticks. "I grew up hearing stories about dragons that my ancestors passed down. The stories they told didn't depict dragons as villains, but as friends, companions, and mentors to the humans."

Adelaide stated the obvious. "No one in Alesfirth tells stories like that."

The prince nodded. "It's rare, but not unheard of. An old

man who used to live near my father and me when I was young, Manfred—the same one who taught us to how to fish—would tell us stories about dragons. He also enjoyed listening to my father's tales about them."

He lifted a stick from the fire and examined the crispy brown fish. "I believe these are done. Here you are." He handed her the stick. "What you don't eat keep for tomorrow or another day, as we agreed to."

Adelaide gingerly picked off a piece of the steaming fish and placed the tender white morsel in her mouth. It burned her tongue, but the fresh, tangy meat was the best meat she'd eaten in a long time. "This is delicious."

Prince Elias popped a piece into his mouth. "Not as delicious as the saltwater fish in Dhalion. It lacks flavor, but it certainly fills up an empty stomach."

Cyr landed on Adelaide's shoulder, cocking his head to eye the fish. She was too famished to offer him any of her hard-earned meal, and he took off and landed next to Prince Elias, who gave him some crumbs.

Adelaide didn't like the prince feeding her bird or the way Cyr shuffled closer to him instead of fluttering away, but the warm meal made her concerns seem paltry.

After they'd eaten all but one fish and the blackbird, which Adelaide stowed in her pack for later, Cyr left their company for that of the tree above.

Prince Elias sighed and stretched out his legs. "Are you ready for that story now?"

"Why are you asking if you're just going to tell it anyway?"

"It's polite."

Adelaide tossed a pine needle into the fire and watched it shrivel up like a red worm. "You're the prince. You don't have to be polite."

He laughed. "Royalty should be politer than anyone so they don't unnecessarily anger their citizens or neighboring countries. Impoliteness is how wars begin."

"They also begin from a neighboring country raiding your village and the king not protecting its people." Adelaide regretted the words as soon as she said them; they were too close to the risky subject of the rebellion.

The prince rubbed his face. "I'm sorry about the attack on Alesfirth, Adelaide. My father and I—"

"Did you not have a story to tell?" She didn't want to hear his excuses or think about that terrible day.

"Yes. As I said, the tale was passed down through my family. It takes place when dragons lived in Klinhun."

His gaze wandered over to the drooping willow trees on the far side of the river. "A young girl was walking in the mountains when she slipped on some rocks near a cliff and fell. A male dragon about her age was flying nearby and heard her scream. He caught her as she plummeted toward her death and returned her to her family. The family offered him a gift, but he refused, for he didn't want to take any of their meager possessions, and dragons have little use for material things.

"The male hatchling and the girl struck up a friendship. She rode him often, which was rare because the Rulers of the Sky believed it dishonorable to carry someone like a horse. Many humans had friendships with dragons in those days, but few had them at such a young age, or as close, for the two did nearly everything together. As the woman grew older, she came to love the dragon's strong, brave heart, and he came to love her gentle spirit."

The prince tossed a pebble into the river and leaned against a tree with his hands behind his head. "Supposedly, a dragon and human had never fallen in love before, and there were problems awaiting the lovers, more than just the obvious physical barriers.

"Many humans, including the maiden's family, thought she should marry a human man because the dragon could hurt her accidentally or any other number of things. The woman, however, refused all the men her parents prodded her toward.

"Most of the dragons felt similarly as the human parents, since they choose a mate by fighting, and the maiden clearly couldn't follow that tradition. But dragons are not involved in their offspring's life after the first ten-to-twelve years, so the male's parents didn't present a threat to the couple.

"The male dragon didn't want to accidentally harm the maiden, so, at a loss of what to do, he left to consult with one of the elders. This dragon—one of the oldest alive at the time—was known for his wisdom, and the male spent a long time with him.

"Then the male dragon returned to his lover, filled with hope. He told her what he had learned, then asked her parents for the gift he had refused when he first saved her life—to spend the rest of his life with their daughter. After he explained what he had learned, and the parents mulled it over, they agreed, for they saw the joy the two received from each other. The parents knew they owed the life of their daughter to the dragon."

Prince Elias waved some smoke away from his face. "The young dragon ripped off one of his scales and melted it. He then took the strand of hair the girl plucked from her head and stirred it into the liquid. He heated the mixture over a fire, and when it bubbled, he offered it to the woman. As she drank, he sang to her—for he had the gift of music—and once she finished drinking, the maiden turned into a dragon.

"The mixture came to be known as the Gift of Dragons and was offered once more to a human because of the love that blossomed between the two species. Many humans desired the gift because of the power, longevity, and freedom of the dragons, but the mixture only worked if a dragon and human loved each other enough to sacrifice something for the other.

"The transformation was excruciating for both species. It's said the humans retained the dragon shape for the rest of their lives, though they could transform back into a human if they chose.

"The gift bound the two races closer than before, but it was also the crack that eventually shattered the peace between the two species, since many humans craved the dragons' power."

He turned to her. "Interesting story, yes?"

It was the strangest tale Adelaide had ever heard. She didn't quite know what to make of it, but it had been captivating. "How did your ancestors come up with such a story? They must have had much time on their hands."

"They didn't make it up, Adelaide." Frustration seeped into Prince Elias's voice. "As I've said, this story was passed from the families who lived alongside the dragons down to mine."

Adelaide looked to see if he was jesting with her. His gaze was as solid as a stump, his blue-grey eyes unblinking. He had to be a few onions short of a bushel. There was no other explanation.

"Well, I'm going to sleep," she said. "Goodnight." Turning her back on his intent gaze, she made her pallet under a nearby tree.

Chapter Fifteen

That night Emma's cloak did nothing to protect her from the nightmares.

Klinian knights pursued Adelaide through dark canyons, swords jutting out of their fingers like claws. One man grabbed her. The more she thrashed and kicked, the tighter his hold gripped her arm. Then Emma stood beside her.

Adelaide pleaded with her sister for help, but Emma stayed silent and still, staring at her with large, glassy eyes. Then her sister fell over, blood seeping from a gaping hole in her chest and dripping down her back. Adelaide screamed, but Emma didn't move.

"Adelaide, wake up! You're having a nightmare."

She jerked her eyes open. The horrible images faded, replaced by Prince Elias's concerned gaze. His hand gripped her shoulder too tight, like the man in her nightmare, and his face bore an uncanny resemblance to that of her captor's.

She shuffled away, sweating and panting.

"How can I help? Do you need anything?"

She needed many things, none of which he could give her. She shook her head and gazed at the fire's remains. The dead embers reminded her of the ashy greyness of Emma's skin on the day she died, so she watched the river instead, trying to push away the grisly images. Happy memories seemed as far away as spring.

Prince Elias sat next to her, pulling his cloak close.

Adelaide huddled beneath her own thin cloak and blanket, shivering more from terror than cold.

"I'll tell you a little bit about my childhood, if that will help," Prince Elias offered.

Adelaide nodded.

"Well, I learned how to fish, ride horses, and disobey my father." His gaze floated far away to somewhere she had never been. "Each time I did something wrong, he would barge up to me, yelling. It terrified me. But once his anger faded, he would wrestle with me or take me to the river to swim, apologizing for getting so upset. He was struggling with many changes and had good reasons for disciplining me." He chuckled at a memory.

"Like what?" She remembered her own father stomping to the river to break a limb when she disobeyed him, which had frightened her out of her dress. But she had a difficult time imagining how a pampered prince could disobey his father.

"Oh, plenty of things. Talking back to him, sneaking out of the house to ride or fish instead of learning my letters, getting mud all over Manfred's house...I could go on and on."

"When we moved to Dhalion, my father's anger calmed. But he never stopped lecturing me about how a prince should behave. When I was better at my letters and disobeyed him, he'd have me fill out papers for him as punishment." The prince made a face. "That was much worse than being thrashed, especially if it was a beautiful day outside. But I love my father. He's always wanted me to be a good king and lead as well as he has."

Adelaide shifted, trying not to think about how the father Prince Elias described was the king she would soon rout out of his palace and crown. The prince had described a much different man than the one she'd been imagining.

The prince spoke to Adelaide until dawn about growing up in the castle: of sneaking away from his lessons to throw rocks off the cliff or talk to fishermen at the docks, shooting his first arrow into a fence post too high for him to reach, healing an injured dove and setting it free, playing strategy games with his father, falling into the sea when Berold tried to show him how to work a boat. He spoke in a soft voice like the bubbling of the river, and Adelaide let the light, peaceful pictures dispel the darkness of the night away.

As the sun warmed the sky with a pink glow, she and the prince waded across the river with Starflare. Adelaide held her satchel high and almost fell in the middle where it was deepest, but caught herself in time. Soon they were on the other side, trembling in their wet clothes.

"I'll build a fire to dry us so we don't fall ill," Prince Elias said as he tied Starflare to a cottonwood and gathered twigs.

"There's no need for that. We should keep going." Adelaide longed for this journey, which took her in the opposite direction of where she needed to go, to end, and to leave this man before more of his words could addle her.

"If we fall sick, we won't be going anywhere for a while. We're staying here until we're dry." He placed some wood in a pile.

Adelaide sighed and helped gather kindling. As soon as a blaze burned, she sat as close as she could without getting singed. The warmth did feel good, and soon her clothes steamed and her eyelids drooped.

"Adelaide, we can leave now. Our clothes are dry." The prince nudged her awake sometime later.

They doused the fire and mounted Starflare. The wind stung Adelaide's cheeks as they rode south, away from the Lentiasa River. She hid from the frigid breeze by ducking behind the prince and trying not to brush up against him.

"We should reach the Caverns at midday tomorrow," Prince Elias announced when they stopped by a rocky outcropping that night.

On this side of the river, the land was scattered with boulders and rises and falls of the ground as if the earth had once been flowing water and had stopped suddenly, frozen in time. She knew from traveler talk that to the southeast of them, too far away to see, lay Tancred Forest, the boundary between Klinhun and the country of Neklosa. The forest also stretched north all the way to the town of Kildare—her next stop after the Caverns.

"Good." Adelaide dismounted and helped make a fire.

They ate the rest of the fish and blackbird. While they devoured the food, the prince said, "Tell me about your family. What are they like? I barely met them when I was at your home those two times."

Adelaide shrugged. "They're like most families—irritating and chaotic."

The prince gnawed one of the blackbird's wings. Adelaide had reluctantly shared the bird with him since he didn't seem to have much food left. She couldn't let him starve even if he might be letting their people starve.

"Is Odo your only sibling?" He asked.

Adelaide gulped down her water as if it could wash the sudden agony in her heart away and spilled some on her leg. She coughed. "Yes."

He looked at her, the water spot on her dress, then her face again. "Odo seems like a good lad."

She fingered the end of her braid, thinking with a pang of her brother's big ears and gentle brown eyes. "He is."

"How old is he?"

"Thirteen winters, though he wishes he was Gunter's age so he could pummel him." Adelaide shook her head, smiling. "He loves trying to beat Gunter up, but I think Gunter likes it better because Odo is one of the few people he can fight and win against." She stuffed a piece of fish into her mouth.

"And you and Gunter are...?"

A corner of her mouth quirked up. "You sound like my mother. We're just friends."

"Good. I have no competition then."

"Only me." She whistled. Cyr leapt onto her shoulder, and she gave him the bones from her fish to clean.

"That is quite enough."

Adelaide shifted, and the dagger in her girdle bit into her flesh, reminding her of her purpose out here. She hoped she wouldn't have to use it on him, on anyone. If only the weapon worked on her nightmares.

She reposed by the fire for a long time after they ate, afraid of what visions sleep might hurl at her. Nightmares had haunted her every few nights since the attack on Alesfirth, but the one last night had been more vivid than usual. Her mind had probably picked up the fears provoked by the prince's presence.

He sat nearby, sharpening his sword with a whetstone and humming to himself. When he finished, he stared up at the stars and sang a song too quietly for Adelaide to make out the words.

His deep, rolling voice eventually lulled her to sleep. No monsters plagued her dreams that night.

When she woke, the smell of sizzling meat filled her nostrils and grabbed her stomach's attention.

"Good morning, fair maiden," Prince Elias greeted her from across the fire. When he stood, she noticed bruises under his eyes as if he hadn't slept. "You're just in time for the morning meal. It might be a little heavier than you're used to, but I hope you'll find it to your liking."

Adelaide stretched and walked over to the fire. "What is it?"

"Deer. I found it before dawn wandering over to the east."

"What did you kill it with?"

"My sword." He patted his gleaming scabbard. "It's good for other things besides killing Gyndilians."

Adelaide warmed her hands over the fire. "You've killed Gyndilians?"

"Nay, but there will be plenty to kill soon if they continue threatening war. Here." He handed her a stick with a slab of steaming meat on one end.

The venison was tough but flavorful. Adelaide only ate this much meat on Festivals; traveling with the prince did have benefits.

They left after dividing up the leftover meat between their two satchels. Prince Elias gave her more, but she didn't complain.

After riding through another cold wind and passing many moss-covered rock formations that reminded Adelaide of giant animals, they finally arrived at the Crystal Caverns.

Chapter Sixteen

"This is what you dragged me all the way here to see? A line of rocks?" Adelaide asked. A spiny ridge rose before them like a giant gate to an unknown land. However impressive the massive slabs of reddish-white rocks were, they weren't worth risking her and her friends' lives for. She wished she had left the prince sooner.

"Nay. We're not there yet." Prince Elias guided the horse around a cluster of trees hunched over like her grandmother's back before she had died. They climbed a slight slope, and the rock walls towered over them on both sides. They rounded some boulders, then stopped before an opening as tall as the rock walls hanging over them and as wide as a large house.

"We'll dismount here. The path ahead is easier on foot."

They alighted amid some juniper bushes. The prince tied Starflare to a pine standing as a sentinel in front of the rift in the rock. Adelaide glanced up at the cloudy sky, but couldn't spot Cyr.

"The entrance is just a little way through here. Follow me." The prince turned and entered the narrow gap between the cliff walls.

Adelaide followed and clutched her torn, stained cloak tighter, for the high sheer rocks on either side cast them in chilly shadow. The path wound down, and cacti and bushes on the ground snagged her dress with brittle hands. Once, Adelaide stepped on something that cracked beneath her foot. She reached down and picked up one of the pieces. It was black, smooth, and curved like an eggshell. What in all of Klinhun? She dropped the odd object and hurried after the prince.

He halted and leaned back against the far rock wall, gesturing to a round, dark opening the size of Adelaide's house that led down into the rock opposite him. "That's the entrance," he said. "Dragons found it long ago when exploring these parts of Klinhun. This area used to be where some of them laid their eggs." He glanced around the canyon's floor. "You can still see fragments of their shells."

Adelaide thought of the curved black fragment she had stepped on. Could it have been remnants of a dragon egg? No, it was impossible. Dragons weren't real.

The prince struck something against the rock and faced her with a lit candle. "The true treasure lies inside. Don't be afraid, there's nothing down there but a few bats and beautiful rocks." He strode into the cave without looking back.

Fear, not of the darkness itself, but of being alone with the prince in there, latched onto her. He could do anything to her in such a place.

She fingered the dagger sleeping next to her hips. She would use it to protect herself if she must. She just hoped her fingers would still know what to do with the weapon in the throes of danger.

Cool, musty air wafted up to her as she stepped into the cave. She followed the faint flickering light of the prince's candle down into the winding tunnel. Water dripped somewhere far away and something rustled above her. Probably sleeping bats.

The half-hidden candle didn't shed much light, and Adelaide stumbled often over loose rocks and hit her head once on the suddenly low roof.

"Be careful." The prince turned back to her, the candle's shadows dancing on his face. "I forgot this is your first time in a cave. Would you care to hold the candle? You'd lose the use of one of your hands, but you'd be able to see better."

It was tempting, but Adelaide would rather keep the use of her hands in case she needed to defend herself. "I'm fine, your highness."

"Very well. We don't have much farther to go."

The prince was correct; after snaking down a few more steps, the tunnel opened up into a large, dark cavern.

Adelaide followed the prince into the chamber. Her eyes widened with wonder.

Every surface of the domed cavern sparkled and gleamed where the golden light caressed it, sending hundreds of mini rainbows in every direction. Even the ground beneath her feet was a solid, scabrous white crystal.

Adelaide placed her hand on the crystalline wall to her right, feeling the beautiful heads poke her hand. If she pressed any harder, they would draw drops of blood.

"Lovely, is it not?" Prince Elias asked.

"Yes," she breathed, not able to keep her eyes off the glittering walls winking at her like an all-seeing star. Emma would have loved this place. Adelaide swallowed past the pain spreading from her heart up to her throat.

"They're beautiful, but rough and painful if handled improperly, much like a certain person I know."

Adelaide turned to him. The candle flame cast his face in shadow.

She fingered the dagger under her cloak, her stomach writhing with fear. But he hadn't done anything yet and the cavern was so stunning; she couldn't keep her eyes off the dancing reflections. "So, what kind of rock is this?"

"The dragons called it Star-Stone, for obvious reasons. I don't believe the humans have a name for it. The rock isn't valuable like diamonds or silver, but just as beautiful. More so, perhaps." His eyes roved over the crystals.

"There's more through here." The prince strode to a crevice in the curved, glittering surface that Adelaide hadn't noticed before because of the rocks' radiance.

Another chamber, smaller and boxier than the first, twinkled like the moon on a river's face. She had never seen such a magnificent sight as these two rooms hidden deep underground and wished Emma could have been there to enjoy it with her. Her sister would have loved the way the crystals came alive when lit from the candle's glow.

"Why haven't I heard of this place before?" Adelaide asked.

Prince Elias shrugged. "The Caverns fell out of memory after the dragons left, probably because humans found gold and silver in the Spearhead Mountains."

"Are there more such chambers?"

"A few. The tunnel we traveled through opens into other caves farther down, but they're smaller, and the Star-Stone doesn't shine as brilliantly as in here." He touched a part of the rock that bulged out and glowed as if lit with fire deep within. "It's legend that the dragons who first found this place were originally looking for hot pools to—"

"Please stop talking about dragons," Adelaide said, studying the play of the candle's luminosity on the crystals.

"Why don't you want to hear about them?"

She faced him. "Because they don't exist. And even if they did, they destroyed our people."

Prince Elias' grip tightened on the candle, but his voice remained steady. "If there was a struggle between humans and dragons, don't you think there would still be evidence of it today, even centuries afterward? The earth would take a long time to heal from such devastation. And do you truly believe humans could win against creatures that can breathe fire, fly, and possess teeth and claws sharper than any sword or spear?"

He breathed deeply through his nose. "Nay, the dragons left of their own accord. They had no desire to harm their friends and companions."

Adelaide stared at the prince, confused and surprised by both his words and strong emotions. Why did he care so much about dragons?

She hefted her satchel higher on her shoulder. It was time to leave this noble with his strange tales of a long-forgotten past and pursue her own future.

"Well, it matters not. They're gone now, and I'm leaving as well. I've kept our deal and must make haste to see about that medicine for my father." She turned and entered the main chamber, the prince's candle behind her barely illuminating its hidden beauty.

Adelaide was loath to leave the serene splendor, but it was time to continue her travels. Alone.

With a last glance at the crystal walls, she entered the dark tunnel, wishing she had asked the prince for the candle before leaving. But it was too late now; she would have to feel her way up.

"Adelaide, wait. I can accompany you to Fernohn. You shouldn't travel alone," Prince Elias urged, the passageway brightening as he drew nearer.

Adelaide entered the solid darkness. He *had* helped her, but he was still the noble she was planning on overthrowing.

With her hand trailing one side of the cave, she made her way slowly and blindingly up, cursing each time she bumped her head on an overhanging rock or sliced her hand on part of the wall. She fell twice but continued on.

Finally, she made it out of the cave, blinking in the sudden brightness. She wound back through the narrow cleft in the ridge, relieved to be in the open air again. When she reached the place Starflare was tied, she tore a piece of fabric from her dress and bound up a wound on her arm where a rock had slashed it during one of her falls.

She glanced up at the sound of a bird's cry. Cyr sat on a branch of the pine tree, staring at her with his dark, knowing eyes.

"There you are." She held out her un-injured arm and clucked at him. "Come on. We're going to Kildare, and not even a prince who talks of dragons as easily as speaking of the weather shall stop us."

Chapter Seventeen

When Elias reached the pine where he had tied Starflare, he kicked it so hard its branches shook. His thick leather traveling boots protected him from the pain he should have felt.

Starflare snorted and stepped away.

"Forgive me, girl." He stroked her nose and sighed. He shouldn't be surprised that Adelaide had left; she'd been fleeing since he met her. But he thought he'd been making progress on building a friendship with her and, yes, had even enjoyed their interesting, albeit rather one-sided conversations.

But then he mentioned dragons, and she had closed up like a turtle, surprising him that she could hide even tighter in her shell. The quick dismissal had pricked him more than it should have.

Elias rubbed his hands through his hair. He should have picked someone else to confide in, but it was too late now. He had to keep trying to earn this woman's trust. Perhaps he shouldn't mention dragons around her until he earned it. Yes, that's what he'd do.

He untied Starflare, made sure the glass vial he always carried in a pocket in his cloak hadn't broken when he kicked the tree, and mounted. "Come on, girl. We have a maiden to catch. But there's no need to hurry; she's only walking, after all."

That night Adelaide made camp near some boulders and chewed a few roots she had recognized from her mother's herb lessons. She was too weary to start a fire, so she drew the blanket the prince had given her close to ward off winter's breath. The ridge of rock stretched ominously above her.

As the cloak of night was thrown over the sky, Adelaide glanced at the empty boulder beside her. Somehow the night felt barren without the prince's solid presence beside her. There would be no songs to relax her mind or strange tales to draw out the poison of her nightmares.

Stop it, Adelaide, she scolded herself. *You're trying to overthrow or kill his father, and when that's done, you might have to kill the prince himself. Don't forsake your sister and your people now.*

Fortunately, Adelaide didn't see Prince Elias the next day, nor the next. At least, she told herself it was fortunate. On the third day after leaving him, she reached the Lentiasa River once more. The sight of the familiar gurgling waters warmed her like seeing an old friend. She found a shallow section and crossed without slipping or cracking the thin sheet of ice encasing the water.

On the other side, wooden and straw houses emerged, and a longing ache for her own home filled her. She hoped her parents weren't too worried about her and that Odo was staying out of mischief.

Outside the second house Adelaide passed, a man around

her father's age plowed the dirt, his sweat-stained tunic rolled up to his elbows.

Adelaide strode over to him. "Excuse me, sir?"

The man stopped and looked at her. "Yes?"

Adelaide stepped closer, the fresh-tilled dirt crumbling beneath her boots. She lowered her voice, her heart knocking against her chest. "I'm from Alesfirth, and some of the peasants don't agree with the treatment they receive. I was wondering if you and the other peasants here in Kildare feel the same."

The man's unruly eyebrows pushed together, and he waved a hand at her. "I don't want none of that talk here. I'm just a simple man trying to earn a simple living for my wife and kids. Now leave and don't come back." He glared at her, and Adelaide clutched her dagger. The man bent over his plow once more and shoved it along the ground.

Adelaide left. The man's cowardice nauseated her and was another reason she had to stand up for her people. Most of them were too frightened to do it themselves. Fear threatened to consume her at times as well, but Emma's memory and that of her starving family and neighbors kept her moving toward Dhalion.

Cyr landed on her shoulder.

"If I don't stand up for them, Cyr, then who will?"

He nipped her fingers as she stroked him, which was all the answer she was going to get from him.

Not far from the short, thick wooden wall surrounding Kildare, a group of five chatting peasants neared her from the direction of the open gate.

Adelaide ambled toward them, her last encounter fresh on her mind. She'd be more cautious this time. "Good day," she said when the group neared her. "I'm not from around here, and I'd like some news about the area."

The group stopped and stared at Cyr. One of them, a short man who reminded her of a tree stump, stepped closer. "Why don't you go to the tavern? There's always news to be found there."

"You look like you know just as much as anyone, and perhaps," she glanced around, but didn't see anyone else in sight besides the guard at the gate who was too far away to hear, "I don't want my words overheard."

The man shifted under her gaze and glanced uneasily at Cyr's sharply turning head.

Another man in the group asked, "What do you want to know?"

Adelaide swallowed. "Only how it fares here with the people. I hail from Alesfirth, and many of the peasants there hurt for food and other essentials."

A few of the women whispered among themselves, their eyes wide.

"Were you there when the village was attacked?" A woman with a mushroom-like nose said. "Do you know how many people were killed? I heard it was two hundred. Do you think the Gyndilians will return? Is it possible they could come here?"

Adelaide wound her braid around her finger. "I'm not here to discuss the attack. If you want to know more about what I'm planning to do about the conditions we live in, meet me on the east side of the gate at nightfall. Then we can discuss—" she stopped at the sound of approaching hoofbeats.

"What is going on here?" A knight rode up on a tan horse with a black mane and tail, his sword clanking against the silver plates covering his legs.

The tree-stump man stepped toward the knight. "Sire, we were on our way back to the fields after the market, when this maiden, who's not from here, stopped us for news of Kildare."

The knight turned suspicious eyes down on Adelaide. "Where are you from? And what brings you here?"

"Alesfirth, sire. I'm on my way to Fernohn to find medicine for my father who has a bad back." Her heart beat like a frightened rabbit's, and she fought to keep her outward demeanor as calm as a hunter's.

The knight's gaze shifted to Cyr. "Where did you get that hawk?"

Adelaide swallowed. She should have sent him away before the knight arrived. Now it would just look suspicious. "I found him near my home when he was a hatchling and nursed him back to health. He's been with me ever since." She fought the urge to clutch Cyr's legs protectively.

The knight frowned. "You shall come with me to see Lord Wymund." He turned to the others. "The rest of you, get back to the fields. There's still several more hours' worth of work before dusk."

The group of peasants murmured their assent, and with curious glances at Adelaide, strode off in different directions.

"Come on." The knight said as he dismounted and grabbed her arm, his other hand holding his horse's reins.

Adelaide walked beside him, her hands sweaty and trembling. She thought through every escape option she could think of, but she wouldn't be able to win against the lord and all his guards with only a dagger. The lord wouldn't believe her story about Cyr, and she couldn't leave him to the nobles.

Only prison or a painful punishment awaited her inside those gates.

Chapter Eighteen

Townsfolk stopped and gawked as the knight led Adelaide through Kildare. The people no doubt wondered what she'd done and if it was bad enough to elicit a hanging.

Adelaide didn't dwell long on the possibilities of her fate; she was too busy scouring her mind for escape options.

"Halt sir, if you please," a voice behind them said.

The knight turned, dragging his horse and Adelaide with him.

Of all the apples! she thought when she saw who the voice belonged to. Prince Elias sat astride Starflare, as regal as if he'd just stepped off a throne. Even though his persistence could be the death of her, a flare of hope ignited at the sight of him. She tried to stamp it out.

"Good day, Prince Elias." The knight bowed to him. "I was taking this lass to Lord Wymund. She has a hawk that can't possibly be hers as she claims. It must be stolen."

Prince Elias glanced at Cyr still perched on her shoulder. The bird darted into the sky, and the prince returned his gaze to the knight. "Well, the bird's gone now, and there's no telling when it will return. I've spent some time with this maiden and can attest that she poses no threat to you or the town. I'll take her from you now."

Adelaide frowned; she wasn't a sack of flour to be traded back and forth between two merchants.

"But, your highness—"

"Farewell, good knight. You should return to your post now. One never knows when a band of Gyndilians might come rushing in." The prince held out his hand to Adelaide, but she mounted without his help. He nodded once more at the blinking knight and turned Starflare away, passing to the right of the stone dais.

"You should stop fleeing me every chance you have. It's quite wearisome," the prince told her.

"I could have rescued myself," although she wasn't sure how. "And besides, I still don't know the real reason you insist on following me. You could just want to add me to your collection of maidens."

The prince ignored her second remark. "Yes, you were doing a mighty fine job of rescuing yourself there, straight to the noose."

"I was trying to decide which course of action to take."

Prince Elias laughed. The deep gushing forth of his joy, and her relief at avoiding potential death, even if it meant being rescued by this infuriating man, made Adelaide smile. He glanced back and a tender look came over his strong-jawed face.

"Watch out!" Adelaide yelled.

The prince turned around and jerked the reins right as a little boy darted into Starflare's path. Starflare bobbed her head up and pranced to the side. The child, unconcerned or oblivious to what had almost occurred, scurried into his mother's waiting arms on the other side of the road. She shot them a glare before vanishing into the maze of buildings.

"What a great rescuer you are, almost trampling a child." Adelaide placed a hand on her stampeding heart.

The prince took a long, slow breath. "I'm sorry. I shall pay better attention to where we're going in the future."

They continued at a slower pace, and Prince Elias didn't look back at her again. She didn't know if she was more shaken from almost trampling a child or from the warm look he had bestowed on her.

They stopped outside the log tavern, and the prince tied Starflare to a post. "I'll buy you a drink to help you recover from that incident. But I also stopped Lord Wymund from punishing you, so I'll only buy it for you if you promise not to run away again today."

His reasoning seemed a bit flawed, but Adelaide didn't plan on leaving town again today anyway. She needed to meet with more villagers since the ones she had met outside town most likely believed she'd be maimed or dead before nightfall. "Very well, if you insist."

"I do."

Adelaide scowled but followed the prince into the dimly lit tavern.

"I'll get us something to drink," he said and made his way to the sharp-boned woman behind the counter.

Adelaide sat on a rickety stool at a corner table, ignoring the curious glances of the other customers—mostly merchants and knights. She was glad there were only two peasants in the tavern, for she wouldn't be able to convince them to join her rebellion since they'd seen her with the prince. She just hoped they wouldn't blab too much.

"Here you are." Prince Elias set a mug of ale in front of her. "It's a little late for the midday meal, but I was able to coax the barmaid to hand over some food left from their repast." He set a plate topped with a loaf of brown bread and creamy white cheese on the stained wooden table. "It's for both of us, so try not to eat it all." He sat across from her and sipped his ale.

Adelaide stared at the food. The prince's generosity and

continued interest bewildered her. What did he want from her? For to act so to a peasant—or anyone that you hardly knew, for that matter—must mean he wanted something from her. But what could a peasant have that a prince would want besides companionship for the night, which he clearly didn't have in mind?

He tore off a piece of bread, put a hunk of cheese on it, and placed it in his mouth. After swallowing, he said, "Now show me your arm."

"My arm? Why?"

"The one with the cut. I want to see how bad it is."

"It's fine." Adelaide reached for some cheese with her uninjured arm.

Prince Elias sighed. "I'm not going to chop it off. I just want to see how badly you're injured."

He probably wouldn't stop pestering her until she did, so Adelaide laid her left arm across the table. The cloth she had wound around it at the cavern two days before was stained an ugly brown.

"How did this happen?" He asked while untying the makeshift bandage.

She watched his large, warm hands probe the scabbing skin, his touch gentle. A ring on his hand—glimmering gold inset with a red jewel—caught the light from the window, throwing dancing rosy rays across the table and throwing Adelaide back in time.

Emma, fifteen winters old, and Adelaide, a winter younger, watch the parading lords and nobles with other wide-eyed children. This is the first time they've seen anything so fine as the king's entourage of bird-bright nobles and rose-plaited horses.

"That one's my favorite," Emma points out a noble dressed in a deep red cloak astride a bay, with matching red thread woven into its mane.

"Why?" They all look the same to Adelaide—a fantasy of

people who seem to have sprung alive from the stories Emma tells every night.

"I love the red. It's so rich and beautiful. I wish I could wear colors that bright instead of these greys and browns." Emma plucks at her light-grey dress.

Adelaide hasn't thought much about the colors she wears. "Why can't you?"

Emma sighs, watching the parade of brilliant people disappear into the city. "Because we're peasants, Ade, and we don't have the money to buy that kind of fabric. All our money goes to the lord."

Adelaide knows this but hadn't connected it to the clothing they wear. "When I'm grown, I'll become rich and give you all my money so you can wear whatever you like." She doesn't know how, but she'll at least try.

Emma smiles and places her head on Adelaide's shoulder. "If any of us could, Ade, it'd be you."

Then, later, oozing red pouring from the gash in Emma's side, draining away her life and the future she could have had.

The sudden onslaught of memories left Adelaide sweaty and shivery. She pulled away before the prince could notice. "I told you it wasn't bad, just a surface wound." She took a piece of the nutty bread and tried to still her shaking hands around its warmth.

The prince sat back, his now-grey eyes as gentle as his hands had been. "It still needs to be covered so it won't become infected. And you didn't mention how it happened."

"I slipped in the cave. I didn't know you were a healer as well as a prince."

"I used to practice healing more when my father and I lived with Manfred. Do you want me to ask the barmaid if she can spare a cloth or—"

"Nay. I can take care of it." Adelaide ripped a short piece off the bottom of her cloak and wrapped the faded wool around the wound.

"That's one way to do it, I suppose." He watched her with a grin. "Now, I—"

"Prince Elias? Your highness? May I possibly have the pleasure of asking your esteemed personage a humble question?" A short man bumbled over to them, bobbing and fidgeting with a tan knitted cap.

The prince turned to the peasant. "Yes? What would you ask?"

The man dropped his eyes to his hat. "Well, it's just that, well, this winter's been a hard one, you see, for my family and I, and, well, I was wondering if..." his voice faltered into silence.

"If I could help?" Prince Elias asked, his face grave.

The peasant's eyes flickered up to him. "Yes, your highness."

"Have you taken your concerns to Lord Wymund?"

The man bobbed his head. "Yes, your highness."

"What did he say?"

"He, well, he didn't say much. He said everyone has had a rough winter, even the nobility, but I, well, I don't believe that's the truth, if you'll pardon me saying so."

The prince rubbed a hand through his wavy brown locks. "Very well. I shall discuss it with him tonight. What is your name?"

"Gaillard, your highness. And thank you, your highness. My family and I are in your debt forever." With a little more fidgeting and bowing, which Adelaide thought might send the man tumbling onto their table, he bumbled out of the tavern.

Prince Elias gestured at the man's retreating back. "See, some people still have faith in the king and prince of Klinhun."

"That's because they have nowhere else to go. Will you truly ask Lord Wymund about that man's situation?"

"Yes, though I fear it won't help." He stared into his mug. "Lord Wymund is a just lord compared to some of the others, but he doesn't often concern himself with individual peasants and their problems."

"That's not surprising." Adelaide wondered if the man named Gaillard would want to join her cause. She didn't know if she could trust such a blundering, timid man with their secrets, though.

Silence like a plague had struck the tavern. Adelaide glanced around. Those who hadn't been staring at her and the prince now did, and she shifted under their curious gazes. She didn't need any more unwanted attention, especially from the wealthy. The prince seemed not to notice; he still gazed into his mug as if it held the secret to the world's woes.

The door banged open, and a group of boisterous knights entered, laughing and punching each other in the shoulders.

"Prince Elias?" One of them said, noticing him. "I didn't know you were coming to Kildare. Does Lord Wymund know you're here?"

The prince glanced up. "Good day, Serle. Nay, he doesn't. I only arrived in town a short while ago."

"And who is this fine lass? She's one of the nicer-looking peasants I've seen lately." A knight with splotchy skin grabbed Adelaide's chin.

She jerked away. "Touch me again, and you'll no longer have any of your fingers."

The knight who had grabbed her crossed his arms and grinned. "She's feisty too. Just the way I like them."

"Leave her alone," Prince Elias growled.

"Yes, your highness. She's all yours." The knight held up his hands. "I already have a lass for the night anyway."

The man named Serle turned to the prince. "If you don't mind my asking, your highness, why are you eating here at the tavern with a peasant?"

The prince glanced toward the door, spinning his empty mug. "I've told you many times before, Serle. Peasants make up the majority of our population and should be treated with dignity and respect."

"As you say, my prince," Serle said, then muttered something to the man beside him, who laughed.

A knight behind Serle asked, "Are you going to hunt with Lord Wymund while you're in town? I hear he recently acquired some new hawks."

Adelaide thought of Cyr and was relieved he had flown away before anyone could capture him. Hopefully, he had enough sense to steer clear of town.

"Nay. I'm not staying long."

Serle glanced at Adelaide, then back at the prince. "You never stay long, your highness."

"There's much to do as ruler of this country." He stood. "My friend and I must leave now, and I'm sure all of you would like a place to sit."

Adelaide ignored the knights' gazes as she followed him. The men whispered among themselves as Prince Elias and Adelaide walked toward the entrance, and she heard the words, "never understand him," and "rough peasant girl" before the door slammed shut behind them.

Outside, the prince stretched his shoulders and gazed up at the cloud-streaked sky. "The knights here wear me out. They act like boys, not men, most of the time. I'm sorry for how they treated you."

She shrugged. "They're knights." She glanced around at the oak buildings cast in the fading glow of twilight, wondering how she could evade him to talk to some peasants before they closed the gates for the night.

"I'm going to take Starflare to the stables and speak to Lord Wymund about that man Gaillard. You may come along if you'd like."

He had just handed her the opportunity she needed. "I have some things I need to take care of, but thank you, your highness."

"Please call me Elias. It sounds so much better," he said.

She looked away from his cloudless blue eyes.

"I sometimes tell stories when I come into town, though now I mainly listen since the villagers aren't too fond of my tales." He mounted Starflare, and Adelaide had to tilt her head more than usual to see his face. "So come to the dais at nightfall if you'd like to listen. The stories are always interesting. The people will most likely be merchants and nobility since the gates must remain closed at night, but it'll be worth your time."

"Will you come find me if I'm not there?"

He grinned. "Do you want me to?"

Adelaide gave him a look, and he chuckled.

Starflare pawed the ground, and the prince stroked her neck. "I won't come looking for you if you don't come, but I will be saddened if you're not there. Despite what you may think, I do enjoy your company."

She wasn't sure what to say to that.

"Farewell for now, Adelaide."

"Farewell."

Prince Elias rode away, his red cloak flapping behind him like a wing.

Chapter Nineteen

There weren't many peasants in Kildare at this time of day, and the few Adelaide saw were on their way home from the market and didn't have time or the desire to speak to a stranger.

She did spot, after wandering aimlessly for a while and earning a few suspicious glances from the guards, two peasants around her age—a male and female—speaking together outside the battered tavern.

"Good evening," she greeted them. "May I speak with you?"

The man eyed her. "What about?"

Since Adelaide knew nothing about the pair except that they were peasants (which was almost enough information in itself), she decided to probe their feelings about the peasant-king situation before diving straight into the rebellion. "I'm not from here and am wondering how Lord Wymund is as a ruler."

The girl's eyes darted about at Adelaide's words, but the noise from the tavern covered their conversation from listening ears.

"Where are you from?" The young man asked.

"Alesfirth. A few of the peasants there don't agree—"

"You're from Alesfirth?" The girl's blue eyes widened with sympathy. "I'm so sorry. We heard about the attack. It was horrible and—"

"I'm not here to talk about the attack," Adelaide snapped. Speaking of that day would unearth too many painful memories. In a softer voice, she said, "I'm here to see if the peasants of Kildare are weary of the lord's and king's selfishness."

The young man glanced at the girl before turning his gaze back to Adelaide. "Life's not easy, if that's what you're asking. I work on the farm all day with my father and younger brother, and we still barely have enough crops to give Lord Wymund, much less enough to feed ourselves. And my sister," he glanced at the maiden, "has recently begun serving in the Lord's hall as a cook for a few extra coins. But it's still not enough, and it's only when we can spare her at the farm."

"Ten children have already been lost this winter. That's double last year's," the girl said, her tired face somber.

Adelaide nodded, her heart heavy. News had reached her family before she left of six dead children due to lack of food. "And there's always the possibility of an attack from Gyndilad, of course. The king has already shown how incapable he is of protecting us from our northern neighbor." She clenched her teeth at the memory of the bodies littering the streets after the attack.

"The rulers of our country don't deserve to hold their positions any longer. So, are you two willing to fight with me and some folk from Alesfirth and Pinhurn to overthrow the king?"

The young maiden stared at her open-mouthed, but her brother stood straighter. "If you have men, as you say. I don't want to watch our people suffer anymore. We're all going to die if the nobility keeps ignoring us, and I don't want this hard life for the family I'll soon have."

The girl stared at her brother. "Maynard, you could be killed. Think of Yvonne."

"That's why I need to do this, Rose. I'd rather die fighting to have a better life than die watching you and Yvonne and Galin and Mother and Father slowly work yourselves to death. We're treated like animals, not people, and it's killing us. It's just not right!" He pounded his fist against his thigh.

Adelaide nodded; this young, fiery man would be a perfect addition to her group. "You're right. But we need more people and weapons before we can do anything. Talk to your neighbors, friends, anyone who might feel the same way and scrounge up any weapons you can find. But be careful. The simplest mistake can lead to your death and the death of hope for the people of Klinhun."

The man nodded, and the girl gazed at Adelaide with fear-filled eyes.

"Meet me in Dhalion in the spring with anyone you've convinced to join us. Others from Alesfirth and Pinhurn will be there as well, and we'll take action to create a better Klinhun."

"I'll be there," the lad named Maynard replied, nodding.

"Good. I'll meet you in Dhalion soon." She strode away.

She ambled around a bit more, but the knights were closing the gate, and darkness had swallowed the sky. Since there were no other peasants to talk to, she made her way to the dais in the center of town. A small fire flickered in the middle of the stone circle, and a few men and women sat on benches around the writhing flames.

Prince Elias sat between a man in an embroidered orange tunic and a woman robed in a flowing purple dress that was partly covered by a heavy yellow shawl. Golden gems sparkled around her naked throat in the fire's glow. The woman and the prince were speaking.

Intrigued, Adelaide stepped closer to the pair, remaining

in the shadows. She didn't know anything about the prince's love life, or if he even had one. She had assumed he didn't, since he spent so much time chasing her and saying he wanted to marry her, but she'd heard plenty of tales about nobles' secret love lives.

"Oh, do tell a story, your highness. Yours is the richest voice of all these men," the purple and yellow clad woman begged, leaning toward him.

"But don't tell one of dragons, unless it's about them killing humans or humans attacking them." A man on another bench said. "Those others you tell are too sappy and boring."

The other men murmured their assent.

"Or you could tell a love story," the woman next to the prince purred, leaning close to him.

Prince Elias rubbed a hand through his hair and gazed at the star-studded sky. "There once was a man, a man with incredible strength and power. But these attributes weren't enough to save the people he loved from a disastrous end of death and despair. In order to do that, he had to leave his beloved people to seek aid elsewhere. He had to give up his power and strength and become someone else. It wasn't easy, but necessary to save them. So he left his home and his loved ones behind and journeyed across the sea to another land.

"Once he arrived at the shores of this land, he met a beautiful woman with the heart of a hawk. She too longed to bring peace to her people but sought it in a different way than the man. She sought to help her people with weapons and quick action.

"Although the two clashed about the best way to save their people, they gradually learned to trust each other. When the man helped the maiden by protecting her and fighting for her oppressed people, she aided him and his people by standing up for them. In saving each other's people, they fell in love and lived out the rest of their days in joy and peace."

Nothing stirred except the shimmering crystal star-specks

overhead and a sense of unease in Adelaide's stomach.

Then a whiny voice broke the quiet. "Is that all?" The young woman in the purple dress pouted. "It barely had any romance at all."

"I enjoyed it," a woman in a green dress across the fire said. "Please tell another, Prince Elias."

He stood. "I'm weary from my travels, and Lord Wymund is expecting me for the evening meal."

"Come with us to the tavern for a drink first," the man beside the prince said. "Lord Wymund will understand. I can send someone to tell him."

"Yes, please come with us," the woman in purple implored. "Father will understand."

"Oh. What are you doing here, peasant?"

Adelaide had been slinking back into the shadows as the men discussed going to the tavern, but not fast enough. Three men had left before the others and spotted her sliding around the corner of a building. They held a candle up to her face.

She rose to her full height—as tall as them both—and attempted to speak confidently without fear leaking through her words. "I was listening to the story, if you must know."

"Why were you doing that?" One of the men, a squinty-eyed fellow, asked. "No one asked you to come."

"I did, actually." Prince Elias marched down the steps toward them. "And I'm glad you came, Adelaide." His face melted into a smile as he looked at her.

The three noble-women watched the exchange, and when the prince grinned at her, their looks turned predatory.

"Why would you do that? Her dress looks like something a servant would clean a table after supper with," the young woman in purple said, stepping closer and scrutinizing Adelaide.

"And look at all that filth on her face. It's probably cow dung. She smells like it too," another maiden observed, covering her nose with a silky pink handkerchief.

Adelaide fingered her concealed dagger, but it wouldn't help her against the poison in these women's voices.

The men had grown bored and were ambling toward the tavern, but the women continued their fun, glancing at Prince Elias every so often, encouraged by his silence.

"Do you peasants ever bathe?" The woman in the green dress wrinkled her pale nose. She stepped close to Adelaide, forcing her to take a step back.

"When we're not working from sunup to sundown to provide you with food," Adelaide said through clenched teeth.

"Don't even attempt to blame us. At least you have work and food." The maiden in purple tugged at Adelaide's dress. "I don't understand how you can wear these rags. Do you, Prince Elias? Peasants are good for only two things in my opinion: work and serving us."

Adelaide bit her tongue so hard she tasted blood. She would have hit the girl, were it not for the knights making their way to the tavern behind her, and that this was apparently Lord Wymund's daughter.

"Their brains are too small they can't do anything else," one of the women taunted.

"If they tried to learn the things we did, their heads would shrivel up."

"They keep bothering my father about how little food they have to eat, but if they labored more and complained less, they wouldn't have that problem. I mean, why is this girl here listening to stories when she should be at home with her family? Peasants are always sly. They can't be trusted. We have to keep pushing them so they don't get lazy."

"I'm amazed any of you females can find husbands. But I guess male and female pigs look and smell alike."

The three women continued to berate Adelaide and peasants in general while Prince Elias stood to the side, a silent, still form in the darkness. Adelaide's anger, at him, not the women, swelled as his silence stretched.

She knew it. He was just like all the other selfish, prideful nobility, no matter how much he said otherwise.

Finally, the women tired of their game and flitted to the tavern. The prince didn't respond to their calls. Adelaide marched into the frigid night, tears blurring her vision. It was time to desert this dung-heap of a town and prince. The knowledge that Prince Elias was just like all the other nobles—no worse, because he had lied outright to her—froze her heart into ice.

Adelaide knew it was cruel, but she longed to make the prince feel a tiny bit of the sharpness searing into her. She stopped at the stables and unsheathed her dagger.

Elias was shaking. Not with cold, not with fear, but with a molten-hot rage erupting deep inside and rushing through him. He had to leave Adelaide this once, though he longed to go after her and speak truth to her, to pick up the lies the women had hurled at her and burn them. There would be time for that later. Now, he had to leave before he killed someone.

He ran into the night that felt as fiery as the sun's surface, a scream rising inside him, demanding to escape.

Chapter Twenty

Gunter's mouth was as dry as dirt in a drought. Someone brought him water twice a day along with moldy bread, but it was barely enough to wash down the crusty food, much less quench his parched throat.

He sat on the stony ground since it was more comfortable than the splintery, rickety bed against the wall. His Gyndilian captors had thrown him into this filthy cell two days after capturing him. He didn't know where in Gyndilad his kidnappers had taken him; they'd kept him blindfolded the entire journey, and he wasn't familiar with the geography of the country. They hadn't traveled far, though, so they must still be close to Klinhun's border.

Gunter kicked at a rat, wishing there were other prisoners nearby. He hadn't heard anyone, though he often perceived shouting outside, horses snuffling and stomping around, and wagons rolling by. If Adelaide were here, she'd have a plan, even if it was desperate and rash.

He remembered when she first told him about her plan to rebel. Gunter had walked over to her house with a basket of mulberries shortly after Emma's death. Adelaide hadn't been home, and as soon as he offered her family his condolences and the berries, he found her at the river. It was the second time he had seen her since the attack—the first had been at the funeral, when she had stared at her sister's grave with a lost expression that clawed his heart.

At the river, Adelaide was hurling a dagger at a tree, mostly missing. But her eyes were narrowed and her face screwed up in concentration, as if it was the most important thing in Klinhun to land the dagger dead-center in the bark.

"Where did you get that?" Gunter asked.

Adelaide retrieved the dagger from the grass. "I took it from the blacksmith's table when he wasn't looking."

"Why?"

She glanced at him, and the anger and longing that sparked in her eyes and the way her hands squeezed around the dagger, as if to choke it, frightened him more than the dagger itself. The Adelaide he knew had been swallowed up by this fierce, enraged one. "I have to do something to help our people. The king didn't protect us from the Gyndilians, even though he knew it could happen. He doesn't care about us, so we need to find someone who does, someone who'll protect us instead of standing by, watching the Gyndilians slaughter us."

"And you're that person?"

She turned and threw the dagger at the tree. It hit the trunk and fell into the grass. "Do you see anyone else taking up the job?"

"How can you help our people with one dagger?"

She retrieved the dagger and shrugged. "Not alone. If I can find enough people who feel the same way I do—which I'm sure I can—we could rise against King Ganelon and put another king, a kinder man, in his place." She stared at the weapon in her hand. "Or we don't even have to set up a king. There might not be anyone good enough."

"But doing what you're suggesting could lead to our death."

Adelaide had wanted to change the peasant-noble situation for a long time, but this was the boldest thing she'd ever said, and the first time she had a specific plan of action.

She stared at him, her voice pleading. He wasn't sure if she was trying to convince him or herself. "I know. But we have to try something, Gunter. A hundred people died at least. And if the Gyndilians attack again, more will die, and our town will be destroyed. Even if the Gyndilians don't return, we can't keep living this way, with the nobles stomping on us, always demanding more. It's killing us, and not just physically."

Gunter went home that day with Adelaide's words reverberating in his mind. The truth of them excited and frightened him, but the hope of changing their lives for the better had triumphed over his fear. Several days later Adelaide told Conrad her desires, and the next day they were planning a rebellion.

A key jingled in the door to Gunter's cell, and he jumped up. The guard always put the food and water in a slot at the bottom of the door, so maybe someone would finally tell Gunter what was going to happen to him.

A thin, pale man with greasy black hair entered the cell. "Come on, boy. The Master wants to see you." He grabbed Gunter's arm.

"Master?" Gunter's voice croaked, and he coughed. "Who's that?"

"You'll soon find out."

The man led him out of the stone building into the chilly air.

Gunter squinted in the harsh sunlight and stumbled while trying to keep up with the man. Once his eyes grew accustomed to the bitter winter light, he tried to make sense of his surroundings. To his right several armor-clad men aimed crossbows at bales of hay near the far end of a barren field. The sight of the odd, yet all-too-familiar weapons took him back to the attack on his home.

He, his father, and Conrad had just taken a break in the fields to eat their midday meal when they heard screams and hoofbeats from the direction of town. They and the other serfs stopped working, looking around in bewilderment, wondering what the clamor was about. Then a man pointed to a horde of figures on horseback riding as if to surround the town, and Gunter's father shouted, "Make haste! Alesfirth's being attacked. Grab anything you can use for a weapon."

After picking up a shaft of wood, Gunter ran with his brother, father, and the other men to town, wishing he could turn back and protect his mother and sister, and yes, hide from the terror invading Alesfirth.

The village was a frenzy when they arrived; Gyndilians galloped over the cobbled street, knocking people over, hacking at anyone in their way, and shooting arrows from the sickly accurate black bows—one of which whizzed right over Gunter's head—women screamed, knights shouted, bodies fell on the living and the dead, blood splayed, and the stink of sweat and gore made him vomit onto the red-painted dirt.

But what most tormented his dreams and waking thoughts was the sound of Adelaide's wailing. Its desperate, shocked sound had sliced through the other noises like a butcher's knife straight into his chest.

When Gunter jerked a step toward the wrenching sound, his entire body quaking, an unhorsed Gyndilian thrust a sword at him. Gunter met the soldier's sword with his stick, and when he yanked it back, he fell and hit his head hard on the ground.

When he came to a short time later, his father stood over him with a bleeding arm, and the Gyndilians were fleeing. Why they left without burning the entire village down, Gunter still didn't know.

His mother and sister had wept when the men returned home, bleeding and pale, yet alive. Conrad and Gunter let their father tell them what had happened while they cleaned up.

The images of mangled bodies and the cries of women, men, and children were harder to wipe away than the blood and dirt. The brothers still couldn't talk about that day. Gunter never mentioned it to Adelaide. He was too frightened the topic would push her farther from him than her sorrow and anger already had.

"Come on, boy. The Master's not patient." The thin, pale man tugged Gunter after him.

The guard led him along a dirt road to a granite building that stretched taller than any Gunter had seen. Two soldiers in silver and black armor stood before the massive oak door, their faces stoic. They stepped aside to admit Gunter and his guard.

The two entered an expansive room with a high wooden ceiling. Rugs displaying various hunting scenes covered the floor. Swords, silver shields patterned with a diving black bird with outstretched talons, and deer heads obscured the stone walls. Just one of those deer heads could feed his family for two days. Adelaide's heart would race at the sight of the weapons. Perhaps he could bring her back one—if he managed to escape.

At the far end of the room in front of a blazing fire, three men supped and chatted at a glossy wood table.

"I brought him as you said, Master." The man pulled Gunter to the table.

A man with a drooping brown mustache and sharp nose stood and walked to the edge of the table, leaning over them. "Very good, Heward. You may leave."

Gunter's guard bowed his head, turned, and walked out the door.

"So, this is the one you brought from near Alesfirth, Warin?"

"Aye, Master," a man with curly dirty blonde hair replied. Gunter recognized the raspy voice from his abduction and couldn't stop a shiver from racing up his spine.

The man called the Master towered over Gunter and scrutinized him with eyes the color of river-silt. Gunter tried to stand tall and straight, but he shook slightly from lack of food and had never been impressive to look at.

"So, what will it be, Master?" The man who had kidnapped Gunter—Warin—asked. Gunter's stomach rumbled at the sight of the juice running down the crisp turkey-leg he held in one hand. "Experimentation or fighting?"

Gunter trembled. *Experimentation?* What were they doing in Gyndilad? And what had the man meant by fighting? Surely they didn't want Gunter to fight for *them*—the ones who had killed his friends and wounded his loved ones. That would be madness.

The Master strode back behind the table, his long black cloak whipping behind him. "Experimentation. He's too short and scrawny for fighting."

"What are you talking about?" Gunter's voice came out too high, and he swallowed. "Experimentation for what?"

The Master plopped a tomato into his mouth. "Wilfrid, return him to his cell. You will leave tomorrow at dawn for Gindar with this worm to begin his life as a test subject." The man looked at Gunter, his muddy eyes filled with contempt. "Then he will never see Alesfirth or anyone he cares about again."

The man named Wilfrid, whose scraggly black beard matched the rest of his scraggly outfit, came toward Gunter.

Gunter's heart thudded through his whole body. They were going to take him farther into Gyndilad, farther away from his family and friends. He couldn't leave Ade alone in Klinhun with the prince following her. He couldn't leave the rebellion either; they needed every man, even a short and scrawny one. It was a doomed and desperate plan from the beginning, but perhaps the spark just needed a little air to blaze into a bonfire.

As Wilfrid placed a hand on his shoulder, Gunter gazed at the Master, hoping he wasn't making a huge mistake. "Wait. There's something I need to tell you."

Chapter Twenty-One

Adelaide thrust all of her grief and fury into the ride, urging Starflare to run until the horse's flanks foamed with sweat and her own legs were limp and sticky from squeezing the horse so hard. She then continued at a walk, seeking to put as much distance between Prince Elias and herself as possible.

It had been almost too easy to steal Starflare; the nobles should take better care of their mounts. The single guard had nearly been asleep on his feet at the stable's entrance, so she knocked him unconscious with a move Conrad had taught her. Her dagger had been unnecessary, thankfully.

Adelaide had put the prince's engraved leather saddle on Starflare and led the horse out past the unconscious guard.

The main gate would have been too heavily fortified, so she crept to the nearest wall, keeping to the shadows and thanking the sky for the peppering of clouds that obscured the moon.

She followed the stone wall, looking for a weak spot or opening. Toward the center of town, a tree's roots had grown under a section of the stone, pushing it up until it crumbled. The barrier was still tall, but shorter than the rest of the wall.

She walked around the entire town, making sure there was no other gap in the stone, then stopped before the collapsed section holding Starflare's reins.

"I sure hope Prince Elias taught you how to jump," Adelaide murmured, gazing at the stone wall that was shorter than her but still imposing in its solidity. She had only jumped once before—over a log on a friend's horse, which had been much shorter than this barrier.

Adelaide mounted Starflare before she lost her nerve, glanced around to make sure no one was nearby, then urged the horse at a gallop toward the suddenly impossibly high-looking wall.

Starflare made it over, but Adelaide nearly didn't. She slipped to the right and had to grab the horse's mane to hoist herself back on. Then she pressed the mare as if each hoof-fall could stamp out the hurt and disappointment the prince had lit inside her.

When dawn snuck into the sky, Adelaide stopped near the gurgling Lentiasa River. The road was only a few paces to the north, on the other side of the river, but she didn't want to encounter anyone.

If someone saw her—a maiden in a torn dress sitting on a saddle inlaid with gleaming silver—they would probably take her straight to the lord of Kildare if they didn't steal the saddle first. She probably should have used a different riding tack, but the prince's had been the closest to the stall and would hurt him that much more.

Adelaide stood for a long moment beside Starflare under the pines, her legs shaking, her chest heaving in time with the horse's. When she could move without fear of falling over, she tied Starflare to a birch near the bank.

She washed her face in the frigid water, took several deep draughts, and filled her animal skin. The pre-dawn greyness was too quiet without the prince's rich voice filling the forest with song. The help he had given her and the stories he had told floated into her mind as she gazed at the whooshing water.

Adelaide shook her head. He was the man she had thought he was at the beginning—just another self-inflated noble—and now she was free to continue her rebellion. This thought didn't bring relief, though, only a surprising hollowness.

After unsaddling and grooming Starflare, Adelaide whistled for Cyr. He landed on one of the birch's silvery branches and peered down at her.

"At least I still have you, right, Cyr?" He rustled his feathers in what she took to be agreement.

Too exhausted to eat the meal she had missed, she fell asleep clutching Emma's cloak to her cheek.

The night after Elias had fled the noblewomen into the forest, he woke early. Thankfully he hadn't killed anyone in his all-consuming rage, but a few saplings outside of town would probably never grow straight again. The only time he remembered being that angry was when he first heard the tale the Klinians told about the Dragon War.

He had been eleven winters old, stepping foot into the King's City of Dhalion for the first time. He hadn't been the Prince of Klinhun then, just a wide-eyed and open-mouthed boy staring at all the novel, fascinating sights.

Men yelled out prices of fish and tossed the still-wet products to grabbing customers. People dressed in vivid colors jabbered to each other while flowing in and out of the stalls like the seawater sweeping the shore nearby. The crowds brought with them the scents of sweat, flowery soap, and sunlight.

His father paused beside the stone dais where a group of elegantly dressed men and women sat or stood, their attention riveted to someone on the dais. Elias stuck his head past a woman in a gauzy yellow dress and saw a man telling a story with profuse hand motions in a booming voice.

The story was essentially the same as the one told at every Fire Festival, except with more killing, blood, and fear.

The mental images of dragons slaughtering innocent humans because they had turned vicious, and the sight of the people nodding and murmuring as if they believed what the man said, shocked the smaller Elias. He balled his fists and stepped toward the group, not knowing what he would do, except somehow make them believe the truth.

His father set a hand on his shoulder to stop him, his own jaw clenched. "Come on, son. Violence won't do any good."

Elias regretfully followed his father away from the crowd, determined to change the story someday.

Now, he missed his father's determination, his leathery pine scent, and their long, late-night talks. He wished he could speak to him about Adelaide instead of waiting for Berold's reply to the message he had sent. Hopefully, soon he could ask for his opinion in person.

Elias walked under a cloudy, cold sky to the stables to feed and groom Starflare. Then he'd find Adelaide and ask for her company. Perhaps she would consent if he tempted her with another free meal. He needed to tell her how sorry he was for the women's remarks last night and why he hadn't vouched for her.

Outside the squat building that housed the horses, a man in the yellow and blue colors of Klinhun lay sprawled on the ground.

Elias stooped and shook the unconscious man's shoulder. "Sir, are you alright?"

The man opened his eyes and stared at Elias.

"What happened to you?" Elias asked. "Were you guarding the stables last night?"

The man placed a hand on his head and groaned. He staggered up with Elias' help. "Ow. That scoundrel hit me rather hard."

"Perhaps you should remain seated."

The man shook his head, then grimaced. "Nay. I'm fine, your highness. And yes, I was on duty here last night."

"Where was the stableman?"

"I'm not sure, but he's very fond of ale and sometimes doesn't make it back to the stable before morning."

"What happened?"

"I was just standing here when a fist came out of nowhere, knocking me out. I didn't come to until just now."

"Did you see your attacker?"

The man rubbed his swollen cheek. "Nay. It was dark and happened quickly. The man must have been hiding in the shadows or something."

Elias swept the ground with his eyes, but no hints hid there. "Do you know if the person took anything?" He stepped into the stable, and the man followed him.

"Nay. As I said, I didn't hear or see anything once I was hit. The man had a strong arm."

Elias' stomach dropped to the floor when he saw that Starflare's stall was empty. He glanced at the shelf across from her stall. Someone had taken her saddle and bridle as well.

He rubbed his hands through his hair, muttering curses. There was no mistaking the culprit. After the escapade last night, no one besides Adelaide had such a strong reason to steal his horse, nor dare such an endeavor.

Elias pulled his wavy locks until his eyes smarted from the pain. Was Adelaide worth all this frustration? Would she ever believe him about the dragons? Maybe he shouldn't have kept his mouth shut last night, but if he hadn't, he would have exploded in a fiery rage, which wouldn't have been good for anyone. Oh, why in all of Klinhun was Adelaide so reckless and narrow-minded?

Elias ground his teeth, contemplating throwing her in prison until her hair turned grey and her teeth fell out. But if he did, he'd be giving up on an alliance between dragons and humans and condemning them both to death.

"Your highness? Is something not to your satisfaction?" The guard asked with chary eyes.

Elias took several deep breaths to calm down.

"Your attacker stole my horse," he ground out. The guard didn't deserve his title if he hadn't noticed that yet, or perhaps he was still out of it from his fall.

The man's gaze landed on the empty stall. "Oh. I am so sorry, your highness. I shall tell Lord Wymund, and we can—"

"No." Elias held up a hand. "Don't tell Lord Wymund or anyone else what happened. This is my problem, and I shall take care of it." Elias didn't want or need anyone from Kildare following Adelaide. He must pursue her until, at least, he recovered his horse. Then he could decide whether to earn someone else's trust or not.

The man gave him a puzzled look, then dropped his eyes. "Yes, your highness."

Elias regarded the five horses munching oats or sleeping. "I need a mount that won't be missed as soon as possible."

"Of course, sire." The man saddled a grey gelding and led him out of his stall. "I believe this one is called Suntaria. He belongs to Oger, who rarely ever rides. He shan't be missed."

"Good." Elias took the reins. "Now get me some provisions as swiftly as you can." He gave him some coins.

The man took them and left.

The prince mounted the still-sleepy horse and waited, wrapping and unwrapping the reins around his hands.

When the man returned, Elias put the food in one of the saddlebags. "Thank you. I'm off to find your attacker. If Lord Wymund asks where I've gone, tell him I left to attend to some urgent matters that have come up in Dhalion." He leaned down to the guard. "Remember, tell no one what happened. The truth will come out in time, as it always does."

The man bowed. "Yes, your highness. Have a good journey."

Elias squeezed the horse into a walk. Outside of town, he stopped, although he ached to kick his heels into the horse's side and fly after Adelaide. But speed wouldn't do any good if he was riding in the wrong direction.

He knew Adelaide wasn't truly going to Fernohn to find medicine for her father; she didn't have enough money or goods for such medicine, and Fernohn was known more for its mining than its healing herbs. Also, that whole incident of telling Gunter to meet her somewhere stank of deception.

So, where would a lone woman with a dagger, a deep distrust of nobility, and a heart raging with pain go?

An idea lit like a twig on fire in his mind, and an abysmal fear filled him. He hoped he was wrong.

Elias turned Suntaria east toward Tancred Forest, where the road wove to Dhalion. He kicked the horse's flanks. Suntaria bolted into the trees as if death were chasing him. And indeed, it might be.

Chapter Twenty-Two

Adelaide stretched. It had been a rough few hours. The monsters in her nightmares had returned with sharper teeth and longer talons, and Cyr, her last protector, had failed at rescuing her from their greedy grasp.

"Thanks for nothing," she teased him where he sat sleeping with his head tucked behind the fluffy feathers on his back.

She felt more refreshed after washing her face in the river, though the water did nothing to wash away thoughts of a certain annoying prince.

Today was her third day in the Tancred Forest, and she hoped to reach the end of it before nightfall. Then, after several more days, she would come upon the Wymar River that flows out of the Spearhead Mountains and follow it north to Fernohn to speak to the villagers. After she convinced some to join her, she would ride along the Wymar River back south. Perhaps she would have time to speak to the outcasts in the Canyon Lands before she finally made her way to Dhalion.

Adelaide's stomach squeezed, and the dagger seemed to burn into her back when she thought of the King's City and what would happen there. But she didn't have a choice; she neared the town more every day, and the peasants in Klinhun were depending on her, even if they didn't know it yet.

She would have to leave Starflare somewhere before entering Dhalion since someone would undoubtedly recognize the horse. Although—Adelaide gazed at the streaks of dirt and sweat marring the horses' black coat and the pine needles populating her mane and tail—Starflare looked more like a peasant's horse at the moment than a prince's.

Adelaide finished eating the squirrel Cyr had brought her last night, wishing she had time to fish. He now stared at her from a low pine branch, awakened, no doubt, from the smell of fire and the squirrel.

"Nay, Cyr. This squirrel is mine, and it's too small to share."

He gave a sharp cry, then flapped over her head before disappearing into the sky.

A few moments later, a branch snapped nearby, and Adelaide immediately thought of Prince Elias. Fear and a desire to see him battled within her, so that she didn't see the form gliding toward her until the person was only a few paces away.

A woman in a deer-skin cloak smiled crookedly at her, revealing four missing teeth. "Good day, dearie. Someone as lovely and young as you shouldn't be traveling all alone."

Adelaide scrambled up, dropped the half-eaten squirrel, and pointed her dagger at the woman. "Don't come any closer."

"It would be much easier if you put that dagger on the ground," a man spoke from behind her.

Adelaide turned and swore.

About fifteen men on foot surrounded her. They must have snuck up through the trees while her attention was on the woman. Had Cyr tried to warn her before disappearing?

The men all wore cloaks crafted from animal skins, and

some of them had what appeared to be animal teeth and claws strung around their necks on leather bands.

Adelaide had heard of robbers in the forest, but hadn't thought they would care about one skinny peasant girl. She reached slowly for her satchel on the ground, her other hand still aiming the dagger at the woman. It wouldn't do much good against sixteen people. But she had to try. "You can have all my coins." All three of them. "They're in here." She held up the sack.

A man with black fur boots and a wide face laughed. "Oh, we'll take your coins, little lass. And your horse, and you."

Adelaide's heart sped. None of the stories she'd heard had mentioned robbers taking live prisoners. They'd always stolen a person's goods, then left them for dead or killed them. Capturing people was too risky, not to mention pointless.

"Why do you need me?" She asked, trying and failing to keep the fear out of her voice.

"Because," the woman grinned, her few remaining teeth as yellow as corn kernels, "our way of life has changed. We no longer merely steal and kill. Now we kidnap. The Gyndilians pay well for Klinian travelers. And that's where we're taking you, lassie, all the way to Gyndilad."

Adelaide's stomach revolted, and she clenched her teeth to keep the squirrel inside. They would have to kill her before she stepped into that cursed country—the country of her sister's killers.

"Griselda, stop telling the prisoners where we're taking them." The man with the black boots scowled at the woman. "It makes them harder to control."

Them? They had taken other innocent Klinians to that cursed country? Adelaide couldn't fathom what these people were thinking, if anything. She gripped her dagger so hard her knuckles almost popped through her skin.

The haggard woman shrugged. "They're going to find out soon enough."

"Enough yapping. Bind her, get the horse, and bring the satchel. No one touches the saddle and bridle except me," the black-booted man commanded.

The men now had daggers and bows knocked with arrows pointed at Adelaide. There was no way she could escape. Even if she managed to mount Starflare, they would injure the horse or her before they could disappear.

She couldn't spot a speck of mercy or kindness in the men's eyes, only cruel brutality. Well, she would make it as difficult for them as she could.

Adelaide hurled her dagger at the closest man. It sunk into his stomach, and he stumbled.

She dropped to the ground, but not fast enough. Agony ripped through her leg as an arrow pierced her thigh.

A man grabbed her shoulder and put a hand on her mouth. "They want you alive and unhurt, but we can always lie about what condition we found you in."

Adelaide kicked back hard with her uninjured leg, squinting against the pain in her right thigh, and made contact with the man's leg.

The grip on her loosened, and she jerked free.

Three men stood before her. She did the first thing she could think of. She fell to the ground again—this time her leg screaming at the hard contact.

Someone grabbed her hair and yanked her up.

Adelaide swung her arms and managed to hit a man's face. Someone grabbed her arms and shoved them behind her. The man tied them tight, and Adelaide gritted her teeth. She lunged to the side, and a man punched her in the stomach so hard she dropped to her knees.

"Just knock her out," the man in boots said as if she was a wily pig.

Adelaide attempted to stand despite the deep throbbing in her stomach and leg, but a fist slammed down on her from above, and the fight was over.

Chapter Twenty-Three

The salty sea air and jovial greetings didn't cheer Berold as they usually did when he returned to Dhalion. Exhaustion dripped off him, and irritation at Elias for forcing him to explain the prince's capricious whims to the king prickled him.

It wasn't unusual for nobles or princes to neglect their duties to chase a beautiful woman, but it was highly unusual for Elias. Even though he was marrying age, he barely looked at women, let alone chased them across the country.

Berold trotted up the stone road he and Elias had often ambled down together. The towering trees on either side waved bare, callous arms at him. A raven cawed from one of the branches. He soon reached the top of the cliff where the brown stone fortress shimmered in the afternoon sun like a sandcastle. He left his horse with the stableman and entered the drafty interior of the fortress.

Despite its chill, Berold found the flickering torches, stained-glass windows, wide halls, and rich tapestries comforting and familiar.

"Where's the king, Frederick?" Berold asked a knight standing beneath a curved entranceway.

"In his chambers, sire."

Berold nodded and climbed the winding stairs at one end of the front hall. Near the top, he entered a hallway covered in thick blue and buttery-yellow rugs. He stopped before a man guarding an iron-enforced oak door.

"I need to see the king, Leifer. It's urgent," Berold explained.

Leifer stepped inside, his chainmail clinking. "Swordmaster Berold Huntington to see you, your highness."

"Let him in," a distracted voice said from within.

The guard beckoned Berold in and shut the door after him.

"Your highness." Berold knelt before the varnished cedar table covered in piles of parchment and quills.

"Please, join me, Berold." The grey-haired man clothed in an azure cloak gestured at a padded chair across from him, and Berold sat gratefully. "I could use a break from this monotony of paperwork, and you must be weary and hungry from your journey. I didn't expect to see you so soon, though your face is a welcome sight."

King Ganelon turned to the thin woman beside him. "Ascelina, please bring some food and wine for our swordmaster."

The woman disappeared through a small wooden door behind her.

"How was your journey?" King Ganelon moved his papers to the side and leaned back, his iron-blue eyes sweeping over Berold. "And where is Elias?"

Berold swallowed. King Ganelon was a fair and benevolent king. He didn't grow angry very often, but when he did, it was frightening to behold. And the man loved his son more than anything in the kingdom.

Berold forced his voice to sound smooth and confident. "He gave me a message for you, your highness."

"Yes? What is it? Don't worry, Berold, I won't pounce on you." The king chuckled, but twirled a quill over and over again.

Ascelina returned and placed a plate of roasted chicken and herb potatoes and a goblet of wine in front of Berold, then left at a nod from the king.

Berold took a sip of the bitter red wine, hoping it would settle his nerves. He set the drink down and cleared his throat. "I found Elias at the Lentiasa River. He told me to inform you that he has discovered the person he wishes to earn the trust of. He's going to stay with her until he gains that trust." Berold didn't know what he was saying, but hoped the king did, or else this visit and his hasty ride would be pointless.

King Ganelon leaned forward, clutching the quill tight. "You found Elias at the river? How did you two become separated?"

"Several days after the Fire Festival, Elias went to see a peasant girl in Alesfirth he had taken a liking to. He told me nothing of the visit, for I was with some nobles at the time. The next day he went back to the lass's house, but told me he was just taking Starflare for a ride. When he didn't return, I went around town asking about him, and when I learned nothing, I went to the serfs.

"Late that night I came to a peasant family who said the prince had come the day before and asked their daughter, Adelaide, for her hand. But later that night she disappeared. When Elias went to see her the second time, they told him what had happened. Elias apparently promised them he would find her and bring her back." *What a foolish thing to promise*, Berold thought.

"Elias had already left to find her when I arrived late that night at their house. Several days later I came upon Elias and the lass—about ten days ago now—at the Lentiasa River. I tried to persuade the prince to return with me, but he wouldn't leave the maiden. He told me to give you the message that she was the person he had chosen. So I left right away, and here I am."

The king stared at Berold as he took some bites of potato,

then asked, "What is your impression of this lass?"

Berold took another sip of wine. "I don't know her well. But from what I've perceived, she, like most people in Alesfirth, distrusts nobility." He remembered the way she had held the fishing pole at the Lentiasa River, as if she wanted to spear him with it, and grimaced. "She's a peasant, of course, and doesn't appear to have much interest in your son."

The king gazed past Berold, spinning his ink-stained quill again. Then he snapped it in half. "I told Elias to choose a male noble, not a lass who has a nice face and a fear of nobility." He stood and strode to the diamond-paneled glass that overlooked the sea. "We don't have time for this," he growled.

While chewing the chicken, Berold tried to puzzle out the king's words, but couldn't. King Ganelon and his son were different from everyone else, but he had become used to their oddities over the years and knew they wouldn't answer him when he dove into questions about their past. They always brushed aside his inquiries or said the knowledge came from stories their ancestors had passed down. This had annoyed Berold when he was young, but now he attached these mysteries to the painful events surrounding the death of the king's wife.

"How does he think he can gain the trust of a woman who's a peasant from Alesfirth? Those villagers hate us more than anyone else in this country." King Ganelon rubbed a hand through his silvery-brown hair. "A war's about to begin here, and it's worse there than I first thought."

"Worse where?"

King Ganelon turned back to him, his eyes bluer than a sunlit sea. "Berold, you must find Elias and tell him to return to Dhalion now. There's no time. The situation both here and over there becomes stormier every day. Elias and I must leave before it's too late."

"Leave? Where would you go?" Berold tried without much success to keep the frustration out of his voice.

King Ganelon waved aside his question. "I don't have time to explain, though I wish I could. Perhaps one day I will." He sat back behind the table and leaned toward Berold. "I hate to make you leave right after you've arrived, but this matter is of the utmost importance, and I trust you the most out of all my knights."

Berold took a large bite of potato, washed it down with wine, and stood. "Of course, your highness. I shall leave at once."

King Ganelon shook his head. "Wait at least until you've had a proper meal, a bath, and some rest. You do smell, after all." He wrinkled his nose, and Berold laughed.

"You may leave tomorrow at dawn. Take your best knights with you. When you find my son, tell him what I just told you, and do whatever you must to bring him back, though try not to hurt him." His eyebrows sunk low over his eyes.

"Of course, your highness."

The king sighed, suddenly looking a hundred years old. "Thank you, Berold. You will be rewarded for your faithfulness." He gazed out the window with troubled eyes, and the swordmaster left the chamber.

This time, Berold would knock Elias out and drag him home tied up hand and foot if he had to. He didn't understand everything that was happening, but the worry in the king's eyes was enough to send fear galloping through him.

Adelaide awoke and groaned. Her head felt like dough that had been kneaded too many times, and her leg roared as if someone had ripped it open with a knife.

She lay in a cave dimly lit by embers. Several of the outlaws that had kidnapped her slept sprawled on the ground under heavy blankets. Her hands remained tied behind her back and were crammed against a rock, making them numb.

Someone had tied her legs with rope, and as she shifted them, a bandage around her thigh tightened where the arrow had pierced her.

Adelaide slowly shifted to a sitting position, wincing as her wound stretched.

A breeze whistled through the dark opening a few paces away, bringing the scent of snow. She shivered under her wool cloak. She had no idea where she was, how long she'd been out, or where her things were, but the longer she stayed with the robbers, the more difficult it would be to escape. She had no intention of being a prize pig handed off to those who had killed her sister and so many others.

Adelaide braced her hands against the rock behind her and heaved herself up. One of the men snorted, and she froze. When no one woke, she hopped toward the entrance.

Bouncing caused the cut on her thigh to split open. Adelaide clenched her teeth to keep her whimper inside. After a pause, she shuffled forward, tripping twice and having to catch herself each time against the cave wall. As she drew nearer the opening, she saw snow pit-pattering from the swollen grey sky.

Before Adelaide could step outside, a man approached her from the opening. His eyes were flat, and a chunk of his nose was missing, making him look oddly misshapen. "Good morning, lass. I'm glad you finally decided to join our merry little company."

"I didn't decide anything," Adelaide replied, her voice scratchy. "You kidnapped me and my horse. Now let me go. I'm not worth your trouble." She wished she had her dagger; she felt naked without it this close to an enemy.

The man stepped closer, and she backed up against the cave wall. "You might not be worth the trouble, but you're worth the money." He fingered a piece of her hair, and she jerked away. "The Gyndilians won't even know all the damage I plan on doing to you." His eyes roved over her, and Adelaide shuffled to the side.

"Leave me alone." She hopped farther away. Her voice and body trembled as much as a newborn horse's legs.

The man grabbed her arm, and she tried to pull free, but his grip was too tight. She wished her legs weren't bound so she could kick him.

"Let her go, Ligart." The man with the broad face and black boots approached from outside, snow sprinkled in his hair and a small deer over his shoulders. "We don't have time for that, and the Gyndilians don't want the lasses ruined."

"They won't know," the knick-nosed man said, eyeing Adelaide as if she was a tasty morsel.

"They're more intelligent than you. And if you ruin her, I'll throw you out of this band." The leader glared at him, and Ligart released her. He stalked farther into the cave.

"Get back to the fire," the leader commanded, and Adelaide obeyed, quivering from the encounter with the knick-nosed man. Her desire to escape escalated with her terror.

The leader, whose name she learned was Hildebrand, might have saved her from Knick-Nose, as she called Ligart in her mind, but treated her like a pesky animal and rarely spoke to her. He jested with his men while the venison cooked. The crisp, smoky smell filled her mouth with saliva.

"Don't give her too much," he told Griselda, who fed Adelaide chunks of the venison since her hands remained tied. "She'll be more compliant if she's weaker. The Gyndilians might pay us more if she is, and we'll be able to travel faster."

After five pieces of meat the woman took the food away, and Adelaide's stomach clenched in disapproval. She hadn't eaten much the day she was kidnapped, which she hoped was only the day before. The woman poured some water into her mouth, and she sucked avidly at the trickle of tepid water.

The woman said nothing to Adelaide while she fed her and changed the bandage on her leg, except, "Here," "Be still," and "This might hurt." No empathy or mercy glimmered in her gaze, but since she was a woman, she might sympathize with Adelaide more than the others.

"Griselda, please let me go. I'm only a peasant, and I won't tell anyone what you're doing," Adelaide whispered, hoping the woman wouldn't hear the lie in her voice.

The woman shook her curly ash-colored hair. "Can't do that, lass. You're gonna make us all richer than nobles." She leaned back and cackled. Adelaide realized the hope of an escape was all on her, which wasn't very comforting, since she didn't have any weapons or the use of her hands and feet.

An image of Prince Elias in his shimmering red cloak bearing a sword flashed through her mind. The image vanished as soon as it had appeared. He didn't know where she was and wouldn't come to the aid of a peasant like her, especially since he hadn't come to her defense against the noblewomen in Kildare.

Once the men finished eating, they rolled up their blankets and gathered their satchels.

"Put the fire out and cover your footprints. We won't be returning here for a while," Hildebrand said, fingering some arrows. A bow and full quiver was slung across his back.

A man with corded muscular arms hauled Adelaide to her feet.

"Ow," she said. "I'm quite capable of standing on my own."

He just gazed at her expressionlessly, keeping a firm grip on her arm.

The men sauntered out of the cave, sacks and weapons slung over their shoulders. None glanced at her except Knick-Nose, who leered.

"Where's my satchel?" Adelaide glanced around the cave, panic climbing up her belly. Emma's cloak was the only thing she had left of her sister besides memories.

"You have no need of it anymore." The thick-set man pulled her toward the entrance.

"I just want the cloak that was in it, to help keep me warm

at night." She shivered as she walked out into the snowy day.

The man marched her through the snowdrifts to Griselda. The men led horses out of another cave, and Adelaide's heart sank when she saw Starflare. She had wanted to hurt the prince by taking his horse, but didn't want the once-lovely mare to end up in such coarse hands. At least they hadn't captured Cyr. She gazed up at the heavy clouds, blinking against the snowflakes, hoping Cyr soared high in freer skies.

"You want this old, tatty thing? You miss your Ma?" Griselda said, holding up Emma's cloak.

"Give that to me." Adelaide strained against the bonds on her wrists, but they didn't give way.

"Here ya go. It won't save ya now." The woman threw it in the snow.

Adelaide knelt in front of the cloak to reach back and grab it. Someone kicked her in the back, and she fell into the snow, face-first. The men and Griselda laughed.

"Not so tough now are ya, all wet on the ground?" A man with old-man eyebrows leaned over her.

Anger flared in Adelaide, and she arched up and bit his nose so hard she tasted blood. The man yelled and punched her cheek, sending her reeling backward. She spit out the man's blood, grabbed Emma's cloak, and stuffed it awkwardly into her girdle.

"You're a beast!" The man she'd bitten thundered, holding his bleeding nose.

She was the beast? They were the ones who had kidnapped her and wanted to sell her to the Gyndilians as if she were a ripe piece of fruit.

Griselda tended to the man, and from atop a russet horse with furry white hooves, Hildebrand declared, "Someone muzzle her so we can go."

The man with the huge muscles gagged Adelaide and lifted her onto a dun. She didn't have enough energy to fight back; her thigh throbbed and her cheek ached where the man had punched her. But at least she had rescued Emma's cloak.

The muscled man sat in front of her. Apparently, he was her own personal guard. Everyone mounted, and a man behind Hildebrand held Starflare's reins since no one rode her.

Two men rode directly behind and to the side of Adelaide and her guard, probably to make sure she didn't throw herself off or to pick her up if she did. And she might have tried if her body hadn't already felt like the lightest touch could splinter it apart. The rest of the men and Griselda rode ahead, in a line behind Hildebrand.

They rode past snow-tousled hills toward the Spearhead Mountains thrusting out of the ground as if trying to rip the sky apart with their jagged edges.

As they rode into the swirling, white landscape, Adelaide kept hearing the man she'd bitten in her head saying, *You're a beast*.

She saw Emma in her mind's eye—a honey-haired woman who always dwelled on the good and gave out kind words. She wondered what her sister would think of her now if she saw her: a woman who threatens people, bites men's noses when they call her names, and plans to lead men to their deaths.

Was she turning into a beast? Sorrow and rage freezing her heart so that not even the memory of Emma's comforting hugs could melt it?

Chapter Twenty-Four

Weary to the depths of his bones and hungry to the bottom of his belly, Elias halted and dismounted Suntaria the third afternoon after realizing Adelaide had stolen Starflare.

"You're a good horse, Suntaria." He placed a hand on the gelding's dappled-grey neck. "But I miss Starflare. She's been with me since my early days in the castle."

She'd been a gift from his father when they moved to the fortress in Dhalion years ago.

King Ganelon had gazed down at the then twelve-year-old Elias. "You can choose any horse you'd like."

The young prince stared with amazement at the horses of all colors and sizes munching grass in the outdoor pasture next to the stable. "I can choose any I wish?"

His father chuckled and ruffled his hair. "Yes, son. Then you can finally learn to ride as you wanted to at Manfred's." Elias had loved Manfred's stocky grey pony, but wasn't allowed to ride him because the pony had been too old.

He gawked at the sleek animals, overcome by his choices. He didn't know so many different kinds of horses existed in the world.

"We have several good coursers," the stableman remarked, pointing out two elegant horses, one with brown spots and the other a cream color. "They are light, fast, and strong, and excellent for hunting."

The stableman gestured to another part of the paddock where several thick-bodied, glossy horses nipped at each other's necks, their manes and tails waving like black banners. "Those, of course, are destriers. They're exceptionally strong and good in war. And then we have a few palfreys," he nodded to a cinnamon-sprinkled horse cropping grass near the fence. "They have a smooth gait and do well over long distances."

King Ganelon turned to Elias. "Well, son, which is it to be? They all look magnificent."

"What about that one?" Elias pointed to a horse the color of a moonless night near the end of the paddock. It pranced back and forth on mud-encrusted hooves, burrs were tangled in its mane and tail, and Elias could count its ribs.

"The nervous black one, your highness?" The stableman asked.

Elias nodded.

"Some knights found her yesterday up toward the Canyon Lands stuck in a pit of mud. They brought her here because they didn't know what else to do with her. She's wild and has a cut on her leg, which makes her even fiercer. My guess is that she escaped from a farm when she was young or was part of a herd in the Canyon Lands."

Elias gazed at the horse with sympathy. He understood how it felt to be taken to a strange place. "She's the one I want."

The stableman turned to face him. "Are you sure, your highness? There are much gentler horses, especially since you've never ridden before."

"She's the one I want," Elias repeated, keeping his gaze on the emaciated horse.

"Bring her over, sire," King Ganelon commanded. "She

shall be his if he desires it."

Elias glanced up at him. "Thanks, father."

"Of course. She's my gift to you." He squeezed his son's shoulder.

The stableman brought the mare over, the horse objecting with each step. When they halted in front of father and son, Elias stepped up to the fence and reached out a hand to the horse's sweaty skin.

The mare balked and danced away.

"Shh. It's okay. You and I are going to be good friends," Elias murmured.

The horse blew out hard but remained still. He patted her flank.

"What are you going to name her?" His father asked.

Elias thought for a long time. While he did, his father glanced up and said, "It's going to be a clear, nice night. Look how many stars you can already see."

The boy looked up at the flaming stars, thought of the horse's night-dark color, and remembered the heat he had felt when he touched her.

Elias turned back to the now-panting horse. "I'll call her Starflare."

"That's an excellent name. I don't think your mother could have chosen a better one, nor a better horse. You have inherited her compassion." His father hugged him.

With one last murmur to his horse, Elias walked beside his father back to the castle.

Now, Suntaria blew out a big breath smelling strongly of grass in Elias' face, and he coughed. "Yes, I still like you, even with your nasty breath."

He tied the gelding to a tree and drank from the clear waters of the Lentiasa River. As he filled up his waterskin, his eyes wandered down the muddy bank. Some tracks a few paces away seized his attention. He went to take a better look.

The hoofprints led away from the pine forest on his side

then meandered down the river before they disappeared in the straw-like grass. The prints appeared only a day or two old, and there had to have been at least five different horses to produce so many, though he couldn't tell for sure because of the way the tracks crisscrossed over each other.

Elias turned into the forest from where the tracks came. After a few paces, he found a pile of horse manure that looked several days old. Next to the manure, something had gouged out a strip of tree bark, and a few horse hairs dangled from the tree's skin where a horse had been tied or had rubbed against it. Another tree nearby had a few hairs clinging to its riveted bark.

Intrigued, Elias walked past the pile of manure until he reached a clearing. He glanced around for any sign that Adelaide had been there. He didn't see anything obvious, so he focused his gaze, taking in every blade of grass, pebble, and speck of dirt.

After a while, he spotted a dark patch in the dirt and the tips of a few blades of grass stained a rusty brown. He leaned down and sniffed; it was dried blood.

He frowned, trying to puzzle out this conundrum. Was that Adelaide's blood or another human's? Or was it merely an animal's?

Elias walked back toward the far side of the clearing and spotted something gleaming silver in the slanting sunlight. He neared the object and realized it was a dagger with a leather handle, its silver blade encrusted with black blood.

Elias' heart thudded as he picked up the weapon. It was Adelaide's dagger—the one she had stolen from his wagon that day in Alesfirth which felt so long ago now. She wouldn't leave a weapon behind that she had so risked much to acquire, especially since any kind of weapon was invaluable to lone travelers.

Elias stared at the weapon in his hand as if it could speak its secrets. Whose blood was on it? Adelaide's or someone else's?

The prints at the river most likely belonged to robbers' horses. He had heard tales of thieves raiding travelers in the Tancred Forest, and had even put an end to some of their raids with Berold's help. Gyndilians didn't dare traverse this far south into Klinhun. At least not yet.

He clenched his hand around the weapon. It was no coincidence there were signs of both robbers and Adelaide near this clearing. If they had met, which seemed probable, then there was no way Adelaide could have escaped, no matter how determined and stubborn she was.

Elias' stomach tightened, and bile filled his mouth. Adelaide would have fought as hard as she could, but she was no match against a group of robbers, even if she knew how to handle the dagger.

But why would they take her with them? For, from the patches of blood he had seen and the dropped weapon, he was sure they had. Adelaide couldn't make it far if she was wounded, and he heard and saw nothing that revealed her presence nearby. To make sure though, Elias ran back to Suntaria, stuffing the dagger into one of his saddlebags. He led the horse in ever-widening circles around the clearing for almost a league, but saw no further sign of her.

Where would the robbers take her? Tancred Forest stretched to the south, eventually reaching the borders of Neklosa—a country on peaceful terms with Klinhun. To the east was Dhalion. The robbers would have no desire to take a hostage to the King's city, where knights swarmed like wasps around a nest. To the west lay the Crystal Caverns and more of Neklosa.

Northward extended the Spearhead Mountains and then Gyndilad. No one would attempt to pass the mountains at this time of year, when they were robed with snow, but robbers knew the mountains almost as well as the forest; it was their favorite place to hide stolen valuables. Elias had pursued thieves up there several times with Berold, and almost always they vanished without a trace.

If the robbers had gone north, they would have had to cross the Lentiasa River again.

Elias spurred Suntaria back to the stream. He rode across the northern bank for a few moments, then spotted what he was looking for: a dozen or so horse tracks leading out of the forest toward the mountains.

Before he galloped in that direction, he noticed a few strands of black hair caught between some rocks in the water.

His heart squeezed at the sight, and though he knew she would never admit it, Adelaide needed him. Hopefully, he would reach her in time.

Four days later, Elias scanned the snow-dusted hills that bowed to the looming serrated mountains—another four day's ride away. His eyes ached from constantly scanning the ground, and his body groaned from lack of sleep; he had pushed himself and Suntaria the last few days, hardly resting so they could catch up to the robbers. He had just found fresh hoofprints and wanted to follow them before another snowfall erased them.

Elias tracked the prints long into mid-afternoon. He now had an idea where they were headed, and urgency pushed him through his exhaustion and the thick snow. But what reason would the robbers have to take Adelaide to Gyndilad? What could the Gyndilians want with her?

A movement in the corner of his eye startled him, and he turned Suntaria around.

A group of five riders raced toward him, their horses' legs throwing up puffs of snow that clung to their shaggy winter coats.

Elias tensed as the riders galloped nearer. He recognized Berold's blue tunic and short brown hair. This did nothing to ease Elias' misgivings because his friend's terse words and abrupt departure at the Lentiasa River was still raw and biting. Elias wished again that he could explain everything to Berold, but it wouldn't ease the pain of what had already happened.

"Good day, Berold," Elias said when the knights stopped near him. Berold and the knights bowed to him. "I hope you're not still angry with me?" Elias didn't have high hopes; he knew how much loyalty meant to his friend.

"Why yes, actually, I am." Berold rubbed his red-rimmed eyes. He looked as weary as Elias felt. "I still believe you're on a fool's mission and apparently so does your father."

Elias frowned. "You spoke to him then. What did he say?"

"He said he had told you to choose a nobleman, not a peasant woman from Alesfirth who loathes you." Berold fingered the several days' growth of stubble on his cheeks. "He said to come back, that the deal is off. There's no time, and it's worse over there than he originally thought. You must return before it's too late, though he didn't mention where you must return to or what this is all about, and I suppose you won't tell me either."

Elias groaned and rubbed his stiff hair. Returning now to Dhalion would solve nothing. If he and his father left Klinhun now, all the people's trust and respect they'd toiled to earn the last nine years would be for naught. It would doom the Klinians to a choking future, not to mention the dragons. And he couldn't leave Adelaide to the robbers; it was his fault she had run away in the first place, and if anything happened to her, her face would haunt him the rest of his life.

Elias clenched his hands around Suntaria's reins. He didn't want to disobey his father, but he wasn't ready to give up on Klinhun or Adelaide yet. "I'm sorry, Berold, but I can't return. Not yet. Adelaide's been kidnapped as well as Starflare, and I can't leave them to an unknown fate. There must still be time to make things right."

Berold glanced at Suntaria, then back at him. "King

Ganelon also told me not to return to the castle without you." He fiddled with his sword hilt.

Elias regarded the other four knights, all of whom he'd trained alongside for years in Dhalion. They tried masking their confusion and embarrassment of the predicament by looking anywhere except at the prince and Berold.

Elias turned back to his friend. "So what are you going to do, tie me up and haul me all the way back to Dhalion?"

Berold's pained eyes latched onto him. "If I have to. You're my friend, Elias, but your father is my King. I must obey him over you, especially in this matter I don't understand."

Elias nodded reluctantly, hating how his friend had to come in between him and his father and that Adelaide was the root of all this turmoil. A thorn of doubt again snagged his thoughts. Was she worth all this pain sprouting among those he loved? He clipped the thought. There was more at stake here than personal feelings and relationships.

He sighed. "I understand where your loyalties lie."

"Then you'll come with us willingly?"

"I wish I could, I truly do, but I can't. Not this time."

Berold—Elias' first friend, the one who had taught him how to be a prince more than Manfred ever could, and had always put up with his strange thoughts and behaviors—stared at him with reddening cheeks, as if waiting for further explanation. When none was forthcoming, he turned to the knights. "Bind him, but harm him as little as possible."

Berold's betrayed eyes scorched Elias, and he had to bite his tongue so he wouldn't tell his friend everything.

The knights urged their horses at him. Elias whirled Suntaria toward the mountains, kicking him hard in the flanks. The horse shot forward.

The men galloped close behind. One caught up and reached out a gloved hand for Suntaria's reins. Elias leaned over and punched the man in the face. He fell off his startled horse.

Elias didn't have time to feel guilty for injuring one of his own men. A knight slipped up on his right and grabbed for his shoulder. Elias swayed away from him, nearly toppling off Suntaria. The knight reached for his arm, but Elias elbowed him in the chest. The man doubled over, his horse slowing.

The last two men had sprinted to cut him off in front. He yanked Suntaria back, then pulled him hard to the right and urged him into a flying gallop.

The two knights rode parallel to him now, drawing nearer with every stride, their faces blank of emotion. When the first drew close enough, Elias jerked his left foot out of his stirrup and kicked the man hard in the side.

"Sorry, Roderic!" Elias yelled as the man put a hand to his side.

The last knight bypassed Roderic, coming up alongside Suntaria's rear. The others would soon recover and close in on him.

"Come on, boy, come on." Elias dug his knees against Suntaria's sides, urging for a little more speed. The horse responded by bursting forward, his legs eating the snow. Whenever they reached Dhalion again, he deserved a long rest and the king's best oats.

The knight fell back and Berold joined him, reining his horse to a stop. "I'll keep looking for you, Elias, until you come back to Dhalion with me!" He shouted, his face red and pinched.

Elias faced forward, his focus now on rescuing Adelaide. He hoped he found her before Berold and the knights found him.

Chapter Twenty-Five

Adelaide spotted Cyr on the seventh day of her abduction. He was merely a speck soaring high in the sky, as if he didn't belong to the earth. Up there, pain, worry, and fear were as brief and fleeting as a wisp of wind. Adelaide envied him his flight and hoped he didn't forget her in his freedom. But at least he was alive and content, and as long as he didn't come to her, he would remain so.

The sight of Cyr brought back memories of home, and she hoped her family was managing well this winter. She longed to see them with every beat of her heart.

"What're you gawkin at?" A man with rotting black teeth asked, brushing roughly by her.

Her muscular guard hauled her onto the dun she had ridden the last several days.

It became easier and easier for the man to lift Adelaide—not that she'd been very heavy to begin with. Since she'd only eaten a few pieces of hard bread or meat—if the men had gone hunting—over the last several days, she had weakened considerably. The bones in her arms and legs jutted out sharper than usual so that she now resembled her family's gangly goats. But hunger was nothing new to her, and the men wouldn't let her die of starvation.

Adelaide was more anxious about the creeping cold. The men huddled next to the fire each night, leaving her to shiver far from the flames with only her and Emma's cloak as protection from the icy mountain air.

As the robbers left the cave they had slept in last night, a deer bounded out of the snow-laden pines into the early morning mist ahead. Adelaide wished she could tell Odo about it, as well as the mountains towering over them. She couldn't keep her eyes off the sheer cliffs frosted at the tips with snow like icing.

The mountains astonished her with their size and impenetrable edges. The robbers were experts at climbing this dangerous terrain; they knew how to avoid the muddiest areas, where to climb the steep ravines, how to navigate the rocks slick with ice, and when to duck under the pines which could unload a sloshy wet pile on an unobservant person's head—like Adelaide's. But sometimes even their adept horses tripped or stumbled in this beautiful, hostile land.

When the sun crawled its way to a spot above them, the group stopped for the noon-day meal in an area surrounded by boulders. Since the robbers continued to keep her hands and feet tied, Adelaide's guard pulled her off the horse. The man yanked her over to a snow-dusted rock and sat beside her. He ate his biscuits without talking or looking at her. He had barely said more than ten words to her and the others the entire time they traveled. But sometimes she heard his booming laugh when the men sat and told stories around the fire at night.

"When can we hunt? I'm tired of his hard bread. It doesn't taste like anything and gets stuck in your teeth." One of the younger men, Hawthorne, stared morosely at the crusty bread in his hand that resembled a tree root more than anything edible. The man complained of something every day.

Yesterday it had been the lack of ale.

"As soon as we get closer to Gyndilad," Hildebrand replied.

Griselda untied Adelaide's gag and gave her some water, which she gulped greedily.

"How much longer until we reach Gyndilad?" A man who had a predator's tooth strung on a piece of leather around his neck asked. "Ten days?"

Hildebrand took a long drink from his animal skin. "I'd say six days if it doesn't snow again. We'll meet the men on the border, as usual, and deliver our goods."

Adelaide's stomach dropped at the news, and she ate without tasting the bread Griselda fed her. How was she supposed to escape in six days? She had been looking for an opportunity every waking moment, but her guards never left her alone, even to relieve herself.

She squeezed her mind for a way out of her predicament, but couldn't think of one that didn't end up with her dead or recaptured. She had to meet the men in Dhalion, but if it came to it, she would rather die than enter the land of her sister's killers.

When the men mounted, panic swirled inside Adelaide. So she fought. When her guard grabbed her, she stomped on his foot and twisted away. Before she could get more than two hobbling steps from him, he grabbed her and heaved her over his shoulder.

She stared at the snowy ground, thinking about how futile her struggle had been. Would her fight against the king be as futile? There weren't many people in the rebellion, and King Ganelon probably had at least a hundred knights at his disposal. But then Emma's face—the face she knew better than her own—came to mind, as well as Odo's, and her father's and mother's. Grief and longing surged through Adelaide like torrential rain. Even if she, Gunter, Conrad, and the others failed and died, at least it would be while fighting for a better life.

She kicked the guard's stomach as he held her, and he groaned.

"Do you need help with your charge?" A man asked somewhere behind Adelaide.

"Nay, I can handle her."

Adelaide thrashed even more to prove him wrong, and the man sat her down so hard on the saddle her teeth clacked shut and the horse snorted. At least the struggle had warmed her up.

"I'll knock you out if I must," the thick-set man threatened.

Adelaide stopped thrashing. She needed to save her energy to plan and execute a *real* escape.

At a shout up ahead from Hildebrand, the horses took off at a trot through the snow-sprinkled rocks and holly bushes.

That evening, the group stopped beneath some trees covered in warty bark. The men started a fire. How they always managed to do so, no matter how soaked and freezing the wood was, remained a mystery to Adelaide.

Griselda untied her gag, and Adelaide opened and closed her jaw to stretch her mouth. She wished they would untie her legs and wrists at least to sleep—her shoulders and ankles continually throbbed, and her wrists and feet had begun to bleed from the tight rope. But after Hildebrand had threatened to leave her gag on all night, she stopped asking.

Griselda fed her a few pieces of bread while the men huddled around the campfire, eating and chatting.

"Remember that one time, Hildebrand, when I strangled that bear with my hands?" A man with a mole on his cheek asked.

"You did not," another man across the fire argued. "I shot it with an arrow first, so it was already basically dead when you got to it. In fact, it was probably already dead."

"It wasn't dead, and you didn't shoot no arrow at it. You—"

A man belched loudly, and the others rumbled with laughter.

Adelaide turned away, remembering nights in the ramshackle barn outside Alesfirth where she would meet with the rebellion. Once, the young men held a belching contest before the meeting began. It was disgusting, and she would never admit it to any of them, but it had cheered her up.

After giving her a last drink of water, Griselda lifted the hood of her raccoon-skin cloak and strode toward Hildebrand who sat some ways back from the flames. The two often had quiet conversations together, and Adelaide wondered if perhaps she was his mother or some other relation. There were several brothers in the group, but she had never heard the men talk about a life other than this one, if they had even had one.

One of the robbers left the ring of friends and ambled over to where Adelaide leaned against a boulder. She tensed. It was Knick-Nose, the man who had threatened her the first night. Since then, he had sent her sly smiles and brushed up against her, but hadn't spoken to her.

"I brought you a gift, fine lass." He held up a tattered, thin wool blanket.

Adelaide's frozen hands trembled at the sight. The last few nights she had curled up into as tight a ball as she could under her and Emma's cloaks, but it still hadn't been enough to ward off winter's starving fingers, and she always woke up half-numb.

"But it comes with a price." Knick-Nose grinned, his eyes as dark as the men's shadows.

"What?" Adelaide's voice cracked from little use.

"A little time alone with me shall suffice."

Adelaide quavered but tried to keep her voice level. "Leave me alone."

"It would be worth it not to freeze to death," he said.

"I'd rather die," she spat. "And if I did freeze to death, then you and your little friends wouldn't get your precious coins."

"Mayhap, but the Gyndilians won't mind if you're missing

some fingers or toes."

Adelaide tried to ignore her terror, wishing for Elias' authoritative presence. She shook her head to remove her desire.

When she glanced up, Knick-Nose had disappeared. She breathed a sigh of relief.

When snores floated to the star-sprinkled sky, and the man on watch faced out into the forest, Adelaide sat up where she had been pretending to sleep. She crawled to the rock she'd leaned against earlier. Keeping her eyes on the guard, she rubbed the bonds against a sharp corner of the boulder. They couldn't tear completely, for the men would notice and just tie her up again. And she couldn't escape tonight because the horses had been moved to another clearing. Besides, Hildebrand slept lightly. But she could weaken the bonds to make her that much more ready for an escape.

When Adelaide felt some of the ropes ripping, she crawled back to the sleeping fire. Afraid of what sleep would bring and shivering too hard to fall asleep, she stared at the wisps of clouds drifting over the stars, thinking of freedom and rebellions. Something else kept creeping into her thoughts as well, no matter how much she tried to banish him: Prince Elias.

The next day around midday, the group halted near a dribbling creek and cracked boulders halfway up one of the peaks. No snow dusted the ground here, but mud coated everything. The horses' hooves made a shlooping sound every time they lifted their legs out of the muck.

A man with loose skin and a thin white beard crawled out from a gap in-between two of the boulders. His bones looked as if they could snap at any moment, and his tattered clothes were streaked with mud.

"Have the dragons come back?" He yelled in a hoarse voice.

"Not today, Henric, but maybe tomorrow," one of the robbers said. The others chuckled as they retrieved their traveling fare and filled their skins with water from the stream.

"No doubt, no doubt." The man sat on a patch of dead grass. He broke off a piece and chewed it. "Tomorrow's the day, no doubt about it." He nodded to himself.

"Who's that?" Adelaide asked once Griselda untied her gag. The man's words of dragons reminded her of the prince. She didn't know if that was a good thing or not, but it did spark her curiosity.

"Old-man Henric," a man near Adelaide said while munching a biscuit. "He's been here long before we began climbing the pass, and he's crazier than a one-footed goose."

"He's harmless. Pay him no mind," Hildebrand said while checking Starflare's legs.

A man with a droopy eye leaned toward Adelaide. "Some say he's lived here before the dragons and humans and that he'll never die."

"Who said that?"

"We did," he chortled.

"Quit talking to the prisoner," Hildebrand commanded. The two men turned away and began discussing what new weapons they'd buy once they deposited her to the Gyndilians. Adelaide wanted to knock their heads together, but could only let the injustice of the situation gnaw at her like a dog with a bone.

Once Adelaide finished eating, she stumbled over to where the old man still sat on the ground mumbling to himself.

A hand clamped down on her shoulder. "Where are you going?" Her guard said. For someone so large, he could sure move quietly.

"Just to talk to the old man. I'd like some different

company for a while, if you don't mind." She jerked away from his grip and continued shuffling to the man. Her guard sat down, watching her.

Adelaide joined the senile man on the ground, ignoring the curious gazes of her captors. "Good day, sire."

He turned cloudy-blue eyes on her. "Sire?" He cackled as if it was the funniest thing he had ever heard, his thin shoulders shaking up and down.

Once he quieted, Adelaide asked, "Did you mention dragons earlier?"

The man scratched his splotchy bald head. "Can't remember now. But they lived here, oh yes they did, if my Pappy's tales were true, and they always were." He spread his hands across the clear sky. "Their scales were all colors, prettier than a sunrise. And when they flew together, it took your breath away, it did, no doubt."

"What happened to them?"

The man acted as if he hadn't heard her. "They had gifts to help the humans, no doubt. And the humans helped the dragons, oh yes they did. But those humans grew nasty and turned on the dragons, oh yes they did. And they all left, over the sun. But they'll be back, no doubt, to help those nasty humans again. Not sure I agree with that last bit, but that's what it is, no doubt."

The man's beliefs, though simple, were strikingly similar to Prince Elias', and she didn't know if Henric had truly learned them from his father, or if he was just plain crazy. Mayhap this man was the one the prince had learned *his* strange tales from.

"So, you believe dragons existed? Was there a war or anything between them and the humans?"

The man looked at her as if *she* was senseless and senile. "War?" He cackled so hard saliva streamed down his chin.

"Let's go, everyone. We need to make it to Spear Cave by nightfall." Hildebrand stood and stretched his arms.

Adelaide's guard lifted her to her feet and pulled her to the group before she could ask Henric anything else. He was still laughing and gurgling when they rode off; he certainly *looked* senseless.

The group reached what was evidently Spear Cave—a large opening in a cliff wall at the end of a steep trail embedded with loose stones—that evening just as the wind began blowing snow at them.

The men clustered around the fire, mostly silent while they ate.

"Could you please untie my hands, Griselda? I don't think I have any skin left," Adelaide said while the woman fed her.

"Nay. Stop asking," the woman snapped and walked away, leaving Adelaide's hands still bound and her stomach still rumbling.

That night, when everyone but the guard at the entrance of the cave was asleep, Adelaide worked on cutting the bonds of her feet against one of the rocks. Like last time, she stopped before the rope tore completely. The action warmed her, but after a few moments of lying still, she was shivering from the freezing air without and her fear within.

The next morning, Adelaide and her captors rode through blowing snow, barely able to see the person in front of them. The freezing wind stung Adelaide's bare hands and face. She huddled down in the saddle, trying to block her face from the sky's wrath.

"I can't see a cursed thing. We need to get to shelter, Hildebrand," a man behind Adelaide shouted over the roaring of the wind.

"I know! There's another cave up ahead."

Adelaide's cloak billowed, letting in the snow, and since her hands were tied, she couldn't pull it close. Her hands and face had lost all feeling, and the rest of her shook uncontrollably.

Finally, they entered a cave much smaller than the one

they had stayed in the previous night. The men huddled together under their fur cloaks and blankets like a pile of dogs.

With a sneer on his mutilated face, Knick-Nose came over to Adelaide's shivering form. Dread rolled through her even though he couldn't do anything with the others so close.

"I've been thinking," he said, stopping in front of her, "since you didn't like my deal the other night and haven't given me what I asked for, I'm gonna give you another kind of gift until you change your mind." He stooped down and punched the right side of Adelaide's face so hard her neck snapped to the left. Bright dots exploded in her vision. Through the pain spreading across the side of her face and into her head, Adelaide found herself wishing for a prince to rescue her.

The next two days the billowing snow and howling wind kept the robbers ensconced in the cave. The men lounged, eating, sleeping, and telling stories of past adventures and people they had plucked valuables from. Adelaide ground her teeth at these stories and tried to ignore the throbbing pain in her face and head from Knick-Nose's punch. At least the wound on her thigh from her first encounter with the robbers was healing. It no longer oozed blood and a crusty scab had formed.

Although no fire flickered, the cave remained warm from all the bodies crammed together. But by the afternoon of the second day, the stench of sweat and old food and the pain of Knick-Nose's continued pinches, jabs, and hits—which the others ignored—caused Adelaide to coil tighter and tighter until she thought she might fling herself at him.

Hildebrand had said earlier that the Gyndilad border was only a few days away. It had to be now or never. Once the group left the cave and put her on a horse in their tight lineup, it would be much harder to flee.

She pressed close to the cave wall all day, waiting for an opportunity, so nervous her stomach felt like it was eating itself.

Then, that night, her opportunity arrived.

Chapter Twenty-Six

Elias peered around a blue spruce and breathed a sigh of relief. Berold and the knights were nowhere to be seen. After they had attempted to take him back to Dhalion, he had seen them only once—camping beneath some firs down in a narrow valley. Although the group had been several miles away, he had continued through the night to remain ahead of them.

Now, five days later, Elias hoped Berold didn't remember which ravine Henric lived in or guess that that's where Elias was headed. The robbers' scarce tracks seemed to point in that direction, and Henric might have seen them. In case Berold was closer than he thought, Elias continued covering Suntaria's tracks and dispersing his fire's embers when he had time and dry wood to build one.

He brushed the gelding's prints away with the edge of his leather boot. If the dark clouds in the north kept moving this way, he might not need to cover his tracks much longer. He hoped the storm wouldn't slow him down too much; every day he didn't find Adelaide heightened the probability that he never would.

Elias yawned and hummed to himself to keep the dark

thoughts away as he rode through the thin ravine, his voice the only sound for miles in the sleepy pass between two bald-headed, old-man mountains.

Soon he came upon a creek and cracked sarsens. After letting Suntaria drink from the glacial stream and sipping some himself, he led the nodding horse toward the boulders.

“Henric, are you here? It’s Elias. I need to speak with you.” He scuffed his boot in the dirt as he waited for his friend.

He’d met Henric five years ago in these mountains while trying to catch a group of ruffians who had stolen a pile of silver from the Fernohn mines.

Elias, Berold, and the four knights who had accompanied them had stopped at this creek just a few paces downstream from where he now stood. He and Berold had trekked into the trees to find the source of a loud splashing noise. Rounding a bend in the creek, they had come upon a naked elderly man washing and singing to himself with his back to them.

“That’s odd.” Berold wrinkled his nose. He touched Elias’ arm. “Let’s return to the men, your highness. It’s just an old cracked man bathing.”

But the song the man sang was familiar. “Wait. I wish to speak to him.”

Elias had walked toward the man, who turned out to be friendly and fairly coherent. The two shared stories late into the night while the knights exchanged curious glances. The prince ignored the looks, since they were nothing new.

Henric had seen much of the world and had much to offer, no matter how strange he appeared and acted. And, more importantly, unlike everyone else in Klinhun, his tales depicted dragons positively, like when the female dragon, Akelda, adopted a human orphan after her own eggs washed away in a storm. Elias had heard most of the stories from his father, but it was encouraging—albeit unusual—to hear them from someone else.

The prince attempted to see his old friend every time he

journeyed into the mountains. He always brought Henric either food or blankets since it was clear the man didn't have much of either.

Now, while waiting for Henric, Elias sang the song that first drew him to the man.

> "Can you hear it?
> Tromp, tromp,
> thick, scaly dragon legs
> shake the ground—
> thunder greeting the earth.
>
> Can you see it?
> Sizzle, spark,
> blue, orange, purple, white
> flames leap into the sky—
> lightning tickling the clouds.
>
> Can you smell it?
> Whoosh, hiss,
> smelly, smoky dragon breath
> whips through the air—
> wind escaping the trees.
>
> Can you feel it?
> Boom, crack,
> Rumble, roar—"

"It's the way the dragons dance." Henric hobbled out from behind a pine tree, singing the last phrase in his hoarse voice. He threw back his head and laughed.

Elias smiled despite his anxiety for Adelaide. "Good day, Henric. How are you?"

"The dragons will come back today, no doubt."

"Perhaps." Elias rummaged around in one of his saddlebags. "Although if they did, it probably wouldn't turn out well for them or the humans."

He retrieved a piece of his least crusty bread and handed it to the man. "Sorry I don't have anything more. I didn't know I'd be visiting you."

The man took the bread. "It's good, no doubt." He sucked on it since he only had a few teeth left.

"Henric, has a group of robbers passed by here in the last few days?"

The man thought for a moment, then nodded vigorously, his thin, white beard flopping. "Oh, yes. Three days ago they were here, no doubt."

Only three days? That was much sooner than Elias had hoped. If he picked up his pace and the snow held off, he could catch up to them in the next day or two. He didn't know what he would do then; by himself, he wouldn't last long against an entire band of robbers.

"Good. And was there a young woman with black hair among them?"

Henric's forehead wrinkled in thought. "Don't remember black hair, but there was a woman, no doubt. She was confused about dragons, oh yes, she was. She had a cold heart, but warmth in her eyes, oh yes she did."

Elias' heart lifted at the man's words that described Adelaide perfectly. He mounted Suntaria. "Thanks for your help, Henric. I appreciate it more than I can say."

The man nodded. "No doubt, Prince, no doubt."

As Elias rode away, he heard the man singing to himself,

> "Can you hear it?
> Tromp, tromp,
> thick, scaly dragon legs
> shake the ground—
> thunder greeting the earth."

◆◆◆

"Since the snow's stopped and we're stuck in this stinkin' cave for another night, we might as well go hunting," Hildebrand proclaimed that evening as he gathered his bow and quiver.

"Finally. Fresh meat!" Someone near the fire yelled.

"Get me out of this tiny, buggin' hole!"

The men hooted and gathered weapons stashed along the cave's walls.

"Shut your mouths!" Hildebrand roared, and the greasy-haired men stopped and looked at him. "A group will hunt with me, and another will scout ahead a few miles north to see if the snow's packed enough for us to leave in the morning." He scanned the men. "Sewall, continue guarding the prisoner along with Griselda and whoever's watching the entrance now."

Adelaide's guard nodded and sat down next to her. It was the first time she'd heard his name.

Once Hildebrand separated the rest of the men into two groups, they left with as much commotion as children on feast days.

When they had disappeared into the darkness, the sudden silence and cold felt like a splash of water. Griselda fell asleep on a pile of deer-hide blankets, snoring much more loudly than Adelaide would have expected from the small, hobbling woman. Her guard sat staring at the opposite wall. Adelaide wondered what he was thinking about, if anything.

"I'm going to the entrance to get some air," she told him. "And don't fret, I won't try to escape. There's a guard there, and I'm tied up, after all."

The man looked at her and nodded.

Adelaide shuffled over to the opening, trying not to think about what she was about to do and how poor her chances were of accomplishing it.

Thankfully, the man at the entrance was not her own personal tormentor Knick-Nose. A skinny man with a wide forehead—the man who had nothing better to do than spend his time complaining—stared off into the bleak midwinter night.

At the sound of her shuffling, he eyed her. "What do you want?" He tightened his grip on his bow, which wouldn't be of much use in these close quarters.

"Don't fret. I just came to get some fresh air. You men stink worse than hogs that have wallowed in mud all day."

He glared at her.

"And," Adelaide jerked her hands apart. The torn ropes gave way. She kicked her feet, and those bindings slipped down as well, "I came to punch you." She hit him hard in the face, but her arms were so weak, it had no effect. Her escape was getting off to a great start...

The man aimed a blow to her stomach, but she dodged and kicked him in the groin. He bent forward, Adelaide kicked his knee, and he fell. She booted him hard in the head to knock him out, but couldn't tell if she had or not.

She stood over him, panting and trembling. He would be alright, but Adelaide might not be. She was weaker than she realized and hoped she had enough energy to ride a good distance that night. At the sound of a step behind her, she glanced up and saw her guard striding toward her.

Adelaide spun and darted out of the cave, the scabbed wound in her thigh breaking open. She stumbled on some rocks near the entrance and fell, cutting her hands. Cursing her bumbling legs, she stood and trotted clumsily through the snow to where three horses were tied to a cluster of aspens. She ran to Starflare like greeting a long-lost friend; she hadn't been able to approach the horse during her capture. Her fingers fumbled with the knot on Starflare's reins, and she cursed.

"Stop. I'll do it."

Adelaide froze. Sewall, her guard, towered over her. He didn't seem to have a weapon. She kicked his leg, but he didn't move or even grunt. He grabbed her. She thrashed and lashed out, but the action had as much effect as a kitten clawing at a wolf.

The man sat her down on the horse.

Realizing where she was, Adelaide stopped resisting. She stared at Sewall, who untied Starflare's reins. "What are you doing?"

He placed the straps in her hands, which now trembled with cold. "I had a daughter once. She too had nightmares."

Then, before Adelaide could comprehend what had just happened, the man slapped Starflare's rear, and the horse galloped off.

Starflare had only taken a few strides when pain exploded across Adelaide's back. She whipped her head around and spotted Griselda near the cave entrance, bow in hand. Sewall still stood by the horses, his mouth agape. It was the first and only expression she remembered seeing on his face.

Adelaide turned back around and gingerly reached down her back with the hand not holding the reins. An arrow was lodged deep in her left shoulder, and when her fingers touched it, a shocking pulse of pain beat down her back, all the way to her legs. She groaned and dropped her hand. The arrow would have to stay in for now.

She tried to maneuver Starflare south—the way the robbers had come up the mountain— and keep her eyes open for the scouting and hunting parties Hildebrand had sent out, but the agony ripping down her body made lucid thinking difficult.

Then, sometime in the night, thick snowflakes spun into her face, and the wind started screaming. Soon Adelaide couldn't see where she was going—everything was a mess of white, whirling flakes.

But she continued riding, desperate to get as far from her captors as she could. Sewall's kind actions seeped into her exhausted, pain-riddled thoughts. She wondered what had happened to his daughter and hoped the others wouldn't hurt him for aiding her.

The snow thickened and the wind stormed. Adelaide hunched over Starflare and squinted against the swirling whiteness. Her fingers soon lost all feeling.

A while later, she realized she'd lost sensation in her entire body. She was afraid she would fall off a cliff or end up back at the cave, but she was so sleepy and frozen that dismounting the horse seemed an impossible feat.

Hours or years later Adelaide opened her eyes, confused. She must have fallen asleep.

Starflare had stopped, and the wind gusted harder than before, infiltrating Adelaide's sodden garments and thrusting into her very bones. She was so cold and tired, and everything was so dark. Perhaps it would be better if she died out here on this mountain. Then she wouldn't have to harm anyone or watch them get hurt. She wouldn't have to hold the weight of Klinhun on her shoulders or suffer this fathomless emptiness stretching inside every breath she took.

Adelaide could no longer feel the cold. Hopefully soon she would no longer feel the despair and guilt haunting her either, only peace and rest more profound than the night promised.

Emma, I'm coming.

Chapter Twenty-Seven

"You shall travel to Dhalion, meet up with this rebellion of yours, kill or overthrow King Ganelon, make sure his son doesn't take the throne, and set up one of those men I told you about who's allied with Gyndilad as the new king. Don't forget to have the new ruler send a cargo of silver to me every two hundred days," the Master said. After a fortnight of living at the Gyndilian camp, Gunter still hadn't uncovered his real name. Maybe he didn't have one.

"Sounds like everyone gets what they want," the Master continued, opening his pale, spidery hands. "You get no war and a new king, and I get silver and an allegiance with Klinhun."

Gunter nodded. He didn't trust the man, but the deal was the only way he could think of escaping to find Adelaide. Perhaps somehow it would ease the tension between the two nations.

The Master smoothed his drooping mustache. "See, we in Gyndilad are a fair people. We merely desire the best for our citizens as you Klinians do."

Gunter stepped aside from the horse snuffling his filthy

cloak. He had slept in the same tiny cell the last twelve nights. And though the Gyndilians had let him eat with them a few times once the Master struck a deal with him, they hadn't offered another place for him to sleep. He was still a prisoner.

"What about the attack on Alesfirth?" Gunter prodded.

The Master waved a hand. "A few of my men weren't happy about the king's timing for the war against Klinhun and decided to take matters into their own hands. They were all punished, don't worry. There'll be no more attacks if you depose King Ganelon and his son. My lord, King Aethelmaer, will make sure of it."

Gunter couldn't tell if the man was lying; his smooth face gave nothing away, not even a twitch. "Fine." He squinted at the sunny sky, hoping for the hundredth time that he was doing the right thing. "And you'll stop kidnapping people as well."

"Of course. Without a war, why would we need Klinhun to give us its people?"

The man made it sound like Klinhun was freely handing over its citizens. Why would Gyndilad have need of Klinians? Gunter remembered what they had said when he first arrived—if he should fight or be used for experimentation. No one had mentioned it again, and when he had asked, he was slapped. He quickly learned to keep his questions and opinions to himself.

Four men on horseback trotted up to them. They didn't wear the typical silver and black Gyndilian livery, but the tattered, dull-colored tunics, cloaks, and trousers of peasants.

"These are the men who will accompany you to Dhalion," the Master explained. "If anyone asks, they're your friends, but they're highly skilled in weaponry, especially the crossbow. They will kill King Ganelon if your rebellion cannot. They will also be communicating with me during your journey and have permission to kill you or bring you back here if you detour in any way from our deal."

The Master held up a finger. "Remember, you are only valuable to us because you are a Klinian and know people already on their way to overthrow the king. Once he's dead and his son is taken care of, you are free to return home."

Gunter swallowed past the lump in his throat at the thought of seeing his family and friends again. If Adelaide knew he had sided with the Gyndilians, she would kill him. Hopefully, she would never find out.

At least he would never have to see these men again once they upheld their deal, if they even planned to. He couldn't quite believe it, but at least he would have help in Dhalion from those in the rebellion if he needed to escape the Gyndilians.

"And what will my friends say when I ride up with four strange men?" Gunter asked.

The Master shrugged. "Tell them you found them along the way to Dhalion, and they want to help your pathetic little rebellion." The man grinned and smoothed his silver and black tunic. "Now, I have much to do, as do you, if you want to reach Dhalion by spring. There should be enough provisions in the saddlebags to last you that long."

Gunter mounted a roan and nodded toward the other four riders who gazed at him with various degrees of disinterest and hatred.

Then he rode out of Gyndilad back into Klinhun alongside enemies who were supposed to be his friends. This would definitely be an interesting and dangerous journey.

Elias fought against the dizzying snow and driving wind as he searched for any sign of Adelaide in the darkness.

"Adelaide!" He called, but the wind grabbed the words and threw them away.

Suntaria stumbled in a thick drift, and Elias patted his

frost-covered flank. "We'll find her. I know we will."

He dismounted to make the going easier for the horse and give himself a chance to thaw his half-frozen legs. But when he stepped down, the snow came up mid-way to his calves.

Horse and man stumbled on, freezing and exhausted. Elias didn't let himself dwell on what condition Adelaide would be in if he found her out in this storm.

When Elias' feet had gone numb, he blundered into an odd-shaped pile of snow he took to be a rock or tree. He stumbled back and blinked as the shape moved. He rubbed the disorienting cold from his eyes. The shape was Starflare. Her head was lowered, her eyes closed, her black coat completely white with snow.

Elias patted the miserable horse. "Where's Adelaide, girl?" He walked to the other side of her, fearing what he'd find.

When he saw her, he gasped. Adelaide lay half-buried in the snow, her head and shoulders exposed. Her face was as white as the snow, an ugly bruise marred her cheek and eye, and snowflakes clung to the straying strands of her braid.

"Adelaide," Elias breathed in relief and dismay. What if he had found her too late?

He quickly dug her out of the cold's greedy grip, whispering her name.

Once she was completely free of the snow, he drew her close and gazed down at her face, hoping it was only lost in sleep, not lost forever. "Adelaide, wake up. Please. You must be alive."

After too long her eyelids flickered open. "Elias," she sighed, then her eyes fluttered shut.

He let out a long breath. But the danger wasn't over; he had to warm her before she froze to death. He held her unconscious body close to him while tying Starflare's reins to Suntaria's. "Thank you for not leaving her," he told Starflare as he mounted Suntaria. The mare nickered.

Shouts broke out of the darkness ahead of him. He turned

Suntaria deeper into the woods, and Starflare followed with plodding steps.

Elias wished he could send his dagger through every robber who had harmed Adelaide. She was too insubstantial against him—thinner than any peasant he'd seen, and other cuts and bruises tainted her skin. But Adelaide probably wouldn't survive if he turned to kill the men; indeed, she still might not.

He gritted his teeth against the unexpected lash of pain at this possibility and clutched her closer to his chest. He urged Suntaria to move faster.

The men's voices faded, and with them, Elias' fury.

Eventually, he found a diminutive cave tucked behind some evergreens and boulders on the edge of the mountain. He laid Adelaide on a blanket inside, then tied Starflare and Suntaria to the trees standing guard in front of the entrance. He covered their tracks with a branch and made sure the horses couldn't be seen from the direction they'd come. He returned to the cave with his tack and saddlebags.

To Elias' relief there was a stack of dry wood in a corner. Apparently, he and Adelaide weren't the only ones to shelter in the cave. He hoped whoever it was wouldn't return anytime soon.

Once a blaze licked the wood, he drew Adelaide—whose skin was as cold as ice and looked nearly as translucent—to the fire. When his gaze landed on the dark purple skin around her eye which had swelled to almost double its size, his rage boiled again. He clenched his hands as the flames of fury leapt inside him, her injured face all he could see.

But giving in to his anger wouldn't help her. He took several deep breaths as his father had taught him.

When he no longer felt like destroying something, he peeled off Adelaide's soaked clothes. He carefully pulled out the arrow lodged in her back, at which she shuddered but didn't wake. He cleaned the hole with melted snow, then wrapped it in a strip from his tunic. He hurried, for her skin was covered with chills, and she wouldn't stop shaking.

When Elias finished bandaging the wound, he placed her as close to the fire as he could without burning her and covered her with two blankets and his fur-lined cloak. He trickled some melted snow into her mouth.

Exhausted, he laid down beside her. With the purple eye and cuts on her face, Adelaide looked much different than when he had watched her sleep that first night outside of Pinhurn. Then, the harshness of her face and demeanor had softened, so she had seemed like a kind, less-fierce woman. Now, the angry bruise on her face—a bleeding-out of the pain in her heart that made her so cold to him and other nobles—cried out to him for help.

Elias wanted nothing more than to place his hand on her face and wish away the bruise, and even more, the deep sore in her heart. But he could no longer do such a thing. He could only wonder what Adelaide had been like before whatever tragedy befell her. He couldn't picture it though; that woman hadn't grabbed his attention or needed him. This one did, even if she forever denied it.

Gazing at Adelaide's pallid face and the shallow rising of her chest, wondering anxiously if she would live through the night, Elias realized something both beautiful and dangerous: he loved her.

Chapter Twenty-Eight

Bone-reaching cold and men without noses and dragons that breathed snow chased themselves through Adelaide's dreams. When she opened her eyes, she glimpsed swaying flame-shadows against a curved roof before falling asleep again.

The next time she woke, someone murmured, "Drink this." When she opened her mouth, something salty and warm slunk down her throat. Darkness took her before she could ascertain anything more.

For a long time, Adelaide slipped in and out of consciousness, drinking, chewing, and swallowing when the voice told her to.

Eventually, she began to feel warm again. Each brief time she woke, another part of her body had thawed. First her face no longer felt numb, then she could twitch her fingers, then her toes. She didn't try moving them more than a twitch; that required more energy than she could muster, but she was grateful her body didn't feel like a solid block of ice anymore.

Once, after sipping the salty warm broth, her throat felt strong enough for speech, and her eyelids didn't immediately droop shut. Flames danced on a smooth stone wall above her and then Prince Elias' blue eyes peered down at her.

"Where am I?" Adelaide tried to sit up, but her head pounded and her arms ached.

"Careful." The prince eased her back onto the blanket. "You were practically frozen and starved to death when I found you. It will take a while for your strength to return. We're in a cave in the Spearhead Mountains, a few days' ride south of the Gyndilian border."

"How long have I been out?" She asked.

"Two days."

"That's all? It feels like much longer."

The prince nodded. "Like I said, you were in bad shape. It's a wonder you were able to escape at all, given the storm and your weakened condition."

"I was fine until I got out in the blizzard. One of the robbers decided to help me for some strange reason, and—" Adelaide stopped, realizing something.

Prince Elias gazed down at her with concern. "What's wrong?"

She pulled the blankets closer around her. "Why am I only wearing my shift?"

The prince dropped his gaze. "Your dress was wet, and I had to, well, take it off so you could warm up. I also needed to take care of the wound on your back. That's the only reason. You can put your clothes back on as soon as you're well enough."

The prince's discomfort eased Adelaide's. She dropped her eyes from his face and loosened her hold on the blankets. "Very well, as long as you turn around when I put them on."

He grinned. "Of course, fair maiden. I am nothing if not courteous."

His familiar smile soothed her spirits. Sleep soon swallowed her up again.

◆◆◆

When Adelaide nest woke and saw Prince Elias hovering next to the fire, she recalled their last meeting in Kildare. A familiar flash of anger ignited inside her. She gathered the blankets around her and sat up, ignoring the sharp burst of pain in her back. "I can't stay here. I need to leave."

Surprise and worry etched the prince's forehead as he turned to her. "What? Why?"

She clutched the blanket and willed her legs to move. They merely trembled. "In Kildare, when those horrible women belittled me, you said nothing, after all the times you said you care for peasants. I was right. You're just like all the other nobles." Despite herself, sorrow bled into her voice.

She stared at the fire's waving orange and red arms. Part of her had wanted to believe Prince Elias; it would have removed so much pressure to save Klinhun. Not to mention, she wouldn't have had to harm him or anyone else. But he had let her down. She shouldn't have let herself trust him.

The prince knelt beside her, and Adelaide wished she could feel those steady, warm hands on her trembling ones. She banished the thought as he spoke. "Adelaide, I didn't agree with anything those women said. Surely after spending all this time with me you realize I wouldn't have. I was trying to keep my anger at bay and not kill them, actually."

The sudden edge of impatience in the prince's voice caught Adelaide's attention. He gazed past her, teeth clenched. "I had never felt angrier in my life than that night, or the night when I realized how the robbers had treated you." He shook his head, and when he returned his gaze on her, there was no denying the tenderness there.

Shadows bulged beneath his eyes, revealing how well he had watched over her the last few days, and Adelaide couldn't ignore the fact that he had saved her life more than once. That would just make killing his father so much harder. No, impossible.

She almost wished she had been right about Prince Elias

that wretched night.

Almost.

♦ ♦ ♦

Adelaide dreamed that night.

She sits by Emma near the Lentiasa River, chatting and chortling about love and life. The river laughs back in its gurgling way. Her sister's hair shines as bright as the sun's rays, and there's no speck of dirt or stray piece of grass on her silky blue dress. Adelaide wears a pale purple one, and it's so light she feels like she's wearing a cloud.

"Ade, can you believe that I'm engaged to Conrad?" Emma asks, her smile nearly as bright as her hair.

"Of course I can. You two have always been mooning over each other. If he had waited any longer, I would have asked for him."

Emma laughs; no amount of teasing can wipe her smile away today. Her face takes on a dreamy look. "He said he'd build me a house in-between his parents' and ours and that there'll be enough space for an herb and flower garden."

"That sounds lovely, Em. The house will need to be large for all the little ones you'll have."

Emma nudges Adelaide's shoulder, blushing a sunrise pink. After a moment she says, "What would be even more wonderful is if I had a double wedding with you and...Gunter, perhaps?"

Adelaide shakes her head. "You know I don't care for him like that. Besides, we're too young. I still have yet to save the country, remember?"

"How could I forget your ambitious dreams?" Emma stands and hoists Adelaide to her feet. "Let's go for a swim."

The sisters jump and grab a branch above them. They leap like a pair of diving birds into the river that has become a serene indigo lake.

Then, Adelaide stands outside a house framed by gardens full of lacy white and purple blooms. She kneels next to a young girl with the same sunny hair as Emma. "How are you today, Herleva?"

"I'm good, Aunt Adelaide. Watch this." She leaps into the air, hovers there for a moment, then lands back on the ground with a grin.

"Good job! You went so high that time."

The girl beams and jumps into Adelaide's arms. Adelaide holds Herleva close, inhaling the peony blossom smell of her curls. White butterfly wings flutter back and forth on her back.

Emma emerges from the house, followed by Conrad. Gunter follows, holding a cake in the shape of a tree with iced pink, yellow, and orange flowers blooming from its branches.

"It's dangerous to let Gunter hold the cake," Adelaide's father says.

Odo bounds over to Gunter, breaks off a limb from the cake, and stuffs it into his face.

"Always hungry." Galiena sighs.

Emma prances over to Adelaide.

"How's the boy?" Adelaide asks, rubbing the bump of Emma's belly.

"Energetic, as always. And we don't know it's a boy."

"It is." She looks over at Herleva, who's chatting with her grandparents. "Your daughter's flying better every day."

Emma puts her arm through Adelaide's and smiles proudly at her daughter. "I know. She's almost as rambunctious as you."

"Herleva, let's show your Aunt and Grandparents what you can do." Conrad beckons to the girl.

She giggles and jumps into Conrad's arms. He throws her up high, and her white wings carry her up into the spring sky.

"She did it!" Emma and Adelaide shout. They hug each other, Em's pregnant belly a precious addition to their embrace as they watch the little girl soar into the sky.

Adelaide's eyes flashed open to reveal the rugged roof of a cave. Like a splash of icy river water, the truth drowned the beauty and peace of the dream.

"No," she groaned, curling up tight and squeezing her eyes against the tears and pain. The dreams she and Emma had longed for would never happen. She would never help plan Emma's wedding, never tease her about her pregnant belly, never see her eyes light up with love for her husband, never be an aunt to her children.

She clutched Emma's cloak and tried to summon the dream back, but it was fading fast. What was the name of Emma's daughter? What color were the flowers in the garden outside her house?

Prince Elias' voice broke her concentration. "What's wrong, Adelaide?"

She stuffed her hands into her mouth to stifle her sobs, but they leaked out like her tears.

The prince drew her close, and she clenched his tunic. His arms and calming whispers reminded Adelaide of her father's arms as he held her when the nightmares first came, but the prince's touch was softer and his smell sweeter.

Adelaide didn't know how long she leaned against Elias, weeping for a life and a sister she could no longer have.

Eventually, she scooted back, clenching the blanket tight. She rubbed her eyes—the bruised one smarting—thankful the tears had finally stopped. She cleared her throat and looked at the prince's chest. "Forgive me, your highness. I had a nightmare, but shouldn't have let it trouble me so."

"Please call me Elias," he said softly. "And never apologize for crying. It cleanses the soul."

Adelaide stared at the hissing embers.

"Who is Emma?"

Her eyes flicked up to his. "What?"

"I've heard you say her name while sleeping, here and outside of Pinhurn, when you had that horrible nightmare."

His face was cloaked in shadow, but his tone was as gentle as if he spoke to a wounded lamb. "I think it will help if you talk about her and what happened. It might ease the pain raging inside you."

Adelaide returned her gaze to the glowing coals. Telling the prince about Emma would be asking him to step inside her heart, and remembering what had happened to her sister would invite shafts of ripping agony into her opened heart.

But Adelaide was tired of the emptiness, the sleeplessness, and the gnawing nightmares. Perhaps they would leave if she gave them a voice and a form. Prince Elias *had* been kind to her and had saved her life several times.

She sighed and met his gaze. "Very well, I'll tell you. But you must promise to look at what I tell you without noble eyes, if such a thing is possible."

"I'll listen to your story as unbiased as I can."

Adelaide dropped her eyes to the fire, staring at the embers as if they were her sister's heartbeats, waiting to burst into flame at her words.

"Emma is..." she swallowed, "*was* my sister. She was only a year older than me, and after I stopped resenting her for being so good, we did everything together. We played chase in Alesfirth when our mother was at the market. In the spring we would catch frogs at the river and place them in Odo's bed just to watch his ears turn red. We would see who could finish their chores the fastest, and in winter we caught snowflakes on our tongues.

"We told each other everything, and if we fought, we soon forgot the argument. We were best friends. Emma was going to be a healer, and I was going to change things for peasants by somehow becoming a knight and fighting for justice. No matter how ludicrous my ideas were, Emma always stood by and encouraged me. We were going to have big families and live next to each other." Fragments of the dream returned, taunting her with false hope.

"She promised nothing would ever separate us," Adelaide whispered. Emma's voice sounded clear in her ear, as if she was back beside her on the grass, watching the stars wink like fireflies.

Adelaide blinked, and she was back in the cave, anger pouring into her—anger at her sister for promising such a foolish thing, that she hadn't spent more time with Odo, that a Gyndilian had killed Emma, and that she hadn't been able to stop it.

"And then what happened?" Elias murmured.

"The attack on Alesfirth."

Chapter Twenty-Nine

Every detail of that horrific day paraded through Adelaide's mind, though it had occurred more than a year before. She twisted her hands in the blanket. "Emma and I had left home early to buy some supplies for our mother at the market. Em stayed near the front of town to trade for food, and I went to the tanner's booth to see how much leather was for my father's boots.

"As I spoke to the tanner, screams erupted from the townsfolk behind me. I turned and saw horsemen with raised swords. I could tell they were Gyndilians from the colors on their shields and tunics, but couldn't understand why they were there.

"I watched as they stabbed swords into passing peasants, one of them an old woman, and another just a...a child." She closed her eyes at the sight of the brown-headed boy falling to the ground, staining the dirt with his blood. So much blood for someone so little.

A hand touched her arm, and Adelaide opened her eyes. Elias watched her with a pained expression.

She returned her gaze to the fire; she didn't need to

experience both her pain and his. "Without thinking, I ran through the crowd toward the gate, toward the soldiers, toward where my sister was just a few moments before. It took a long time to reach the food stalls because people were running everywhere and Lord Lambert's knights were beginning to fight the Gyndilians, though most of the worthless knights fled.

"When I finally found Emma, she was...she was..." Adelaide squeezed her eyes shut against the sight of her sister's unseeing eyes. "They had killed her. One of the Gyndilians had killed her, and I was too late. She was already gone." Adelaide stared down at her lap, too weary to cry.

Then hot anger fractured her sorrow and pain like cracking glass. She hated the Gyndilians who murdered her sister, but she loathed the one who had allowed it to happen. The one who hadn't fulfilled his duty to protect his people when they needed him. The king, who unfortunately was Prince Elias' father.

"You have suffered much, Adelaide, more than I first guessed." Prince Elias' murmur interrupted her heated thoughts. "No words I say can bring your sister back, though I desperately wish they could." He clenched his hands. "Some of the Gyndilians are worse than wolves."

The fury stuffed into his words and his blazing eyes shocked Adelaide. Perhaps he did care about the people of Alesfirth. But then why had he and his father done nothing about the attack? Why were there still so many starving peasants in Klinhun?

Elias leaned toward her, and although he didn't touch her, his eyes did. She shivered. "If I ever have the chance, I will kill the men who slew your sister. But please remember that my father and I weren't the ones who killed Emma that day."

"Nay, but it was your father who put the knights in place who fled. And you and your father never came to help our village recover. It was as if the attack never happened. And what about before the attack? There had been rumors of Gyndilians building a garrison for years, but no extra knights ever showed up in Alesfirth."

"We sent them," Prince Elias said, his voice bitter. "As soon as my father and I heard those rumors, we sent knights. I don't know where they went, though I wouldn't be surprised if they bribed a lord of another village to take them on. Alesfirth's never been a favorite among knights or nobles.

"As for the attack, my father wanted to go, but his advisors thought it might be a lure to draw him there, so they told him to stay. I was in Findar at the time, discussing where that nation stands with us. My father and I sent several wagons full of supplies to Alesfirth, but they must have been stolen along the way."

Adelaide shrugged. She hadn't seen or heard any sign of wagons. She couldn't know if he was telling the truth about them or the extra knights.

"You don't have to punish the Gyndilians. It won't solve anything," Adelaide said. "Besides, you don't even know who did it."

"I know, but it would make me feel better. And Klinians need to see that we uphold justice in this kingdom."

"Justice?" Adelaide scoffed. "People in Alesfirth and the other villages have their hands cut off from stealing bread when they're starving. If you want to uphold justice in Klinhun, then replace the lords with people who actually care about the townsfolk."

"We've tried. But once people taste power, they become greedy. They nearly always use their positions to their advantage and treat those they rule with disrespect. There have been a few good lords and kings, but not nearly enough."

Elias leaned closer, his grey eyes alight with anger. "And who would make a greater king than my father? He's not perfect, but he genuinely loves the people of Klinhun and listens to them. Any king on the throne would somehow disappoint his people. The people of Klinhun need outside help to rule justly, for on their own they will fail."

Adelaide leaned back, shocked by the prince's tirade. She had refused to think about what would happen after her rebellion overthrew the king, for that had always been the most important and dangerous part. But what if another king took the throne and ruled with a tighter fist than King Ganelon or those before him?

"What kind of help?" she asked.

"Help from something much bigger than themselves, like, dragons."

Adelaide frowned. "Elias, they aren't real. The sooner you realize that, the better it will be for everyone."

"Perhaps they are, perhaps not." He grabbed his sword and scabbard from the floor. "I'm going to hunt. You need some meat to strengthen you. And Adelaide," he looked at her, "I'm sorry again for what happened to your sister. I would have liked to meet her. I also can't help but tell you, I think you're beautiful." He leaned down toward her.

Frightened and startled at his proximity, Adelaide did the first thing she thought of: she smacked him in the face. She regretted it at once, but even more so when she saw the hurt in his eyes.

Before she could apologize, Elias bowed low. "Forgive me, Adelaide. I was too brash, especially after all you've gone through. I merely desired to give you a kiss on the hand. But next time I shall ask first."

He walked stiffly out of the cave. Adelaide sat stupefied by his humble seriousness and lack of anger at her response. He was most assuredly unlike any noble or man she'd met before.

Adelaide sighed and walked with trembling legs to where her dress—now dry—lay beside the fire. She put it on. Then she grabbed Emma's cloak and smelled it. But the lavender scent of her sister had disappeared long ago, replaced by smoke and sweat.

What should I do, Em? Adelaide asked the cloak, as if her sister hid in the wool fibers.

Something had to change in this country, but what? Elias' words about dragons floated to her mind, but she dismissed them. Even if there were dragons alive somewhere, why would they help the people who abhorred them?

She just needed to reach Dhalion as soon as possible and speak with Gunter and the others. Perhaps they could come up with a way to depose the king without harming him. After that, Adelaide had no idea what they would do. As Elias said, putting another king in Ganelon's place could just continue the cycle of problems facing the peasants now.

Weary from telling Elias about her past and reliving the powerful emotions they invoked, Adelaide returned to her nest of blankets, Emma's cloak clutched in her hand.

Elias breathed in the crisp, pine-filled air and stretched. As he trod through the muddy woods, Adelaide's words swirled through his mind like snowflakes, and his heart weighed as heavy as the mountains piercing the sky above him.

No wonder she rarely smiled. She had faced more sorrow than anyone should have thrown at them in life.

As he ruminated over Adelaide's tale, he was both amazed and envious of her deep love for her sister. He had never felt that close to anyone in his life, not even his father.

He ducked under a branch laden with snow. Adelaide would probably never care for him as much as she cared for her sister, but at least she trusted him enough to finally tell him the truth of her past. And she had called him Elias, just Elias, probably without even realizing it. His heart leapt just thinking about it.

He had gained her trust just when he had to break it.

Elias rubbed his face at the thought of seeing the distance and suffering in Adelaide's hazel eyes once more. But it couldn't be helped; he was out of time.

Chapter Thirty

The smell of sizzling meat woke Adelaide sometime later.

"Good evening." Elias leaned over the fire toward her. "How are you feeling?"

"A little stiff." She stood gingerly, wincing as the arrow wound in her back tightened.

"How's your wound?"

"It doesn't hurt much anymore."

He edged toward her. "May I see it?"

Adelaide froze, then nodded. It was better for him to tend the wound than to die from an infection. She uncovered her shoulder. The prince stood close behind her, examining the wound with his fingers. His tender touch and warm breath on her neck sent shivers up her spine.

"It's healing well and already has a scab. We'll continue washing it with warm water and keep the cloth covering it clean."

After cleansing the wound and giving Adelaide a new piece of cloth to tie around it, Elias sat beside the fire, his eyes on the flames.

Adelaide tied the bandage around her shoulder and

straightened her dress, her eyes on the prince's contemplative stance. She sat beside him, still trembly from his touch, but tried not to let her emotions show. "Thanks for rescuing me from the snow and healing me. I would have understood if you let me die."

Frustration yanked down his brows as he faced her. "When are you going to learn you're a valuable person? And not just to me, but to all of Klinhun."

Adelaide glanced away, embarrassed that he could see inside her so easily.

"I didn't have much of a choice, anyway," he said in a lighter tone. "If I hadn't, you probably would have come back to haunt me."

Adelaide's mouth twitched into a smile. "Probably. And the fear of it would have killed you."

"Oh, no doubt."

Her stomach gurgled as she watched fat drip from the dangling meat and sizzle in the flames.

"Before we eat, I must bring you a visitor I found while I was hunting." Elias strode to the cave's entrance.

"Visitor?" Adelaide asked, but he was already outside.

A moment later Elias returned with a large brown hawk on his shoulder.

"Cyr!" Adelaide cried, stumbling over and rubbing the bird's feathers. He shrieked and flew to his normal spot on her right shoulder—thankfully the uninjured one.

"How did you find him?" She wondered, relieved to have the hawk back, safe.

"He landed on a branch in front of me out of nowhere, as he enjoys doing, scaring me so much I dropped the wood I'd been carrying. I persuaded him to land on my shoulder. Once I returned here, I took him to a branch near the horses, where he's been since you woke up."

Adelaide raised an eyebrow at Elias' brief tale, surprised that Cyr would allow the prince to carry him. But she said nothing and went to sit by the fire, Cyr on her shoulder where he belonged. "Let's eat. I'm ravenous. What is this, anyway?"

"Venison." Elias held up one of the sticks of blackening meat. "It should be ready by now."

He handed her the charred stick, and Adelaide stuffed a large chunk of steaming meat into her mouth. It burned her tongue, but she didn't care, she was so hungry. She gave the tougher, burned parts to Cyr, who swallowed them whole.

"How did you manage to escape from your kidnappers? The question's been gnawing at me since I found you."

Adelaide chuckled at the sight of meat juice and tiny black bits smeared across Elias' cheeks and stubby beard.

"What's so funny, fair maiden?"

"You have food all over your face. Aren't princes supposed to eat with delicacy?"

"This *is* me eating delicately." He wiped off the bits of meat and juice with his sleeve. "So, how about those kidnappers?"

"I killed them all with one rock," Adelaide said with a straight face.

Elias's brows furrowed. "How did you manage that? Did it bounce off the wall or something? Weren't there about ten of them?"

Adelaide burst into laughter. She felt strangely light after telling him about Emma and the happy surprise of Cyr's presence.

Elias stared at her, then laughed too. Cyr ruffled his feathers.

"If anyone could kill ten people with one rock, it would be you," Elias said once he regained his composure.

"I'm not sure if that's a compliment, but thanks."

"Truly, though, how did you escape? And how did they kidnap you in the first place?"

In-between bites of venison, Adelaide recounted what had happened after she left him in Kildare up until her escape in the snowstorm. She left out the part about Knick-Nose threatening and bruising her because she didn't want to ruin the peaceful atmosphere. But Elias had seen her face, and by the flashes of anger in his eyes, she guessed he knew what she wasn't saying.

When she finished, she took a long drink of water from an animal pouch Elias proffered her.

"Oh, my." He gazed at her with appreciation. "It's no wonder you were in such bad shape when I found you. Berold and I have attempted rooting out robbers in these mountains several times, but they know the terrain better than anyone and hide extremely well.

"I never knew they were selling people to the Gyndilians." He stabbed one of the now-empty meat sticks at a smoldering log. "I'll have to tell my father so we can gather more knights and put an end to their schemes. I won't allow them to kidnap innocent people in this country."

Adelaide couldn't ignore the evident love in the prince's words for his people. And how she now owed him her life. She had wanted to stay as far from him as possible, yet had ended up closer to him than she'd like to admit. Could her life become any more complicated or ironic?

She gave another piece of venison to Cyr. "How did you find me?"

"The morning after those women treated you so horribly, I went to the stable and saw a wounded guard and Starflare gone. It wasn't difficult to guess what had happened." He raised his eyebrows at her.

Adelaide shrugged, her cheeks warming. "The guard deserved it. It'll teach him to pay better attention in case a real enemy, like a Gyndilian, ever comes along. I was doing him a favor." She licked her greasy fingers. "And at the time I thought you were an arrogant noble."

"And now?"

"I'm still trying to figure you out. But don't worry, I won't steal Starflare again."

"Well, that's progress." Elias stretched out his legs. "When I noticed you were gone, I figured you would have gone east, since that's where you were originally headed. Two days outside of Kildare, I saw hoofprints on the south side of the Lentiasa River. A few paces away, I noticed other signs of horses, and in a small clearing, I found this." He reached into a sack and pulled out Adelaide's dagger.

Her heart thumped in relief, but also with unease, for the weapon reminded her of the violent job her friends still counted on her to fulfill. She had planned on using it on the prince, who now held it so comfortably—he who had rescued her. Did he recognize the weapon? It was his, after all. Would he arrest her now?

"I'll give this back to you without repercussion if you promise not to kill anyone I love with it," Elias said, his face grave.

So he did recognize it. But if he knew she had stolen it from him, why was he giving it back? Adelaide's eyes flicked from his face to the dagger and back. How much of her plans did he suspect?

Her heart hammered and sweat trickled across her palms. Why didn't he ask why she stole the dagger in the first place? Perhaps he didn't want to know.

She had already come to the realization that killing King Ganelon wouldn't solve the country's problems or ease the pain of Emma's death, so she said truthfully, "I promise," and reached for the weapon.

Elias handed it to her, and she tossed it into the air several times, enjoying the familiar feel of the warm leather handle before sliding it into her girdle.

"So, what happened when you saw the dagger?" Adelaide prodded.

"I knew you wouldn't leave the weapon behind, so someone must have kidnapped you. I went back to the river to see if the horses had crossed it.

"It was clear they had, so I followed signs of you and the robbers north to the Spearheads. A few days ago I saw Old Man Henric, and he mentioned that he'd seen and talked to you. What do you think of him, by the way?"

"He's interesting and different, that's for sure."

"Like me?" Elias winked.

"Yes, but more odd."

"So you don't think I'm peculiar anymore?"

Adelaide scrutinized the prince from his muddied leather boots to his tousled brown hair. He didn't look much like a prince or act the way she had thought they did. And yet, he didn't act like a peasant either. "I didn't say that, just that you aren't as odd as him."

Elias nodded. "That's fair. So after I talked to Henric, I knew I was on the right track. Two days later I found you, unconscious and nearly frozen to death. And you know the rest."

Elias' persistence in searching for her—a mere peasant—astounded her. Surely it wasn't just because he cared for her as he claimed; he hadn't known her *that* long.

She dipped her head toward him. "Well, I am much obliged." She stood, dislodging Cyr, who glided outside.

"I still need to get to Fernohn, though, as soon as possible." Even if she no longer needed to speak with the people there about the rebellion, she had to keep up her pretense. She still had friends to protect.

"To get that medicine for your father?" Elias asked with a raised brow.

"Yes," she said a little too fiercely.

"Very well. I shall accompany you to Fernohn, then to Dhalion to see the King's City and the sea."

Adelaide opened her mouth to protest; it would be difficult to locate the others in Dhalion with Elias around. On the other hand, his presence would be useful if she stumbled into another nest of robbers, especially since her dagger hadn't helped much the first time.

"Very well." Adelaide surrendered. "But I don't need a personal guard every moment of the day."

"Nor do I desire to be your guard every moment of the day." Elias placed another log on the fire. As the flames mesmerized her with their dancing rhythm, Elias' voice captivated her with a song about his favorite topic—dragons. It brought tears to Adelaide's eyes.

"A maiden, lovely and sprightly,
saunters through spring-green meadows,
plucking bouquets of flowers gaily
to fill her home of sorrows.

Stooping to pick a beaming daisy,
"Ah," she says, "What's this?"
Something red and cheery
lays in the grass like a stolen lover's kiss.

The maiden cradles the scale close,
her cheerful bouquets forgotten,
and skips home to show the dragon-rose
to her curious-eyed son.

The boy strokes the scale in awe,
but the father knocks it to the floor.
"Those proud creatures just sleep and gnaw,
impressing anyone with a roar."

The man takes a bottle to his bed,
and the maiden picks up the smooth scale.
She puts it beneath her son's head
as she tells him that night a tale.

Over the years, the gift gives her son good dreams,
keeps their soup warm in wild winters,
softens her son's plague-brought screams

and eases her husband's painful blisters.

When the woman's gentle son
grows and marries a neighbor lady,
and her husband's last life-yarn is spun,
the maiden holds the scale humbly.

She decides to thank its giver
for all it had done for her family,
for making their lives slower
and keeping her hope lively.

The woman keeps the scale close
while scaling cliffs covered with dragon signs,
stumbling through wind that blows
and rows of rock as sharp as spines.

She searches long and hard,
but never finds the owner of the treasure
bestowed on her family that was marred.
Instead, she finds the dragon's bower
and dies in its protective cover."

The prince's voice and the peaceful images lulled Adelaide to sleep. No nightmares haunted her dreams that night.

The next morning, once they ate the rest of the venison, Elias grabbed Adelaide's hand and pulled her to her feet. "Follow me. I have something to show you."

"What?"

"I want you to be surprised. Come on."

Adelaide followed Elias out of the cave, making sure her dagger was tucked into her girdle, more out of instinct than fear.

Cyr dropped out of the sky, landed on her shoulder, and nicked her ear.

"Yes, it's good to see you too," she told him.

She strode beside Elias, who kept rubbing his hand

through his hair and remained oddly quiet, not even humming.

The sun shone, melting the snow, but patches remained beneath the pine trees and rocks, and mud squished beneath their feet in the open spaces. A bird chirped nearby, reminding Adelaide that spring stepped nearer every day.

After walking through the woods for a while, Elias halted at a grass-strewn clearing halfway up the mountain. Adelaide huffed and sweated like it was the middle of summer.

"Are you alright?" Elias asked. "I probably shouldn't have brought you up this steep climb so soon after finding you in the snow. You're still recovering."

Adelaide waved his concern away. "What are we doing here?"

He turned and walked around the glade, gazing in-between the trees as if looking for hidden robbers or bears. After making a complete circuit, he came to a stop facing Adelaide in the center of the clearing. "I'm going to convince you that dragons are real and the only hope for this country."

"How?"

Elias rubbed his hands through his hair so hard that Adelaide wouldn't be surprised if he was bald by the time they returned to the cave. "Just watch."

He closed his eyes. A soft golden glow emanated from his skin and clothes and spread outward as if he had turned into a candle. The light grew until it encompassed his entire body and Adelaide could no longer see him, just a glowing shape like a man-shaped star hovering over the grass. The light expanded until the entire clearing filled with a steady, golden-white glow, turning the trees and grass vapid and stale.

Adelaide blinked, and there, in front of her, where Prince Elias had just stood, was a dragon.

Chapter Thirty-One

Adelaide gawked at the red-scaled legs supporting a golden back lined with sharp spikes as long as her body. They marched down the thick red-gold tail curling around the creature's bulk and up to its serpentine golden neck. There, atop its giant triangular head, they created a crown of three horns sharper than any dagger. Shorter spines edged along its square jaw, and gold wings tipped with red lay flat against its sides, jutting out at sharp angles.

The dragon—with its blazing scarlet scales shifting to a kingly gold near the top of its body—resembled a sun rising out of a blood-filled day into the light of hope and victory.

Adelaide, it's me, Prince Elias, a familiar voice said in her mind as the dragon gazed at her with one of its crystalline eyes—eyes the color of the sky, the same shade as Elias'.

Adelaide jumped at the intrusion into her mind. "What...how...?" She couldn't even think what to ask; her thoughts, like her body, had frozen at the sight before her.

I told you dragons were real. Elias' tone stank of smugness.

"Um, yes," Adelaide stammered. "But you neglected to say that you *are* a dragon." She couldn't keep her eyes off the massive creature. All the tales she'd heard and songs she'd sung had gathered into the beast before her. But it didn't open its maw to destroy or devour her...yet. It just stood there, staring at her with those familiar, yet too-huge eyes.

The dragon's belly rumbled, causing the ground where Adelaide stood to tremble. She took a few tottering steps away.

I needed to gain your trust before I could tell you something as strange as this. If I had told you I was a dragon the first day I met you, you wouldn't have listened to anything else I said.

She hadn't listened anyway since he was a noble. But it was true; she would have run even farther and faster away if he had told her he was a dragon. That didn't make it easier to believe now, though.

Adelaide, I listened to your tale with open ears, so please listen well to mine. The dragon flicked its golden-red tail, knocking down a few trees. The creature didn't seem to notice the branches cracking or the soil raining down on its tail spikes. *If I had shown you I was a dragon when I first met you, you could have told someone about me. Depending on if they believed you or not, things could have become dangerous quickly.*

Staring at the dragon and hearing his words inside her head, Adelaide felt like a worm brought out of its familiar world of dirt into the blazing heat of day. "You're not going to scorch me, are you? Or accidentally knock me down like those trees behind you?"

A whooshing, warm blast of air rushed out of the cave-like nostrils and tousled Adelaide's hair and clothes. *Why would I kill or hurt you after saving your life? After trying so hard to earn your trust?*

She shrugged. "I don't know. Somehow you've turned into a fire-breathing creature, and I don't know anything about them except that they supposedly killed Klinians centuries ago. And how can I possibly trust you now? You just turned into a dragon." She waved a hand at the beast, her voice rising. "If you hid this from me, you could be hiding anything."

Another, smaller puff of steam escaped the beast's nostrils. *Adelaide, I told you at the caverns that the dragons didn't kill anyone. One of the humans wove that tale to grab more power for himself and to take out his rage on the dragons."*

Adelaide loosed her own breath of hot air and sat. A question that had always niggled at her became more persistent now. Why had Elias always been so interested in her? It had seemed odd as a prince, but as a dragon it made no sense. "Why did you want to gain my trust so much?" Her eyes widened at a sudden thought. "Wait. Does this mean your father is a dragon as well?"

Yes. King Ganelon's the tenth ruler of the dragons. His father was the king who chose to leave Klinhun rather than fight the humans.

Adelaide whistled. If what Dragon-Elias said was correct—and there was no reason he would lie—it was a good thing she hadn't attempted to injure his father. He could've just morphed into a dragon and blew her or her friends out of existence as easily as blowing out a candle.

"Wait." Adelaide held up a hand, even though no words had intruded into her mind. "Did you say your grandfather was the king who led the dragons out of Klinhun?" She couldn't fit the realization that dragons still existed, let alone that the one standing before her was the grandson of the dragon who left their country centuries ago, into her head.

Dragon-Elias bobbed his thick head once. *We live a long time compared to humans.*

"Indeed." She kneaded her aching head. "So, if your father is the King of Dragons, why are you here in Klinhun, where every citizen, except for that Old Henric man, hates the thought of you?"

Dragon-Elias laid down like a large cat, his tail curling around him. His snout lay on the ground only a few paces from her. She tensed but didn't move.

This is a long story, so make yourself comfortable.

Adelaide propped her head on her hand. Cyr shuffled on her shoulder. She was surprised he hadn't flown off at the sight of the dragon. He was acting as if he saw such huge, frightening creatures every day.

As if noticing the direction of her look, Elias thought to her, *Did you know birds are the dragons' fellow friends of the sky? We can speak to one another.*

After a moment of silence, Cyr landed on one of the dragon's tail spikes and preened his feathers.

Adelaide frowned at the hawk. "Very well, Cyr, but if you get burned, it won't be my fault."

I asked him to come over. Would you like him to return to you?

Adelaide didn't bother answering. Elias hadn't lost any of his irritating characteristics as a dragon.

Cyr soared back to her shoulder and nicked her ear as if apologizing.

See, he does love you, the voice in her head said.

Adelaide scrunched up her face at the gold-scaled snout. "I suppose you can't speak out loud?"

The dragon moved his head from side to side.

"That's a shame. It's quite bothersome to hear you inside my head." She rubbed Cyr's tail feathers, and he stretched out his head in pleasure. "Since you listened to my tale the other night, I'll listen to yours without interrupting, but only if you ask my permission before speaking to Cyr again."

A hiss of smoke leaked out of the dragon's nostrils. *You would make a deal with a dragon? You are either braver or more foolish than I thought.*

"Being burned wouldn't be the worst way to die. At least it would be fast." She glanced away, thinking of Emma's torn body. "And it would save me from so much pain," she whispered.

Adelaide—

"Now tell me everything." She shoved the smarting pain aside and prodded the creature with her gaze. "You have a lot of explaining to do, your highness."

Very well, most stubborn of maidens. I'll begin when the end started—the end of peace for both humans and dragons.

A human man, whom the dragons call the Destroyer, since he destroyed all that was dear to us, became jealous and angry when the dragons refused to use their gift to turn him into one. He hated that the dragons possessed the sole power to rule Klinhun, though they never neglected the weaker species.

Adelaide glowered at the term, 'weaker,' but Dragon-Elias didn't see it.

This human believed he deserved more power. Since he couldn't receive it from the dragons, he let his anger rule him and turned to other means.

He convinced some of his friends that the dragons were cruel for not letting the humans reign, and they did so only because they hoarded all the power for themselves. So the men left their village one night, cornered a young dragon, and killed it. They took the dragon's body to some villagers nearby, proclaiming that the dragon had attempted to kill them in a wild fit, but they had overpowered it. They showed some wounds on their body as proof, which they most likely inflicted themselves, so full of hatred and foolishness were they. A low growl erupted from the dragon's throat, and Adelaide cringed.

"How could a group of men kill a dragon?" she asked. Now seeing the massive size, impenetrable scales, and teeth that could slice her as easily as slicing cheese, she couldn't believe humans had killed one, let alone hundreds, as the stories said.

The men targeted a solitary young dragon. And you must remember, this was the first time, at least that we know of, that violence existed between the two species. So the men's actions took the dragon by surprise. Although we look fierce and frightening, most of us don't engage in violence unless we have to. We were created to look after and live peacefully alongside the humans, so it goes against our nature to harm them.

"Really?" Adelaide had never heard that dragons were created to look after humans. "How do you know that?"

He lifted one of his shoulders. *It's written in our very beings. We also pass the knowledge down to our hatchlings through songs. I'd love to share them with you sometime.*

"Very well. But first finish this tale."

Well, this group of bitter men spread more tales of dragons hurting people. They showed wounded humans as proof and also burned corpses as if the dragons had done the damage. The dragons could tell from the scent of the corpses that the humans were lying, but the group's ploy of frightening people worked.

Fear took root in the humans, and many didn't listen to the dragons.

After several of these so-called attacks, a throng of humans confronted the dragons. My grandfather, King Aloysius, knew their claims of the dragons' destructive behavior were false. There were also harsh consequences if dragons ever voluntarily hurt a human.

But more and more humans accused the dragons of vicious acts as news of attacks spread throughout Klinhun. The dragons felt betrayed by the humans' lack of faith in them after all the years they had protected and lived with them, but there wasn't much they could do. King Aloysius and the eldest dragons met to discuss the matter. They debated long and hard, but kept returning to the same conclusion.

Before any of their kind could retaliate against the humans, they decided to leave rather than fight.

Dragon-Elias' eyes crinkled at the edges as he bowed his head. *So the dragons left to cheers from the humans who longed for them to leave, and tears from those who didn't want them to depart. But those humans also knew it must end this way if the two species were to avoid a disastrous war. For if a war occurred too many humans—possibly even all—would die. The dragons couldn't live with the possibility of killing those who had once been their friends, those they had protected. And so, the dragons left.*

They flew to a volcanic island they named Niclond, several hundred miles south of Klinhun. They still live there, hoping one day to return to Klinhun—their true home—and to those they once called friends.

Chapter Thirty-Two

"The dragons live on an island?" Adelaide couldn't believe that dragons besides Elias and his father had survived after all this time. And on an island, of all places. How could there be room for such huge creatures on what she imagined to be a tiny piece of rock?

Elias bobbed his head.

"Why don't they return here? They could rule the humans by just opening their mouths and roaring."

Amusement rippled through Elias' thoughts. *You already know the answer to that. Everyone here believes the dragons are evil, arrogant creatures. They wouldn't wait to find out if it was true. They would attack the dragons, and then the dragons would either have to retaliate or leave again, which would just bring us to the predicament we're already in.*

You must understand, Elias' slate-blue eyes held hers, *the dragons don't merely want to rule. If they did, they would have returned ages ago. They want to restore their friendship with the humans. Only then can both species truly prosper.*

"So, why do people today sing and tell so many terrible stories about the dragons if they're not evil?" Elias had hinted at the reason before, but now that Adelaide knew dragons were real, she could properly listen.

The human who plotted to steal the dragons' power, the Destroyer, set himself up as the new king. He circulated stories that he and his allies invented to turn people against their friends. As is their want, the stories became fiercer and bloodier over the years until people no longer recalled the wise, caring nature of the dragons but only their claws, teeth, and size.

The Destroyer outlawed all the favorable tales and songs of dragons. At the end of his life, he created the Fire Festival to memorialize them as destructive creatures. Because he held the power to destroy a village with his new army, everyone obeyed him, even those who didn't believe him.

Adelaide knew what it was like to live in fear of a king. It incapacitated and chained you so you couldn't do anything you believed in or hoped for. But when Emma had been murdered, the shackles of fear had loosened.

King Aloysius, the dragon-king, Elias continued, *kept in contact with a human through a dragon who flew to the sea near Dhalion once a year.*

"Dragons have come to Klinhun? I've never heard of or seen them before."

That's because the dragon messenger and humans guarded their communication with their lives. It has been the dragons' only communication with Klinhun for centuries.

Before King Aloysius died many years ago, he gave my father, the next in line, the knowledge of how to turn a dragon into a human. It hadn't been tried before and was thought to shorten a dragon's life, but King Aloysius had been exploring the option ever since the Destroyer broke our relationship with the humans. He had hoped it could help unite us.

King Aloysius made my father promise to keep the knowledge a secret and only attempt it when it's evident that the two races must be united again. Only my father, me, our human friend here, and the current dragon messenger who keeps us updated, know of this secret. And you too, now, of course.

"Who is the other human?" Adelaide hoped it wasn't another noble; she didn't think she'd be able to stomach that. "And I don't know how you changed yourself, just that you did."

That's all you need to know. And the human friend is Manfred, the man I told you about.

Adelaide nodded, then another thought occurred to her. "But if the dragons on the island don't know you can turn into a human, where do they think you and your father have been all these years?"

Exploring the outer chain of islands and what could be east of Niclond. He shifted one of his red-scaled legs closer to his belly. *After my father became King, there was a large volcano eruption on our island, and some—*

"Wait. What's a volcano?"

The dragon's deep, rumbling laugh rolled over her. *I forget sometimes how small your world is.*

Adelaide frowned but let the comment pass.

A volcano is a large mountain filled with fire. Sometimes the fire spews out the top and down the sides, incinerating everything in its path. Niclond has two volcanos.

Adelaide's eyes widened as she tried to imagine fire-exploding mountains, but she couldn't fathom it any more than she could the sea.

You're not keeping your side of the bargain of not interrupting, Dragon-Elias said.

"Well, I didn't know you'd be telling me about mountains that exploded with fire."

I'm a dragon. You should always expect the unexpected. Now, back to my tale.

There was a volcanic eruption that destroyed much of our island, and though dragons are impervious to fire, it wiped out many of the animals we eat. Even before that happened, our population had been growing too large for Niclond. The outlying islands are even more barren.

Quarrels broke out over land and food, and several dragons became ill from lack of good meat. The eruption just exacerbated all of this. So my father decided it was time to try bridging the gap between the two species. We needed a place to stretch our wings, and from what Manfred told us, the humans needed us.

We told the others we were going to explore the islands and the area east of Niclond. We only told the dragon-messenger our true plan, and he promised to keep it a secret. To our knowledge, he has.

"Why didn't you tell the dragons about your true destination?" It seemed like an unnecessary deception.

We didn't want to keep our whereabouts a secret, but we didn't want to raise the dragons' hopes when we didn't know what awaited us. Some would have tried to hinder us from leaving or tried to go with us. It was easier and quicker for us to keep it a secret, especially since dragons take so long to make decisions. Every moment is vital to our survival.

Dragon-Elias scratched at his crimson neck scales with his massive golden claws. *Once we told the dragon-messenger our plans and he assured us he wouldn't tell anyone where we were going, my father and I left Niclond. We promised to return as soon as we found somewhere to stretch our wings. We vowed to keep in touch with the dragons through the messenger. When my father and I reached the shores of Klinhun, we turned ourselves into humans. It was the first time a dragon—albeit in human skin—had stepped onto this land in over five hundred years.*

Adelaide stared at the creature, soaking in all he had said. She had so many questions, but the one that first popped into her mind wasn't about anything he'd said. "What about your mother?"

He gazed out at the trees encircling the clearing. *When I was a hatchling, several boulders from the volcanic explosion crushed her.*

Adelaide didn't know how old a hatchling was, but it sounded young. "I'm sorry, Elias. That's horrible." She swallowed, remembering the haunting pain of Emma's death and shuddering at how horrible it would have been to lose a mother.

I was too young to remember much, but I miss her every day. Sometimes I wonder if I would have been a better dragon or man if she had been with me as I grew up.

"You couldn't have been a better man," Adelaide said, then glanced away, embarrassed she had said her feelings out loud.

Something hard brushed her knee, and Adelaide looked up to see the end of a knobby wing touching her before it pressed back against Dragon-Elias' body.

I appreciate you saying that, Adelaide.

She said nothing, astonished at how much her opinions of him had changed over the last few weeks. She had hated him, then as he had continued to help her, she had begun to trust him.

But if he had hidden his true identity all this time, even for good reasons, could she still trust him?

The dragon's copious blue eye gazing at her was so huge and complex that she could lose herself in there forever. Elias blinked, breaking her trance. *My father and I came to Klinhun when I was nine winters old, and we went to live with Manfred. He had been our only contact with humans for several years. Before him, it had been his father. Manfred—*

"So everything you told me about your childhood was a lie?" Confusion and doubt crawled across Adelaide's skin like bugs.

His head swayed back and forth, sending a gust of air through Adelaide's messy braid. *Nay. It was all true, some of it just happened when I was in this form. Manfred taught my father and me how to be humans, and not only humans, but the proper etiquette and behavior of a king and prince. He had worked for the previous king as a gardener and had picked up much knowledge over the years.*

So when the human king, King Clerebold, died when I was 12 winters, my father and I moved to the castle. My father was able to convince everyone he was the dead king's brother, and I frightened the dead king's son enough that he and his mother fled to Findar. They won't show themselves around here for a long time. If they ever return, my father will take care of them.

"You threatened the young prince when you were only 12 winters old?" Adelaide didn't know why she was surprised; she was looking at a dragon, after all. But when she pictured it, she saw a child-version of Elias, tender and unruffled, incapable of any harm.

Don't be so surprised. I'm a dragon, after all. I'm capable of atrocious things, more than you are with that dagger. Remember, I had to restrain myself from killing those awful women and the robbers when I saw what they had done to you. His front claws dug into the ground, leaving marks deep enough for a grave.

Adelaide scooted back from those dagger-sharp, arm-long talons.

Dragon-Elias drew his claws back under him. *But I don't wish to harm people. I don't enjoy causing pain.*

Adelaide believed this more easily than anything else she'd heard or seen that morning. "So, you became the Prince of Klinhun and your father the king for what purpose?"

To gain the trust and respect of the people so they'd believe us and not try to kills us when we told them we were dragons. Then the dragons could return and rule peacefully again, and the tyranny of the nobles would end. We hated the deception, but it had to be done to save both species. He let out a puff of steam over Adelaide's head, filling the clearing with the smell of smoke and meat. *But it has taken much longer to gain the people's trust than my father expected. The kings and nobility's lies and wickedness have sunk deep into the country, causing more damage than we realized.* His bottomless blue eyes fixated on Adelaide as if seeing into her depths.

My father has kept in contact with the dragon-messenger as he promised. Life on Niclond has deteriorated. There's even more overpopulation and lack of food than when we left. Life here has also declined, as you well know. We could be at war with the Gyndilians any day. If the dragons had remained in this country, protecting it, the Gyndilians wouldn't dare be so bold to attack this land.

His spiked tail lifted in the air, then fell back at his side with a thump. *Last autumn, the messenger from Niclond told my father a dragon had proclaimed himself as ruler, since my father could be dead, for all they knew. The dragons forced him to leave the island. But my father knew it was only a matter of time before another dragon tried to rule in his stead.*

So he gave me a year to find someone and earn their trust so I could convince them dragons weren't evil and eventually reveal my identity. We thought it would be easier and quicker to earn one person's trust than an entire country's. He snorted, gazing at her with amusement. *Little did I know how hard of a nut you were to crack.*

His words breezed right over her head, so focused was she on his and his father's larger plan. "What would have happened if you hadn't found someone or they didn't believe you?"

My father and I would have returned to Niclond to think of another solution. But I doubt there is one.

He contemplated the sky for a moment, then lowered his head back to Adelaide. *You are the one I chose, Adelaide, to help my species and yours, that day I came to the Fire Festival.*

She should have been expecting something like this, what with Elias' words about how hard of a nut she was to crack and his pursuit of her all over the country, but his declaration still punched her stomach.

She had never considered Elias' motive of pursuing her would entail acting as an ambassador between two species roiling with rage and enmity. And why in all of Klinhun had he chosen her? She was a peasant who hadn't even believed dragons existed.

Doubt latched onto her mind. Did he care about her as a person at all? Or was all he had done these last few weeks, even saving her life, just to win her trust and save the dragons? If so, what a fool she had been to think he might care for her.

"You became my friend and followed me all over the country just to save your dragon friends?" Adelaide stood, her thoughts churning. Cyr bolted from her shoulder. "You used me." Even if she didn't know anything else, she knew this much. If she didn't care how Elias viewed her, then why did this knowledge hurt like thorns digging into her heart?

The dragon shook his head, but with what emotion, Adelaide couldn't tell. *It's true, I suppose, that I want to use you to bridge the gap between our two species. But what was I supposed to do? You were—and still are—my last chance to help Klinhun and the dragons. You are important, Adelaide, but the saving of the humans and dragons is more important than either of us.*

And if there's one thing I've learned from spending time with you, it's that you care deeply for your people and want the best for them. Reuniting with the dragons is the only way to rescue peasants from the nobility.

He bent his head and growled at her like a dog. *But do not say I don't care about you, because I do. If you cannot see that, then you are blind. I have come to love you, Adelaide. And a dragon's love is just as strong, if not stronger, than a human's.*

Adelaide pressed her hands to her eyes. It was too much. First, Prince Elias was a dragon. Then he wanted her to help him save two species. And now he supposedly loved her.

It didn't matter; Adelaide was already entangled in too many nets. She was just a peasant, after all, with already too many people's lives resting on her shoulders. She didn't need the dragons' hopes on her as well. She couldn't help them, so it was best to leave this prince, dragon, and man while she still could.

"Leave me alone, Elias," Adelaide whispered, her heart stuttering.

She turned and darted through the forest, away from the dragon and his desperation, away from the tearing emotions his words of love had fanned into life inside her.

Chapter Thirty-Three

Elias stared at the place where Adelaide had fled into the forest. The leaves she had pushed aside in her haste trembled, and the acrid scent of her anxiety snaked over to him.

He throbbed at the panicked look in her eyes and her swift departure. But what did he expect? For her to kneel before him and promise her undying love? He had just taken her world and all she knew about him and spun it like a child's wooden top.

Even so, she had taken the news about him and the other dragons surprisingly well. Of course, it was hard to disbelieve someone discussing dragons when he turned into one before your eyes. Elias just hoped Adelaide hadn't lost all her trust in him and understood why he had kept the truth from her until now.

He stretched his red-specked golden wings so they rose to the tips of the trees forming the clearing's edge, wishing he could fly to retrieve Adelaide. He hadn't flown since he went for that swim in the lake near Pinhurn. Even when he had shifted into a dragon that night in Kildare, he hadn't dared flown, just blasted boulders and trampled trees in his rage.

His entire body ached to taste the wind on his tongue, to dip and dive through the clouds—to be free. But he couldn't risk anyone seeing him, not now when there was a greater exigency and opportunity for dragons and humans to live together once more.

Elias sighed, steam whistling out of his nostrils. He closed his eyes, imagining the weaker human form that he had grown unexpectedly used to over the years.

A glowing warmth followed by excruciating pain invaded his extremities, stomach, chest, and finally, his head. No matter how many times he did this, he never became accustomed to the torment.

Just when Elias thought his body would crumble from the inside out at the agony, the ripping anguish vanished.

He opened his eyes and blinked. It always took a moment to adjust to the loss of his heightened senses and size. He wiped the sweat off his face and straightened his cloak. He hurried back to the cave, worried that men would bind and take Adelaide away again.

She wasn't there, but there weren't any signs of robbers, so she must have left on her own. Elias gathered his things, put out the fire, and tried to cover up the evidence of their stay as much as possible. Now that Adelaide had run again, he wasn't ready for Berold and his knights to find him. Would she ever stop running? He sure hoped so; this was exhausting, even for a dragon.

At least she had kept her promise and taken Suntaria this time instead of Starflare.

"Come on, girl," Elias murmured to the black mare once he had saddled and mounted her. "We need to catch that maiden again. Hopefully, this will be the last time."

◆◆◆

"What should I do, Cyr?" Adelaide contemplated the hawk preening himself on a birch's branch near a moss-cloaked creek.

It was only early evening, but Adelaide was too weary to ride any further, and what was the point if Elias would just catch up to her? His dragon abilities probably made him ride faster than a normal person.

And she hadn't been able to keep thoughts of Knick-Nose and his rotten-apple smell out of her mind as she rode through the tree-lined ravines. *Perhaps*, a tiny voice inside her argued, *it wouldn't be so bad if Elias did find you.*

Adelaide ignored the voice as she scrutinized Cyr. "You've apparently talked to him and still like him. But he didn't lie to you about who he was just so he could enlist your help." Adelaide had lied to Elias too, but never about who she was or her feelings toward him; he knew she had loathed him.

Cyr gave her as much attention as a rock, so Adelaide turned aside, her thoughts shifting to Emma. But she didn't know what her sister would do in her predicament. Would she agree to help the dragons, since it would also be helping her people?

"But how can I even help Elias and the other...dragons?" Adelaide found it hard to admit, especially out loud, that the creatures existed after laughing at any mention of them her entire life. "And what about Conrad, Gunter, and the others? They're expecting to kill or dethrone the king when we meet in Dhalion, not bow before a dragon. They won't believe me if I tell them Prince Elias and King Ganelon are dragons in human form." It sounded strange even to her, and she had just seen Elias transform before her eyes. And she couldn't tell Elias about her friends, because he could imprison or scorch them, though she didn't believe he'd actually hurt them.

But the real reason she didn't want to tell him about the rebellion, she realized, was far more personal and selfish. She was terrified of seeing the pain and disappointment that would cloud those beautiful blue-grey eyes.

In the end, she was no better than him—probably worse, because she had expected to kill him and his father. And he had only wanted to help her and save their people.

Adelaide sunk onto a boulder beneath the weight of this knowledge and placed her head in her hands. The knowledge didn't change much. She still had to go to Dhalion and somehow convince those in the rebellion that they don't need to get rid of the king, and that Prince Elias isn't so terrible once you get to know him—at least in human form.

Adelaide groaned at the impossibility of that conversation. But it was much easier to think about than solving Elias' dragon problems, which threatened to overwhelm her in a downpour of terror. So dousing the rebellion would come first.

She turned to Cyr, who was cleaning the delicate white feathers under his russet-brown wings. "Thank you so much for your wise counsel." He didn't look up.

She stuck her tongue out at him before striding down to the creek's mossy bank. She filled her animal skin in the current, then gazed at her rippling reflection. Perhaps wild, crazed-looking women attracted dragons, because that was the reflection staring back at her.

The skin below her right eye, where Knick-Nose had punched her, was slightly red but no longer swollen. Most of her long black hair had escaped her braid and was knotted together like weeds. Her torn, once-tan dress was now dark brown from the dirt of her journey.

If she didn't take better care of herself, she would soon end up looking like Old Man Henric, and her friends from Alesfirth wouldn't recognize her. She could almost hear Emma tsk and say, "Sis, you look as if you've wallowed in mud all day."

Adelaide took a quick dip in the stream's freezing waters, then washed her dress. While waiting for it to dry, she wrapped herself in a blanket she had taken from one of Elias' satchels and ate the rest of the venison he had cooked the night before.

She wondered if he had killed the deer as a dragon. It must be horrible to be trapped in human flesh when one was used to possessing strength greater than a human could hold and not able to tell anyone about it. Worse though, would be to have wings and never to be able to use them.

As an icy sliver of moon rose overhead, Adelaide changed back into her damp dress, pulled the blanket over her, and laid her head on Emma's cloak.

Late that night, she awoke breathless and sweaty, the cloak clutched tight around her shoulders. The nightmares hadn't ended when she spoke them aloud, and she wished that Elias, dragon or not, was there to ease the darkness with his solid presence.

But then she remembered the word he used that had helped drive her away: love. Like fire, it was dangerous if one came too close.

The next morning, Adelaide woke to chirping sparrows and a numb leg from sleeping on it wrong. She stood and stretched, contemplating what to eat.

"Good morning, fair maiden. I thought you would already be in Fernohn by now."

Adelaide turned and saw Prince Elias riding toward her, grinning.

Seeing him back in his familiar human form comforted Adelaide and melted away some of her confusion from the day before. She smiled. "Well, I have been recovering from a near-death experience."

"Does that mean you'll stop running from me every opportunity you have?"

"Probably not, especially if you try burning me to death," she jested.

But apparently not with enough lightness, because Elias

scowled. "How many times must I tell you I would never harm you for you to believe me? What else can I possibly do to show you that I care about you?"

"Since you asked, you could tell me the truth and not use me for your own gain." Her epiphany from yesterday came hurtling back, and she glanced away, her heart prickling.

"I'll never keep secrets from you again, but I didn't use you. I can make no better promises than that, since I'm not perfect, human or dragon."

"Nor am I," Adelaide murmured while watching Cyr soar circles over their heads.

"Well," he said while dismounting, "your hair looks especially lovely today. Why do you not wear it like that more often?"

Adelaide forgot she had left her hair down last night to dry. She combed her fingers through the locks, then braided the black strands, trying to ignore the heat creeping down her cheeks to her neck. "It gets in the way when I ride."

Elias nodded and took out some tough pieces of bread from one of his saddlebags. "I still have some biscuits left. They're not very tasty, but you took the rest of the meat, and I'm guessing you don't have any left." He glanced at her, and she shook her head.

He then gave the biscuits all his attention, as if they'd run away if he looked anywhere else. "I was hoping you would come to Dhalion with me to speak to my father about what to do with the dragons and humans. And to prove to him that he and I don't have to leave Klinhun."

He handed her a biscuit and took a bite of his. "In case it helps you decide, we'll need to stop in Fernohn on the way for supplies."

Adelaide raised an eyebrow. "That does make it more tempting."

"I thought you needed to go there?"

Adelaide shrugged, fear and shame tying her mouth up in knots.

While they ate, Adelaide scrutinized Elias' face for any sign that beneath his skin lay scales and fire. She didn't see any, but she did see signs of sleeplessness: dark half-moon circles under his eyes, redness dotting his irises, and lines furrowing his brow.

"Are you enjoying staring at me?" He asked with a shy smile.

Adelaide's cheeks warmed, and she glanced away. "I was just thinking about how horrible you looked. Did you get any sleep last night?"

"Nay. I had to find you before any kidnappers could."

"Well, it looks like you haven't slept for several nights." She couldn't help thinking again about how much he had sacrificed for her. She probably wouldn't be alive right now if he hadn't saved her from the cold.

"I didn't get much sleep when you were ill either." He waved a hand. "But it matters not. Dragons don't need much sleep."

"But you're human too," Adelaide protested. Then an idea slithered into her mind. An idea to leave this dragon-man for good. The plan tasted bitter and made her insides squirm, but it was necessary. She couldn't risk Elias finding out about the rebellion—for the sake of her friends—and the chances that he would escalated the closer they came to Dhalion.

She lifted her chin and said, "We aren't leaving until you sleep for a while."

"Who's the prince and dragon of this pair?"

"Just because you're a prince and dragon doesn't mean you should make all the decisions, especially those about your own health." Adelaide almost laughed at the stunned look on Elias' face. He probably had never been so contradicted in his whole life.

After clenching and unclenching his hands several times, he said, "Very well. I'll take a short nap, but it's because I need one to better protect you, not because you told me to."

Adelaide sighed, smiling. And he called *her* stubborn. “Very well, your highness.”

Elias shot her a look, rolled out on a blanket, and was asleep in two breaths.

She gathered her things and neared the horses. Before she left, she glanced at the prince. There was no evidence of a scaled, fire-breathing beast in the gentle rise and fall of his chest, the bristly stubble lining his stubborn jaw, the wave of his brown hair, and in his large, now-still hands. His lips were turned up in a slight smile even in his sleep, and she wondered what he dreamed about.

Memories from their time together rose in her mind like the sun: his deep voice rolling over her in song, his strong arms around her when he held her after a nightmare, the sweaty, smoky scent of him, the proud look on his face when she thanked him or praised the food, the way his eyes always strayed to the skies, as if he was soaring up there on those golden-red wings of his—a deep longing and pain etched in his face.

Adelaide lowered her things to the ground, and then herself. She was tired of trying to evade him, of trying to convince herself he was as wicked as other nobility. In their whole time together, he had tried to protect and take care of her. He had hidden things from her, yes, but so had she. She could ride with him at least to Dhalion and then somehow find her friends when he went up to the castle.

And so, this time, Adelaide stayed.

Chapter Thirty-Four

When Elias woke and noticed her there, his smile lit up his whole face. Adelaide pretended his look hadn't just sent her stomach spinning by tightening Suntaria's saddle.

Once Elias gathered his things, they mounted and rode toward the mining town of Fernohn. They traveled east, through the valleys of the snow-melting mountains. Cyr soared above, and Prince Elias informed her he could speak to the hawk in his human form as well as a dragon. But thus far he seemed to be upholding his end of the deal not to speak to Cyr unless Adelaide agreed.

Elias didn't discuss his feelings for Adelaide, for which she was grateful. She did catch him gazing at her occasionally when they rode side-by-side. She tried to ignore the looks and the heat they sparked inside her.

As they rode, their conversations centered mostly on Emma and dragons. Adelaide found it easier now to speak about her sister, especially since the prince always seemed so interested in her.

"What's your favorite memory of your sister?" Elias asked the day after he joined her at the creek.

Adelaide ducked under a pine bough and received several pine needles in her hair. "That's a difficult question. There're so many."

After a moment's thought, she chuckled. "This once, when Emma was twelve and I eleven, one of our neighbors wanted to get rid of a goose that had been eating her plants. My sister always had a soft spot for unwanted or injured animals—she was the one who helped me take care of Cyr—so she asked our mother if we could bring the goose home. My mother didn't want to, since a single goose isn't worth much, and we already had a lot of animals to take care of. But Emma could be persuasive when she wanted to."

"Like someone else I know," Elias said.

Adelaide shook her head, shame pouring in. Emma had persuaded people with kind words and tender expressions, whereas Adelaide persuaded people by threatening them with her dagger and harsh words. In that way, they were nothing alike.

"So," Adelaide continued, "Mother gave in to Emma, and we went to get the goose. We put it outside with the chickens, and Emma named it Quacker because of the sound it made."

"Very creative." Elias chuckled.

"Yes, Emma was always so original." Adelaide grinned and steered Suntaria around a patch of mud. "Later that day, Quacker came waddling on his short little orange legs into our cottage, nipped at everyone's feet, then grabbed Emma's only cloak and attempted to eat it. Emma tried grabbing the cloak, but the silly goose half-flew, half-waddled away with it in its beak. Geese can move faster than you think.

"Em chased that bird all through the house and outside, her face red from yelling at the animal and at me to help, but I was too busy laughing. It took her almost the entire morning to catch that foolish-brained fowl, and when she did, her cloak was ruined. I had never seen her so excited to eat goose as she was the next day. After that adventure she stayed away from geese, making sure her garments were far from their beaks."

Elias laughed, and Adelaide joined in, the laughter a better panacea than tears.

When they had caught their breaths, Adelaide asked, "Do you have any siblings?"

He shook his head. "My sister died before she hatched."

For a moment, with his deep laughter gushing out, and his solid presence on the horse beside her, Adelaide had forgotten he was a dragon. His words jolted her back to the truth. "Oh. I'm sorry."

He shrugged. "Only the strongest dragons survive to adulthood. And I never knew her. But it sounds like it would have been fun to grow up with siblings."

"Fun and annoying." She recalled Odo's million questions and Emma's habit of commenting on her outfits and hair. "What was it like growing up on an island with exploding mountains?"

Elias's gaze traveled far past the cloud-swollen sky. "Thrilling. My friends and I would chase each other over the tops of the volcanoes, trying not to let the smoke touch us." He sighed wistfully. "We also flew through the jungle, but if I tried that now, I'd get stuck since the trees grow so close together. I also loved swimming in the ocean, which is warmer and clearer than the sea near Dhalion."

Adelaide tried to picture his words, but she had never seen an ocean, jungle, or volcano, and he was the only dragon she had met, so it was difficult to imagine his childhood. "It sounds...interesting."

His mouth lifted at the sight of her puzzlement. "It was good. But as I told you, we didn't have much prey, and some dragons talked about limiting hunting territory for different clusters, which would make the dragons cranky and dangerous." He scowled. "That was one of the reasons we came here, and why it's so imperative to change the humans' minds about us."

"I'm still confused why you need my help. What can I possibly do for a bunch of irritable dragons?" Adelaide could barely help her own people, let alone powerful, fire-breathing creatures that she hadn't even know existed until a few days ago.

"I'm not sure yet. But you think like a human, and a skeptical human at that, so it's a start."

That night and the next three Elias turned into a dragon when they stopped so Adelaide could grow accustomed to his dragon-form, and because he wouldn't be able to once they reached Fernohn. Adelaide didn't doubt these reasons, but she thought it might also be to show off his power and strength. The transformation shocked her less each time, but she never completely overcame her awe.

I wish I could fly, Elias said one night while gazing up at the star-studded sky, his long neck arched back.

"Why can't you? It's night, and there's no one around." Adelaide watched his scales shimmer in the firelight as if alive.

He lowered his head to look at her. *Because I don't want to leave you alone at night out here.*

She crossed her arms. "I will be fine for a few moments. I did escape the robbers by myself, you know." Well, almost by herself.

I know. You are very capable, but I'm unwilling to take the risk when there's a host of outlaws attempting to kidnap any Klinian they see and take them to Gyndilad.

"I could have taken them if I had had more daggers."

Laughter rolled through Elias, shaking the ground. Adelaide smiled at the sight of his long, red-spiked tongue hanging out like a dog's, and the disbelief that she was here, sitting next to a fire-breathing dragon. She didn't think there could be anything stranger in all of Klinhun or its neighboring lands.

Chapter Thirty-Five

On the sixth morning after leaving the cave where Elias had nursed Adelaide back to health, they came upon the mountain town of Fernohn. Wooden buildings sat like loose teeth at the base of a snow-dusted mountain, and the Wymar River ambled down the far side of town with the slow and steady gait of an old man. The mines in the cliffs above the town stared out like sightless eyes.

As Adelaide and Elias neared the village below, Adelaide noticed a thick cloud of smoke hanging over the town. Screams soon pierced the chatter of squirrels and birds. The sounds whirled her back to the attack on Alesfirth, and she clenched the reins. "What's wrong?"

"I'm not sure. Come on." Elias urged Starflare into a gallop, and Adelaide followed him down into the hazy town.

"What happened here?" Elias asked a man covered in coal dust at the edge of town. Only the man's eyes and mouth peeked out of the black grime covering him.

The man bowed, then nodded to the mountain on their right, where gray smoke billowed up into the air. Behind the man, flames flickered through the thick miasma. "One of the mines just exploded, your highness. Half of the mountain came down, killing and trapping many miners. The explosion caught some buildings on fire too."

"How many people are trapped?"

"We don't know. We're trying to get them out now."

Elias nodded. "Go ask whoever's not busy to bring water from the river to put the fire out. And make sure the women are tending the wounded."

"Yes, your highness." The man bowed and ran into the thick smoke.

"Adelaide, come with me." Elias turned Starflare toward the cliff and smoke. For once, Adelaide obeyed without saying anything.

The smoke was clearing when they reached the damaged area, but it revealed nothing agreeable. Heaps of broken rock, silt, and splintered wood lay all over the ground. Above the piles of debris was a huge crater of different hued layers of rock, as if someone had taken a huge bite out of the side of the mountain. Adelaide couldn't even see the mine's entrance below the mountain with all the debris strewn everywhere.

People covered in ash and dirt were attempting to shift wood and boulders out of the way of the mine. Others helped bleeding people maneuver out of the wreckage. A few villagers just stood still, shocked and crying.

Elias and Adelaide dismounted, and the prince told a boy with red ringlets, "Take our mounts to the stables and make sure they're fed and watered. Ask the stableman to bring over a wagon to take the wounded to the healers."

The boy bowed and trotted away with the horses.

"Where was the mine?" Elias asked an older boy beside him.

"Under all this." He gestured at the debris.

Elias nodded and helped the townsfolk by moving rocks and logs, calling for people, and listening for signs of survivors amid the wreckage. Adelaide was surprised, even after all he had told her and done, by his quick efficiency and willingness to help. No one else seemed surprised to see the prince digging his hands into coal-dusted filth and pulling out miners. She wondered if he had aided them before. Elias now resembled the prince he had told her about—the one Adelaide wished the country had. She couldn't seem to look away from his dirty, helping hands.

"Are you going to help or just stand there?" A man covered in grime asked her.

She joined in, moving splintered wood and rocks into the pile several paces away that the townsfolk had begun. Sweat soon stained her forehead and ran down her back despite the late-winter chill.

"I think someone's still alive over there!" Elias shouted, trotting over the boulders to a spot near the blasted cliff.

Adelaide and several men scrambled over to help him shoulder cracked boulders and split branches out of the way. They soon saw smudged clothing. After moving another rock, a scraped face and an oddly-bent leg came into view.

Elias took the unconscious, bleeding man to the cart, and when he returned, Adelaide whispered, "How did you know that man was under there? He was too far away to hear."

"I have better senses than most humans because of my more...wild attributes." He winked at her.

Adelaide didn't know what to say to that.

"Please!" A woman wailed nearby. "Have you found my husband, Leofolt? He should be here. He's not dead, I know he's not. Please."

Elias went over and placed his hands on the woman's shoulders. "What does he look like?"

"He has," she sobbed, "he has yellow hair and freckles. He wears a dark gray tunic when he works in the mine."

"We haven't found him yet, but we will," Elias said with confidence before returning to the vast pile of rubble.

The woman slouched, staring at nothing as tears streamed

out of her swollen eyes.

Adelaide turned to the weeping woman. “Why don’t you come with me to tend the wounded? Someone will let you know when they find your husband.”

The woman said nothing but let Adelaide lead her through town toward the structure that people were walking back and forth from with the injured. When they passed the pile of dead that the people had excavated from the rubble, she turned away, Emma’s lifeless body and the others from the attack too-vivid in her mind.

They passed a charred building on their right. Near the top of a building beside it, flames still flickered, fighting for life against the water villagers tossed up at it from buckets.

The healing house was full of men with bandaged arms, legs, chests, and faces lying on straw beds and the floor. Some of the conscious men moaned, pain as evident as snow in winter on their faces. The building reeked of blood, sweat, and coal dust.

“We’d like to help,” Adelaide told a white-haired woman who bustled from patient to patient like a hungry bee.

“Good.” The woman glanced up at her from beside a man with a half-burned face. “A lot of women left to put out the fire. Do you have any experience with healing?”

“Some.” Her mother had taught her the rudimentary herbs for fevers, headaches, scratches, and the like.

“Rub this on the burns.” The woman thrust a tube of ointment at her. “Then give them water to drink. We have skins full of river water over there.” She nodded to a corner of the room where a woman drooped in a chair.

“Aline,” the healer spoke to the woman beside Adelaide. She had stopped crying and now merely sniffled. “You can help me.” The woman followed the healer to a patient who had just been brought in, and Adelaide moved to do what she had been told.

Until mid-afternoon Adelaide remained in the healing

house, taking care of the patients and doing whatever the white-haired healer instructed her. The sight of so much suffering turned her stomach; Emma had always been better suited to this work.

When some women returned from putting out the blaze, Adelaide went in search of a drink, her throat a dry riverbed.

Someone had set up wooden benches on the stone dais in the center of town. Several men with dirt-smudged faces sat on them and chatted while raising mugs to their lips. A woman rested beside them, gazing out at the now-deformed mountain where Elias must still be searching for survivors.

Adelaide strode toward the building across from the dais that had the painted sign of a tankard hanging from it.

"Lass, you must come up here for a drink."

Adelaide turned. The woman on the dais was looking down at her. Adelaide climbed the steps and took the drink the woman offered her.

"It doesn't cost anything today."

"Thanks." She took a swallow. The cool, tangy ale soothed her throat and warmed her stomach.

The woman patted the empty spot on the bench beside her. "I wanted to be out here where all the action is."

Adelaide joined her, grateful to rest her feet.

"You're not from around here, are you?" The woman's light-green eyes considered Adelaide.

"Nay. I'm from Alesfirth."

"You're a long way from home, then."

Adelaide nodded.

The woman glanced at the charred building toward the far end of town. "Well, I'm glad you're here. We need all the help we can get with Lord Giffard gone."

Adelaide guessed Lord Giffard was the noble in charge of the village. "Where is he?" She took another sip, wishing she had something to eat as well.

"Supposedly, he's up north in the Spearheads," she

gestured to the snow-dusted mountains on their left, where Adelaide and Elias had just descended, "looking for prospective places to mine. But no one really knows if he is or not. He's always taking off somewhere with his knights, sometimes taking his wife and sometimes not. He won't tell anyone about his travels, and his wife keeps to herself.

"Although," the woman leaned toward Adelaide and whispered, "my suspicions are that Lord Giffard has a house up in the mountains, and he and his friends go there to drink and gossip like old hens. Apparently, the hardships of leading this town are too difficult for him." She snorted and took a drink from her mug of ale.

"Why is he still lord if he always disappears?"

"King Ganelon has tried banishing him, but he keeps creeping back. The king can't lock him up because he doesn't have any evidence that Lord Giffard is actually forsaking his duties on his little jaunts. The king could just take him away for no reason, like other kings have done, but he won't."

"Why not?"

The woman flattened her white dress when a gust of wind attempted to lift it. "He actually cares about justice. He and his son have done a good job so far with this country."

"What?" Adelaide spluttered, nearly choking on her ale. She had never heard a peasant say such a thing before.

The woman looked at Adelaide with a knowing smile. "King Ganelon and Prince Elias are the best rulers we've had in a long time, possibly even since men defeated the dragons. But no one knows much about those early rulers."

"What makes you say that?"

"What? About the kings? They lived longer ago than our memories reach. Everyone in Klinhun knows that." She gave Adelaide an odd look.

"No, about the king and his son being such good rulers."

"Oh, that. Well, for one thing, King Ganelon lets us keep half of the minerals we mine, where, before him, King

Clerebold took all of it. King Ganelon also sends us wagons of goods in harsh winters. It's not his fault that Lord Giffard and his knights keep it all for themselves. We have no way of telling the king so he'd believe us, or we would."

The woman laid her leaf-green eyes on Adelaide. "I've also heard that King Ganelon sometimes sends wagons of goods to other towns, but robbers or lords retain the supplies and lie to the king about it." She splayed the hand not holding her mug. "Now, I don't know if that's true or not, but I wouldn't doubt it if other lords are like Lord Giffard."

Adelaide remembered what Prince Elias had said about sending supplies to Alesfirth after the attack. She had seen wagons rattling into Alesfirth before, but assumed they were full of maintenance items for the town or other such things belonging to the nobles. She had never looked into one until she stole the two daggers from Prince Elias' wagon, and then she had only been interested in weapons. It wouldn't surprise her if Lord Lambert had taken the goods from the wagons for himself; he always reserved the best produce from the market for his hall.

"The king would have no way of knowing the lords are lying because he doesn't come to the villages often, and even if he did, there would be no evidence left," Adelaide mused.

The woman nodded, her grey-streaked braid flopping against her shoulder. "I don't know Prince Elias very well—he could be a lazy, woman-chaser most of the time—but right now it appears he's a hard-working man. At least he's not sitting around on his bum like these other men." The woman nodded to the men on a nearby bench who belched and waved their mugs in the air, slopping ale on their tunics and the ground.

"Has Prince Elias come here before?" Adelaide asked.

"A few times. He doesn't usually stay long, just stops by for a drink before moving on with urgent business, probably to chase robbers and the like. But when he stops at my tavern, he always listens to the latest news and asks the few peasants who wander in about their lives."

She nodded to herself. "Yes, I believe he's a good prince. What do you think, dearie?" The woman's keen eyes pinched Adelaide.

She regarded the broken mountain, where Elias worked. What the woman had told her about him and what she knew of him seemed to match. "He's definitely a different kind of ruler. It seems he cares about his people—at least more than past rulers have. He *tries* to be a good prince. And perhaps that's what matters most."

As she acknowledged these things to herself, her treatment of Elias the previous few weeks smothered her in guilt and horror. She drained the rest of her ale in one gulp, coughing at the rush of fiery liquid.

"Are you well, dearie?" The woman gazed at her with concern.

Adelaide set her empty mug on the bench and nodded. "Quite. Thanks for the ale." She stood.

The woman brushed away her gratitude. "Of course. Thanks for your help. If you want to come by before darkness sets in, some of the townsfolk will have food to share on this difficult day."

Adelaide nodded. She wasn't one to turn down free food. She made her way back to the healing house, but there were more than enough women now to help. So after receiving directions to the stables, she checked on Starflare and Suntaria.

The stableman wasn't around, probably off helping at the mine. The horses both greedily munched their hay, and Suntaria nickered when she came near.

"It's good to see you too, riding friend." She rubbed his ears and watched Starflare, who continued munching. "Just because I stole you, doesn't mean you have to ignore me." The horse twitched her tail, and Adelaide scrunched up her face at her.

Although the stableman had already groomed the horses, Adelaide brushed them again, cleaned out their hooves, and filled their water buckets. She made sure the saddles were clean and that all of Elias' saddlebags sat together against the wall. She peered into one to see what he carried while he traveled, but saw nothing more exciting than blankets, oats, and fishing line.

When Adelaide left the contented horses, the sun had sunk, and a crowd of people gathered on the dais. The smells of roasting meat and baking bread drew her like a bear to berries.

Before she mounted the dais steps, a loud squawk caught her attention. Cyr landed on her shoulder. "Good evening." She ruffled his head feathers. "Try not to get stolen or land me in trouble here like you did in Kildare." He rubbed his beak against her hand.

On the dais, dirt-streaked and exhausted men and women huddled around two small fires, whispering and watching the meat cook. Most were peasants, but a few people dressed in embroidered robes stood off to the side, talking together.

A woman a few years older than Adelaide held out a plate with chunks of yellow-white cheese to her. "Would you care for some food?"

Adelaide took a piece and procured a mug of cider from the woman she had spoken to earlier, who nodded at her before twirling away to give someone else a drink.

Adelaide sat on a bench, content to watch the people around her and fill her belly. A little while later a man announced that the venison was ready. Adelaide grabbed a piece off the burned stick before too many people crowded the meat and returned to her spot on the bench.

People soon swarmed the dais, sorrow lining their faces. Men patted each other's shoulders and women hugged children and other ladies to their chests, tears spilling down their cheeks.

Adelaide only spotted three knights in the crowd and guessed the others had gone off with Lord Giffard. The town would experience much more tragedy than a destroyed mine if the Gyndilians or a large group of robbers chose to attack while the lord and his knights were away carousing or whatever they did.

While Adelaide watched two boys chase each other around the adults' legs, thinking of Odo and how he and their father would soon begin plowing Lord Lambert's fields, a hand landed on her shoulder. She jumped, and Cyr soared off into the fading light.

"Don't worry, it's just me, though that might give you more cause for alarm." Elias sat beside her and stretched his arms. His tunic and leggings were completely covered in dirt, as was his face and hair.

"How did the work fare?"

He yawned. "We finally moved most of the rubble aside. I think there were twenty-three dead and six survivors." He rubbed his face, and Adelaide again was staggered at how hard he had worked beside his people.

"Just a moment," she said and went to fetch some food.

When Adelaide returned with a plate of meat, bread, and cheese, a man was speaking to Elias, his two children watching the prince with wide eyes. The man noticed Adelaide standing awkwardly nearby with the plate. He bowed, told his children not to gawk, and left with the children, who flicked glances back at Elias.

He glanced at the food Adelaide proffered him and back at her, surprise scrawled on his face.

"What? I can be nice when I want to be." She handed him the plate.

"I'm sure you can. It's just that you haven't done anything like this for me before."

"Don't let me regret it."

Elias chuckled. "There's no chance of that happening." He

tackled his food, telling Adelaide about the people they'd rescued and asking her what she'd done in-between bites of food. Before he finished eating, a bow-legged peasant climbed atop a bench. Everyone hushed.

The peasant man turned to Elias—who put his empty plate aside—and proclaimed, "Prince Elias, I know you often have your own plans and work to do. I regret to say we frequently turn our anger on you for how things are done in this country, even though they've been that way for centuries. But I know I speak for everyone in Fernohn tonight when I say we are grateful for what you've done for us today and that we can call you our Prince and some-day King."

The man clapped. Then, one by one, adults and children stood, turned to Prince Elias, and brought their hands together.

Elias gazed at each face, tears welling in his eyes, until they landed on hers. Adelaide couldn't keep her gaze away from the crowd for long, struck that so many people respected and loved the prince. But when his gaze alit on hers, Adelaide couldn't look anywhere else.

For saving her life, for not giving up on her when she ran away, and for helping these people, Adelaide stood and clapped.

Tears now flowed from Elias' blue eyes as he stared at her. His grin never winked out.

After the applause ceased, people came up to thank Elias. Adelaide let the crowd push her away from him to the back. She didn't want to block the way to their prince.

When the moon shone as brilliantly as a new silver klin, the crowd departed to gather and bury their dead. Elias left with them after giving Adelaide a sheepish grin. She remained on the dais; she had no desire to see another funeral. She could still smell the freshly turned dirt outside Alesfirth, hear her mother's wails, feel the sweat on her brother's hand clutching her own, and sense the stares of the crowd as she dropped wildflowers onto the pale body that no longer resembled her playful, sweet sister.

She sat on the dais for a long time, lost in the past, staring at the peasants' candles that seemed to float through the air. When she later went to sleep in the stable, she heard low, haunted singing and didn't know if it was from the funeral nearby or her memories.

◆◆◆

Elias wished Adelaide had joined him at the burial, but understood why she didn't.

As he followed the crowd outside of town, the wagon carrying the dead creaking beside him, he kept seeing Adelaide standing and clapping for him, a proud smile on her lips. He never wanted to forget the image.

The shell she put on for protection was cracking, her heart gradually softening, but not nearly fast enough for him. He could only hope it continued, because he couldn't bear the thought of loving her while she just saw him as her prince and dragon-friend, if she even saw him as that much. There were still risks in loving her as a dragon, but others had done it long ago, and surely it would be easier since he could turn into a human as well. He hoped his father would approve.

The cart and crowd's halt brought Elias back to the somber setting around him. He helped the townsfolk dig graves and place the dead in them. When people had tossed flowers or other treasures onto their loved one's bodies and said their last goodbyes, Elias cleared his throat. This—speaking in front of large crowds—was the part he hated most about being a human prince.

"I don't personally know the men who died here today," Elias declared. "But from the love displayed in you all toward them, I know they were beloved sons, dedicated fathers, and caring husbands. Without the daily risking of their lives in the mines, this town wouldn't be able to function, and many would starve." He wondered how many people still starved because the work wasn't enough. "Let us never forget their hard work and sacrifice. Let us strive to follow their example each day."

He held up his flickering candle, and the others followed his example. He led them in a common threnody as several men stepped out to cover the bodies with dirt, giving them forever to the earth.

"Closed eyes,
silent heart,
rest well,
rest forever.

Brother, son,
father, friend.
The day is gone,
the night is here.

Cherished soul,
precious life,
greet the darkness,
enjoy the peace.

Loved one,
blessed one,
protect us,
guide us.

Closed eyes,
silent heart,
rest well,
rest forever."

Chapter Thirty-Six

Gunter awoke shivering and terrified. He had dreamed that the king and prince had pounded on the doors of his cottage, demanding food and threatening to burn their homes if they disobeyed. Gunter's mother and father handed over every grain of flour and morsel of cheese. Their family shrank until they became no more than sacks of bones, and King Ganelon and Prince Elias grew as round as pillows. In the nightmare, Gunter lived near Adelaide's family and saw Prince Elias order her to hand over whatever food they possessed. She shook her head, and he thrust a sword into her stomach.

"Come on, runt. Are you going to lie there as if you're dead all day?" A gruff accented voice interrupted the images assaulting Gunter, and he opened his eyes.

Leofric was nudging his side with a booted foot.

"Do you think this pathetic rebellion of his actually exists?" Ligulf asked his brother, Leofric. "If so, it can't last long if its members get captured so easily." He gazed down at him with disgust.

Gunter groaned and sat, sore from riding practically nonstop the last four days. He rubbed heat into his arms and, as he did every day, wondered where Adelaide was and how she fared. Hopefully, no prince or king had stabbed her yet.

"Rough night, runt?" Baldwin brushed aside his greasy, sandy hair.

Gunter ignored him and bit into a chunk of crispy meat from the day before that was so burned it didn't taste like anything. He had become used to the Gyndilians' teasing over the last few days that seemed to stretch for a year. As long as they didn't beat him, he could live with it.

"Dreaming about your pretty lady again?" Baldwin's grin revealed crooked yellow teeth.

Gunter squeezed the piece of meat he held until it crumbled. He hadn't mentioned Adelaide to them, but from his age, embarrassing cries in the night, and urgency to reach the King's City, they had guessed. His anger, which he couldn't hide, only sharpened their taunting of his supposed love for a mysterious maiden.

"If she's as little as you, your first child will look more like a puppy than a person." Ligulf elbowed his brother, and they burst into harsh laughter. Baldwin smiled as he rolled and dusted the snow off his blanket.

Gunter ground his teeth together so he wouldn't retort, which is what the men wanted. He had shouted at them about something they'd said about Klinians the first day of their journey, and their eyes had lit up with glee and their insults had sharpened.

"We're entering a town today, correct?" Dunstan shouldered his crossbow then hid it under his thick, patched cloak. The man was the only one who didn't tease Gunter—at least not to his face. In fact, he rarely spoke to Gunter at all, and when he did, it was with cool politeness.

"Yes," Baldwin replied. "So men, put on your smiles and don't do anything to give us away. If you do, the Master won't be pleased, and you know what that would mean."

Leofric blanched. "Torture."

"Or death, if he's in a good mood," Baldwin said.

Gunter shivered, wondering again how he had become accountable to such a dangerous man. He stood and hefted his satchel. "Why do you call him the Master? Do you truly not know his name?" He directed his question to Dunstan, the least hate-filled man.

Dunstan's abnormally large blue eyes scrutinized him. "Supposedly because he's a master with a blade. No one knows if that's the real reason, though, because the Master doesn't take kindly to people probing into his past."

Gunter nodded, wondering if the Master didn't want people shedding light on his past because he had secrets to hide.

"Enough of this nattering. Let's go," Baldwin said as he saddled his red roan.

"Which town are we heading to today?" Gunter asked.

Ligulf glanced back at Baldwin. "Should we tell him?"

"The Master didn't say anything—"

"We're heading to Lenast, a town on the other side of these mountains," Dunstan interrupted. To the others, he said, "It won't hurt him to know. He can't do anything with us near him."

Ligulf and Leofric grunted their approval, but Baldwin frowned at Dunstan.

"Why does Gyndilad wish to go to war with Klinhun?" Gunter shifted on the black horse they had given him and winced. He couldn't remember aching this much before, not even on the first day of harvest when the men cut and hauled bushels of wheat into the lord's storerooms.

"To gain more land and wealth since Klinhun has more mines and better ports than Gyndilad. Then we shall be wealthy and dictate what other nations do." A greedy grin twisted Leofric's face.

"That's part of the reason." Dunstan swerved his horse around a boulder. "The other is because our king believes it to be the best recourse for our nation."

"Is the Master your king?" Gunter doubted it, but wanted to know for certain. He didn't know much about the neighboring country; when you didn't even know if you would have any food to eat that day, learning about your neighbors wasn't your first priority.

Baldwin chuckled. "Nay, though he may wish it sometimes. He's one of King Aethelmaer's most loyal men. Now shut your mouth, runt, before I shut it for you." He leered at Gunter. "You're not learning anything more about our country."

Gunter shut his mouth, wondering how much the men were allowed to hurt him.

The group remained silent as they passed through a sheer valley between serrated peaks swathed in snow. Not too much longer and they'd be in Dhalion preparing to kill the king. Part of Gunter hoped Adelaide did the task before the Gyndilians forced him to. Then guilt knifed through him for desiring such a selfish thing.

His heart ached for his friend. Where was she? Had she been able to keep ahead of the prince?

When the sun kissed the sky in a rosy-lipped farewell, the men climbed out of the steep pass. A town lay about a mile below, candles winking through the wooden slats of cottages.

"Does everyone remember the story?" Baldwin asked from the front of the line, leaning back so he wouldn't fall off in their steep descent.

"We're poor peasants from Pinhurn traveling to Fernohn to seek work since our crops died last spring, and it's been a harsh winter," Leofric recited.

Baldwin nodded. "Good."

They had consulted Gunter the day they left Gyndilad

about a plausible reason for traveling this time of year. Gunter had heard that the towns closer to the mountains had faced a harsh winter and remembered men from Pinhurn walking by his hut in the summer talking about a drought. Most people didn't travel in winter, but Dunstan had said they could make their journey more reasonable by throwing in a sick wife or other relative.

"Don't forget to let Gunter do the talking. Our accents could give us away," Dunstan, who rode behind Gunter, reminded the men. "And be sure to keep your swords hidden. We're pretending to be peasants, after all."

"Do I smell bad enough to be a peasant?" Ligulf leaned toward his brother, offering his shirt for him to smell.

Leofric wrinkled his nose. "You always smell bad."

Baldwin peered past the sniggering brothers to Gunter. The fading sun cast the Gyndilian's face in deep shadow. "If you say anything that puts us at risk, runt, I'll gut you like a pig. My sword will be behind you the entire time, even if you can't feel it."

Gunter believed him; he had seen Baldwin's hunting skills the day before. He'd taken down a deer with one blow after the others had cornered it. Gunter—a weak, trapped animal himself—nodded feebly.

"Good. Come on." Baldwin led the way into town.

There was only the creaking of the horses' saddles, the crunching of hooves in the crusty snow, and the curling mists of their breath in the night air.

"You can do this," Dunstan murmured behind him.

Gunter jumped, then berated himself for his cowardice.

They halted in front of a cloaked guard standing before a short wooden gate embedded in a crumbling stone wall. "Who are you and what business do you have here?" The guard said, peering at them. "The gate is closed for the night."

Baldwin nudged his horse behind Gunter's, who imagined the man's thick fingers wrapped around his blade, hungering for Gunter's pain. He forced the thought away. "We hail from Pinhurn and seek shelter for the night." His voice trembled, and he covered it with a cough. "We're on our way to Fernohn to seek employment in the mines."

"Who are these men with you?" The guard's head swiveled to take in the still forms.

"My brothers." Gunter decided that would make more sense if they had to use the sick relative lie. "Our farm suffered much in the drought last summer and part of our house has collapsed from the snow."

The man stared at them a long time, his eyes pools of night. Gunter's heart pulsed down to his toes.

The guard finally, thankfully opened the wooden gate behind him. "The stables are at the back of town. You can sleep there. Make sure you leave town on the morrow."

"We will," Gunter replied, sighing in relief as they entered the sleepy village. The snow-covered peaked roofs reminded him of a mini mountain range. People stared at them out of the windows they passed.

"Could we get a drink?" Leofric gazed longingly into the candle-lit tavern full of laughing and singing men.

"Of course not," Baldwin said. "Drink will only loosen your tongue, and you or Ligulf would give everything away."

Leofric didn't take his eyes off the raucous room but didn't argue.

Once inside the musty stable, the men unsaddled, and Gunter attempted to unclench his frozen fingers.

Baldwin unrolled his blanket on the straw. "You might want to speak up more at the next town. That guard probably wondered if there was a man inside that old cloak of yours."

"At least he didn't give us away." Dunstan glanced at Gunter appreciatively.

Gunter nodded at him. It was the kindest thing any of them had said to him.

"The next town won't be until Fernohn, and then it'll be

Dhalion," Baldwin said.

"Where we meet the king." Ligulf rubbed his hands, a glint in his eyes.

"Here." Dunstan handed Gunter a familiar-looking dagger.

Gunter just stared at it, aware of the others' voracious eyes on him and the weapon.

"If you're going to overthrow that king of yours, you should have the skills to do it." Dunstan glanced at the others. "Calm down. He's probably not skilled enough to hurt me even standing this close to him. I'll take it from him as soon as he's done."

When Dunstan returned his attention to Gunter, his gaze softened. "Go ahead." He nodded to the barn wall a few paces away.

Gunter picked up the weapon and attempted to ignore the stares of the Gyndilians and their tense breathing as he aimed at the wall. When the dagger landed in the straw, a burst of laughter erupted behind him. Frowning in concentration, and to think of anything other than the men weighing him, Gunter remembered cold nights like these when his parents and Elysande snuggled together because they didn't have enough blankets. He remembered Conrad working in the fields until his hands bled so their mother might have enough left over from paying taxes to trade for flour. He remembered the prince shoving his spear into Adelaide's stomach in his dream.

Thunk. The dagger hit the wall, right where he aimed it, silencing the laughter behind him. Gunter grinned. No longer would he stand helpless and weak while the nobility hurt his loved ones. Now he could do something to protect them.

Chapter Thirty-Seven

"Good morning, Adelaide," Elias greeted her when she meandered out of the stables to scrounge up some food the morning after the burial. "Did you enjoy sleeping with the horses? You resemble one a bit, with all that straw in your hair."

Adelaide smoothed down her braid and found only one piece of straw stuck in the black strands. She tossed it at Elias, who dodged out of the way. "It was nice, actually. Where did you sleep?" She took an oat-and-barley roll from him. It was still warm and delightfully softer than the biscuits they'd eaten the last few weeks. "With the nobility on their feather beds?"

At the hurt dripping off his face, Adelaide regretted her words. Before she could reel them back in, he spoke. "Actually, I slept with one of the peasant families. They were very hospitable and gave me one of their beds."

"Oh. Good." Adelaide took a bite of the roll. It tasted as good as it smelled—nutty and sweet. "The people of this town seem to respect you and your father."

"More than we deserve. We've helped the villagers a few times, but not as much as we should." He glanced at his hands.

"It's easier to help them than the towns on the west side of Klinhun since they're closer to Dhalion. But that's no excuse for not doing more for the western towns, especially since they mistrust us more than other villages, particularly the one farthest north." He raised an eyebrow at her.

Adelaide smiled around her last bite of bread. "Yes, the people there are frighteningly bad tempered."

Elias chuckled. "Indeed." His smile vanished. "But as I said, they have reason to be."

Adelaide opened her mouth to argue since he seemed so forlorn, but what could she say? That the wagons his father had sent had been taken by the lord? He probably already knew that, and it would just make him more downhearted.

"I have to meet some of the miners and knights near the dais. If you get hungry later, there's food in here from the family I stayed with." He handed her a woolen satchel. "Don't go wandering off, now. I don't have time to chase you down."

"Don't worry, I would have already left if I'd wanted to."

Elias laughed and strode off toward the center of town.

Adelaide ambled around while chomping an apple she found in the satchel. She chatted with some of the townsfolk who weren't too preoccupied. It would have been the perfect opportunity to coerce people into her rebellion, but after learning the truth about Elias, his father, and the dragons, a revolution was pointless.

At midday, as Adelaide listened to a middle-aged woman gush about her daughter's upcoming marriage to the blacksmith's son, the drumming of several horses approaching snatched her interest. Perhaps it was the lord returning. Was he as pompous as Lord Lambert? After a farewell to the woman, she went to find the source of the commotion.

Along the tree-lined Wymar River, five horsemen cloaked in the blue and yellow colors of Klinhun galloped toward town. As they drew nearer, Adelaide recognized one of the riders as Elias' closest knight and friend, Berold.

He and the other knights stopped in front of her, breathing heavily. Sweat stained the horses' flanks, and the men's once-kingly garments now resembled peasant clothes with all the dirt and tatters. Not to mention, the men reeked of sweat and horse.

Berold, gasping, glanced around at the stable and chandler's shop behind Adelaide. "Where's Elias? He must be here if you are."

Adelaide crossed her arms, wondering why the man thought they were so attached when she had still been contemplating overthrowing him the last time she saw Berold. "He's at a meeting with some townsfolk."

"Why?"

"One of the mines exploded yesterday. He said he'd be at the dais."

"Very well." Berold urged his horse into a trot, the others close behind. Adelaide followed at a run, curious why the horsemen were in such a hurry to see Elias.

Near the dais, the woman with the betrothed daughter stared at the passing knights, her eyes popping. "Oh, my. This looks like official business. I have to tell Avice and Geva." She scuttled away, her hands fluttering at her sides.

Atop the dais, Elias sipped a mug of ale while surrounded by exhaustion-lined men. He rose when he noticed Berold dismounting. The other knights remained by their horses at the stone steps, but Adelaide climbed up after Berold.

"It's good to see you, my friend, even after our last encounter." Adelaide took a step closer; was Elias referring to their conversation at the Lentiasa River? Or something else? "I had to find Adelaide before anything happened to her," his gaze flicked to her, "but now that she's safe, you and your men may accompany us to Dhalion. I must speak to my father about some important matters as soon as possible."

Berold's face pinched as if he was in pain. "Elias, there's something I have to tell you."

The prince's eyes hardened like stone. "What? What's wrong?" The fingers clenching his mug drained of color.

Tears now shone in Berold's eyes, and Adelaide felt the first whisper of fear. What if there had been another Gyndilian attack? What if her parents and brother were somehow in trouble?

"My men met a messenger from Dhalion on the road just south of here who recognized us. I told him I would deliver his message since, well, since it would be better if I did." Berold swallowed loudly. "Elias, your father, King Ganelon...he's dead."

Adelaide gasped.

Elias stared at Berold as if he hadn't heard the words.

Berold glanced away, fiddling with the handle of his sword. "He was apparently found dead yesterday morning in bed. The physicians don't know how he died. The council sent a messenger to tell you as soon as they found out. Since no one knew where you were, they sent someone to the closest town first."

Berold gazed with conflicted eyes at Elias and squeezed his shoulder. "I'm so, so, sorry," he whispered. "Your father was a good man and king. He was like a second father to me at the castle."

All the color bled from Elias' face, leaving it a sickly white. His mug fell from his hands, hitting the stone dais and splintering into a hundred different shards. The liquid stained the grey stone a dark umber.

Elias let out a low moan that ripped Adelaide's heart into a hundred pieces. He tore out of Berold's grasp and fled down the steps toward the edge of town.

Berold made as if to go after him, but Adelaide stepped in front of him. "I'll go."

He narrowed his eyes. "You? You've known him only a few days, and you've never even seen his father."

Adelaide straightened, wishing she was taller so she could

make eye contact with him. "I know Elias well enough." Berold didn't even know he was a dragon, after all.

Without waiting for his reaction, Adelaide turned and ran after her prince.

She followed the sound of a throaty roar—which she hoped the others believed came from a mountain lion—several miles outside of town to a lofty oak peering down at the whirling brown river.

Elias, in his gold-dipped crimson form, sat under the oak, his back and wings somewhere up in the branches. His neck and head stuck out from between two high limbs as he cried tears as large as pebbles that hit the ground like a rainstorm.

He didn't move when Adelaide approached. She didn't know how to comfort a dragon, so she sat by his front right leg and placed her hand on a warm, ruby scale, trying to dodge his tears.

She observed the cottonwood trees shielding the river, unable to believe the king was dead. Yes, she had been planning the possibility before leaving Alesfirth, but the knowledge of death felt much different than the idea of it. She probably wouldn't have even been able to kill him if it had come to it. Besides, he wasn't just a far-off king anymore; he was Elias' father.

If she had wanted to continue the rebellion now, she would have to kill the king's heir. She glanced up at Elias and shuddered. There was no chance of that happening now, after all he had done for her. But there was a chance Elias could still die—at the hands of the men she had stirred up in her imprudent, reckless rebellion. They all believed he was a vile prince, and it was her fault. Adelaide's stomach churned when she contemplated how she had poisoned people with words to end this good man's life—a man she hadn't even known.

As Elias wept for his father, Adelaide's thoughts inevitably turned to Emma. As always when she remembered her sister, she felt as if someone had wrenched her heart out of her body, cut it in half, and shoved it back inside, demanding that she live with only half a heart. But the pain didn't throb as much as it had just weeks ago.

Adelaide pulled Emma's cloak out of her satchel and reflected on the memories it stirred within her: the girls chasing each other through the house and giggling, racing to town while their mother shouted at them to stay close, putting horse manure in Odo's boots to watch his face turn flaming-red, talking about boys while twirling their feet in the Lentiasa's soothing waters.

The tears came slowly, then quickly as Adelaide knew, again, that she would never make any new memories with Emma. Her sister was truly gone, forever.

Sitting beside Elias weeping for his father, Adelaide wept deeply for her sister, freeing the tears to stream down her face unencumbered for the first time since Em's brutal death. She clutched her sister's cloak to her chest as if it could stem the aching pain inside.

As the sun sank, sending out pink and orange streaks, Elias took a deep breath and let it out slowly. His voice was ragged and weary in her mind as he gazed at the sky. *Thank you, father, for living well. I'll never forget you and all you taught me, but I must...* he lowered his huge head. *Farewell, father. I will do my best to make you proud.*

He stretched his head up, past the tree's branches, as high as he could without taking off—his neck a long, gleaming line of gold scales and spikes against the less-beautiful simmering sky. He made a low-pitched thrumming sound deep in his throat that caused bumps to rise on Adelaide's skin.

He sat like that for a while, the thrumming spreading through the air until it felt as if Adelaide's very bones vibrated. Then, after a glow of warm light, Elias was human again. His eyes were red and his hair disheveled.

"Thank you for understanding," he said to Adelaide, then he strode back to Fernohn.

Adelaide stared at his diminishing form, then at the cloak in her hands. She saw Emma's honey-eyes pleading with her. It was time to let her sister go.

With tears blurring her vision, Adelaide tore the filthy cloak into tiny pieces and flung them into the trees beside the river.

"Farewell, Emma," she whispered.

Chapter Thirty-Eight

"So, Elias, are you going to tell me what you've been doing all this time I've been looking for you?" Berold asked the next morning as he, Elias, Adelaide, and the prince's knights rode along the Wymar River toward Dhalion.

Elias inched out a smile at Adelaide. Even though it was frail compared to his normal blazing grins, she wondered how he could attempt one at all. She still felt shaken and drained from watching the last bit of Emma disappear on the breeze.

"You shouldn't have to ask, Berold," the prince said. "I was rescuing this fair maiden from robbers who treated her no better than animal quarry."

"Why didn't they just take her money and leave her behind?" Berold scrutinized Adelaide as if trying to see her value.

She fingered her dagger, entertaining thoughts of tossing it at the man. Elias made an odd growling sound in his throat, drawing Berold's attention back to him. "They were taking her to the Gyndilians, to sell her." He clenched his reins so hard the color fled his skin.

"Truly?" Berold looked at him askance. "Does your father

know about this?" Realizing his mistake, the knight's face paled. "Oh. I'm sorry, Elias. I'm truly sorry..." he stammered.

Elias gazed into the forest surrounding them, his eyes a somber grey. "He's dead, and the sooner I face that, the better it will be for me and our kingdom." Quieter he said, "And nay, I don't think he knew."

Berold nodded, and Adelaide tossed her braid over her shoulder, straining to think of a way to change the subject.

Berold spoke before she could. "When would you like the funeral to take place?"

"As soon as we arrive. I want to invite all the townsfolk, including the peasants."

Berold's eyes widened, but he didn't object.

"How long until we reach Dhalion, Elias?" Adelaide asked.

"Where's your respect?" Berold scoffed. "He's 'your highness' to you."

"I told her she can call me that, Berold. She's a close friend."

Adelaide and Berold frowned at each other. She hadn't even realized she had been calling Elias that; after opening up to him near the cave, it just seemed natural.

"We'll be there in about ten days." Elias' face lightened. "I can't wait to show you the sea, the castle, everything. It's so much different than any other part of the country. You're going to love it."

"I should after all you've said about it," she teased.

Disgruntled, Berold jumped into the conversation before Elias could reply, talking about certain nobles and knights at the castle, smiling smugly that Adelaide knew not what they were discussing. She didn't mind; she was merely glad he saw her—a mere peasant—as competition for Elias' attention in the first place.

As the group made their way south, Adelaide noticed more and more signs of spring's gentle breath. Patches of green popped up out of the brown grass, a rabbit hopped among the bushes, and a chirping sparrow darted in front of them with a twig in its beak. This, and the knowledge that King Ganelon was dead, making Elias the target for her rebellion, quickened Adelaide's desire to reach Dhalion.

Elias seemed eager to reach home too, pushing them to ride from dawn to dusk every day, stopping only once at midday. Berold continued to act like an arrogant swine around Adelaide—refusing to look at her when she spoke and speaking about peasants as if they were dirt. Adelaide's hands and tongue were sore from stifling her desire to stab him with her dagger and words. She often only made it a few moments before something rude escaped her lips.

"I wish you and Berold would try harder to get along," Elias said while rubbing his beard one morning as they prepared to leave. Adelaide had just called the knight a rotten apple for an offhand remark about the peasants in Dhalion. He then had shouted that she had proved his point with manners worse than a week-old fish's, before promptly trodding off into the trees.

"It would be easier if he didn't hate peasants so much." Adelaide stabbed a log in the fire until it gave a wheezing hiss.

"He doesn't hate peasants. He just doesn't care much for them."

Adelaide speared Elias a look; those were the same in her mind.

He sighed. "Berold just hasn't been around them as much as you or I. He was raised differently—in the city with other nobles—where they practically train you to look down on everyone else." He tilted his head as he swept a glance at her. "You do goad him on, though. You're not helping lift his opinion of them."

"Well, what do you expect? Apparently, I'm no smarter than the ground he walks on." She stabbed the log so hard it creaked apart to reveal a throbbing red inside.

"Adelaide." Elias touched her arm. "Look at me, please."

She reluctantly did so.

"You know I don't think of you or any peasant like that." His eyes glowed a bright blue, and Adelaide wondered if it was from the fire crackling beside them or the one that burned somewhere deep inside him. "Peasants work harder than nobility and make almost everything we need to live. Without them, Klinhun would fall apart." His gaze flicked away, and he swallowed before turning back to her. "You are a beautiful, intelligent, brave woman. Anyone who can't see that is a fool, Berold included."

Adelaide fingered her braid, embarrassed, and returned her attention to the fire.

Elias stepped away. "I'll find Berold and speak with him about treating peasants with more respect."

He departed, and Adelaide wished he would return; his presence comforted her. She swatted the wish away. All that mattered now was killing the rebellion she had begun and returning home. Elias could find someone much better suited to helping the dragons. She wanted to see her family so much it physically hurt; they probably believed her dead by now.

Where a wooden bridge crossed the Wymar River, joining the Southern Road to the travelers' path, they dismounted and watered their horses and themselves.

It was warmer here closer to the sea, and Adelaide hadn't worn her cloak the last several days. The air pressed against her as if it wanted to squeeze her into a water droplet.

"This is the final stretch," Elias said, mounting. "From here it will take us two days at most to reach Dhalion." He pointed at some purplish-gray trees on their right. "The sea is somewhere past those."

Adelaide craned her head, but saw only branches and bark. "Are we going to be able to see it?"

He shook his head. "Not until we reach Dhalion."

"Come on, Elias," Berold urged. "We must bury the king and coronate you as soon as possible. The people shouldn't be without a king for long, especially in these tense conditions with Gyndilad."

The prince nodded, and they turned their backs on the Wymar River and turned their faces to the King's City.

Throughout the day Adelaide strained her eyes in the direction where Elias had pointed, searching for the sea. Several times she met his gaze, and he winked before turning around.

Then, mid-morning of the second day, she saw it.

The needle-covered trees suddenly ended, exposing a brilliant cerulean sky and even more brilliant white-flecked indigo water far below that flowed on and on, father than she could see. The water rippled in the breeze and shimmered as the sun's mirror, dazzling her eyes.

Mesmerized, Adelaide dismounted and walked to the edge of the cliff. Far below, waves swayed and slapped the jagged rocks, sending a giant spray of water up onto the sheer cliffs. The sea sloshed back again, preparing for another onslaught, as if longing to break through the bounds of rock and fill the earth with its salty spray.

Snowy birds crying shrilly wheeled over the hissing sea, sometimes diving in to reappear moments later with fish dangling from their beaks. Over the sound of the birds' cries and the splashing of the water striking the rocks below was the constant sound of lapping as the tops of waves hit the sea. It was relaxing, yet solemn, reminding Adelaide of a song about a sailor her mother used to sing to lull her and Emma to sleep when they were little.

She breathed deep, letting the tang of salt and hint of pine fill her lungs. Cyr launched off her shoulder, soaring and dipping over the never-ending waves.

Elias came to stand beside her. "So, what do you think?"

There were no words to adequately describe how small she felt standing up on the cliff over so much water, nor how it soothed her. So she just went with her first thought. "It's big."

Elias chuckled, though the sound had lost its bounciness after his father's death. Now it just sounded hollow. "Indeed. Every time I see it I'm reminded how insignificant I am."

"Elias," Berold strode over, "we need to leave if you want to make it to the castle by the evening meal."

"Speaking of the castle," Elias turned to Adelaide's left, "there it is." He pointed to a spot where the cliff abruptly dropped away before rising again to another bluff surrounded by trees. A cinnamon-colored stone castle thrust up out of the lush forest, its tiled turrets as blue as the sea.

Adelaide couldn't see much of the castle from this angle, but what she saw was enormous: the trees encircling it looked like twigs compared to the reaching fingers of the turrets, and the outer stone wall appeared as sturdy as the cliff it sat upon. Her whole village and Pinhurn and possibly even Kildare could fit inside the mighty fortress. She laughed inwardly; her rebellion would never have made it past those thick, well-fortified walls. She had never imagined the castle could be so huge.

"Not as an amazing sight as the sea, but it has survived storms and wars. And it's even more awe-inspiring up close." Elias turned to the horses.

Adelaide gazed at the beast of a castle a moment more, then whistled for Cyr.

The dirt road they followed twisted away from the edge of the cliff and veered steeply down. Adelaide had to lean so far back in order not to fall off Suntaria that her back began to ache.

As they neared the town and sea, the scent of salt and the sounds of lapping water, creaking carts, and people's voices swelled.

In mid-afternoon, a wall built of the same sandy brown stone as the castle, though much shorter, rose before them as the road leveled off. Knights clutching bows with swords strapped to their sides and quivers slung over their backs perched on top of the semi-circular fortification.

The group stopped in front of the hefty iron-inlaid gates barring the city. A knight from above clothed in chain mail over a yellow tunic and blue trousers peered down at them. "State your name and business," he commanded.

Elias glanced up. "It's me, Theobold."

"Forgive me, your highness. Just a moment." The knight strode to the side, pulled down on something, and, with a loud groan, the gates swung open before them.

Chapter Thirty-Nine

The streets of Dhalion were cobbled in dove-grey stone. They led down in winding paths, presumably to the sea, which Adelaide couldn't see at the moment for all the sandy-stone buildings. Each blue-tiled roof sprouted a chimney, and every cottage appeared twice as large as her home in Alesfirth and much sturdier.

Every few paces trees and flowers beamed at her from brightly-painted clay pots along both sides of the road. Some of the trees' branches dripped with pink blossoms and green buds.

Elias noticed her gaze and said, "Those are peach trees. You'll have to try one of the fruits when they're ripe. All of this is my father's doing." He gestured to the potted flora. "He loved plants. There are also cherry trees along some of the roads, which also produce tasty fruit." He gazed at a pot full of red, cup-like flowers with a thoughtful, sad expression.

"What are peaches and cherries like?" Adelaide asked, partly to distract him and partly because she just wanted to know. Berold clicked his tongue in annoyance beside her, though she couldn't see why. Surely not even all Klinian nobles knew what these fruits were?

"Peaches are round, fuzzy, and yellow-pink. Cherries are smaller, red, and waxy on the outside. Both are delicious. We're also trying to grow apricots and plums as Neklosa does."

Adelaide didn't bother to ask what apricots and plums were; it would just further reveal her ignorance, and she probably wouldn't be able to picture them anyway.

The city's swept stone streets and waste-less corners surprised Adelaide. As they meandered through the orderly town toward the far cliff, people turned to look at them. Many adults waved at Prince Elias and welcomed him home from his travels. A gaggle of children ran behind the entourage, laughing. People gathered on either side, bowing to Elias as he rode by and whispering to each other, possibly guessing at the identity of the skinny, filthy maiden beside him.

Adelaide attempted to sit straight and tall, as if all the attention and collision of color lining the streets was normal. She didn't think she had seen so many hues at once, even during festivals in Alesfirth when the nobility wore their finest. Here, the noblewomen were decorated in every combination imaginable: canary yellow dresses encircled with red girdles, round, soft purple hats atop twilight dresses, spring-colored cloaks with orange-embroidered hems. The noblemen wore vivid fluffy hats and tunics. Even the peasants she spotted wore cloaks the rich shades of tomatoes, pine needles, and straw.

The group halted beside delicate bunches of purple, white, and orange flowers lining the dais in azure pots.

Elias squeezed Adelaide's arm and whispered, "Time to be a prince." He rubbed his hands through his dirty hair and mounted the steps. Berold trailed him.

The entire town now seemed to stand around the stone pedestal, gazing up at their prince. Parents hushed children in their arms and patted the heads of those clutching their clothes. A few adults hobbled on canes, and others wiped dirt or what appeared to be fish guts from their tunics.

"Good day, people of Dhalion," Elias proclaimed. "I'm most glad to return home from such a long journey, but all is not right." He swallowed and brushed a wavy lock of hair out of his eyes. "My father, King Ganelon, died while I was gone."

Gasps escaped from the crowd, and they exchanged stricken looks with one another. Apparently, the knights or anyone who knew of the king's death had waited to share the news until the prince could deliver it in person. Adelaide thought it quite considerate of them.

Elias continued in a surprisingly steady voice, "As each of you know, my father, although not perfect, was a man who lived and worked every day for the people of Klinhun to have a better life. He cared about all of you and did until the day he died." Elias breathed deep as if to keep himself from crying.

"His burial will take place at dawn, and I invite all of you to attend. He will be laid to rest under a tree north of town instead of under the castle, since he loved green and growth more than cold, dead stone. As King Ganelon's sole heir, I will be crowned king on the night of his burial. All of you are welcome to attend the ceremony." He bowed, then strode down the steps with Berold.

When he mounted Starflare, he said for only Adelaide to hear, "I detest speaking in front of people."

Adelaide grinned at the absurdity of such a statement from him—the next king. "You sounded much like what I imagine a king would."

"Thank you. That is high praise indeed."

"Shall I call you King Elias after your coronation on the morrow?" The title felt awkward and too stilted in her mouth. It put up a larger barrier between Elias and her than the 'Prince' title had.

He groaned. "Please don't. Everyone else will soon enough. I don't need you and Berold to as well."

"Why do you dislike it so much? You *are* the rightful king."

"Yes, but it reminds me of the vast distance between the people of Klinhun and myself."

As they made their way past the crowd, Adelaide saw tears in many people's—both peasants and noble's—eyes as they watched the prince pass. Their expressions and responses to King Ganelon's death shook Adelaide. Not long ago she had planned to take these beloved rulers away from their people, thinking it was what the peasants wanted. How arrogant and naïve she had been.

She searched the crowd for her friends, but didn't see any familiar faces.

Prince Elias, with Berold riding on his right, and Adelaide on his left, led the way out of Dhalion under more of the sweetly fragrant blooming peach trees. The castle on the cliff above stared down imperiously at them.

"What do you think of the city thus far?" Elias gestured at the cinnamon-colored buildings around them. "I wish I could show you more of it, but alas, there's no time. Perhaps another day."

"It's nice." Sunlight bounced off the shop and house windows shuttered in vividly painted wood. She had never seen glass windows before and thought they were lovely, if unnecessary.

"I can look around Dhalion more on my own. Once you're king you'll have much more important things to do than entertain me." The words prickled when she said them, as if she had eaten a thorn bush.

Elias frowned. "I'm not entertaining you. I enjoy being with you, as I've told you many times. I've risked too much for you not to understand the depth of my feelings."

Or had he risked his life for the dragons? *No*, Adelaide berated herself, *he has risked his life for you.*

"That may be," she said, "but what will your people think if you continue spending most of your time with a peasant maiden who isn't even from here?"

Elias opened his mouth, but Berold spoke before he could say anything. "Forgive me for interrupting what's no doubt a stimulating conversation, Elias, but shouldn't we discuss the details of your father's burial and your coronation? We must arrange matters with the steward once we arrive at the castle, after all."

"Always the practical one, Berold." Elias tried to smile, but it faded before it found his eyes.

Berold reached over and patted his arm. "I know it must be hard to discuss, but we have to."

Elias nodded, and the two conversed about flowers and horses. Adelaide returned her attention to the scenery. The cobbled street clattering beneath their horses gleamed red, violet, and yellow when the sun struck the stones. The path inclined out of town and wove up the cliff toward the castle. Tall, skinny trees with high limbs and white-grey bark lined the road, and to their left stretched a silent, shadowy forest.

To her right, not far below, the buildings of Dhalion shimmered like waxy chocolates she had seen in one of its shops. They ended where the sea began. A sprinkling of boats bobbed precariously near rocks offshore, and she could make out one or two tanned men in each craft. She wondered what it felt like to float on so much water in such a tiny craft. How did they avoid the ragged rocks looming nearby?

At the top of the bluff, the road ended at two massive wooden gates strengthened with iron. They and the stone on either side stretched taller than the trees surrounding the castle, and Adelaide had to crane her neck to see the top of the gate.

After a moment, the gates creaked and lowered slowly to the grass in front of the company. The doors stopped with a jolt that rattled Adelaide's teeth. Cyr shifted on her shoulder, and she instinctively touched the dagger at her back, even though it wouldn't help her in there. Not so long ago she would've longed for an opportunity like this—an easy way to sneak into the castle and overthrow royalty. Now, she only felt out of place and nervous.

"Come on." Elias rode over the boards into the castle grounds.

The huge stone structures Adelaide had glimpsed from the cliff dominated the area inside the gate. Even the massive fortified gate surrounding half the fortress appeared child-sized in comparison.

Directly in front of them loomed a domed archway leading to a squat building that stretched almost all the way to the far-left end of the wall. On either side of the building turrets shot into the air, their pointed blue-tiled roofs a deeper shade than the afternoon sky.

The castle steadily grew taller the farther back it expanded, with more towers, domed arches, and triangular roofs, until it ended in the highest tower near the cliff—a blue-nailed finger trying to shove back the sky.

"That's where my room is," Elias remarked, seeing her eyes linger on the spire.

"It's very...tall."

Elias leaned toward her and lowered his voice. "And also the easiest tower to fly out of without being seen."

She stared at him. His eyes glimmered with amusement. It was hard to imagine him doing something like flying now, in his human form. She still didn't know what the other part—the dragon side of him—was capable of.

Cyr soared away to examine this new expanse of sky, and the group stabled their horses in the largest and cleanest stable Adelaide had ever entered. Then she, Elias, and Berold climbed the stairs leading up to the domed archway enveloped by hungry ivy.

Inside, long, vaulted windows covered the opposite wall, and rugs stitched in swirling ruby and gold patterns concealed the floor. An opening in the wall on the far left stretched into a hallway lit with torches. At the end of the room on their right, a stairway wound up in a tight spiral.

Adelaide could barely breathe. The rich-colored tapestries of hunting scenes and couples staring ardently into each other's eyes, the clear-as-air windows opening onto gardens and fountains spouting water, and the soft, spotless rugs, was more opulence than she'd seen in her life. She had heard stories of the extravagant wealth of nobles and seen evidence of it herself in Alesfirth, but nothing like this. She felt naked and dirty standing on the plush rugs—the filth of her one-room peasant home clinging to her skin.

Elias turned to Berold. "Could you give the steward my requests for the burial and coronation? If he has any questions or concerns, he can ask me later. I have some matters to attend to."

Berold nodded and with a glance at Adelaide, strode toward the hall on the left.

Elias turned to her. "I'll show you your quarters for tonight, then go—"

"Excuse me?"

"I want to show you where you'll be staying tonight."

"Elias." Adelaide wove her fingers together. "I can't stay here."

He waved a hand in the air. "Of course you can. After everything that's happened to you, I won't let you go that easily. You're my guest."

"Elias," Adelaide exhaled, "I'm a peasant, not a noble. I can't and shouldn't stay here." The thought of sleeping in this luxurious castle while her parents slept on straw atop dirt floors repulsed her. "I can't sleep in a nice bed when I know my parents and brother aren't."

Elias' gaze melted with sympathy. "I know it's hard. For the first few months after my father and I moved here, I would sneak out of my window and sleep on the cliff, letting the sea and stars lull me to sleep. But you're a human and my guest."

He took a step toward the stairs at the far end of the room. "Just humor me, please. You can sleep in the stables tonight if you wish, just don't tell me about it. I would, at least, like to imagine that you're warm and comfortable."

"I can be warm and comfortable in a stable," Adelaide said, especially the nice huge one here. But she followed him up the stairs, down a hallway, up another flight of stairs, past two wooden doors, down some stairs, and on and on until she was completely lost.

They passed several windows colored and molded into peaceful scenes: a green boat sailing on a wind-tossed wave, a hummingbird hovering over pink roses, a little girl picking blackberries. Adelaide lingered over these beautiful glass pictures until Elias touched her arm.

They trod on patterned rugs and passed woven tapestries of fishing and hunting scenes, coronations of dead kings, and ogling lovers. They passed guttering torches, vaulted ceilings, elaborate sword and shield displays, and several yellow and blue flags tacked up—free to wave in the wind no more. But Adelaide saw nothing of dragons. When she asked, Elias said he and his father didn't own such things, and why would the past rulers, who hated the creatures?

When she spied what was to be her room that night, she decided she would most definitely sleep with the horses.

A silver pitcher and cup sat on a polished oak table in the middle of the room. A large circular, fluffy rug embroidered with orange, yellow, and red flowers encompassed the entire floor. To the right, flames crackled in a stone fireplace. At the back of the room lounged a silk bed with too many pillows to consider sleeping in, all swathed in a sheer pink curtain. Adelaide's family could sleep in the bed without ever touching each other.

She turned from the gaudy bed and gazed out the circular window that looked out on the ebbing sea.

"So, what do you think?" Elias asked from the doorway.

"Must I answer that?"

"No, I suppose not." He glanced at the table. "Would you like me to have a young lady draw some water for a bath or for you to drink?"

Her eyes widened. He was attempting to be nice, in his luxurious way, but it was too much. "No. I'm quite capable of—"

"Taking care of yourself. Yes, I know." They stared at each other. Elias' grin was wide enough to cause Adelaide to blush like a love-sick girl as she remembered all the times she hadn't been able to care for herself, but Elias had.

He eventually glanced away and cleared his throat. "I shall come fetch you when the evening meal is ready, if you're still here."

"I don't need to eat with—"

"I insist, and don't you dare go anywhere until after." His voice contained all the authority of a prince, and even she didn't dare retort as he left the room.

Adelaide walked to the window, feeling lost.

Chapter Forty

"Here you are, fair maiden." Elias placed a plate of fish saturated in a creamy white sauce sprinkled with herbs in front of Adelaide. The smell tantalized her stomach.

"Why are you serving the food, your highness?" A woman in a low-cut green dress that exposed a glimmering gold-jeweled necklace said from across the table. "You should be resting. You just returned from a long journey."

Elias sat at the head of the glossy oak table in the high-ceilinged hall. "I consider being with my people restful, Ermina." He turned to Adelaide, who sat on his right. "This dish is a fish that lives nearby, what the townsfolk call a white sea bass. It's the fish I told you about."

Adelaide nodded and squared her shoulders. She felt as out of place with these lavishly dressed nobles, fine food, and elaborately carved plates as the fish probably felt at the end of a fishing line. Her eyes kept meandering past the piled plates to the high windows that looked out into gardens bursting with bushes, fruit trees, and flowers. Amid the plants, ivory fountains of fish and horses spouted water into lily-pad dotted ponds. She couldn't believe someone would spend so much money on such trivial ornamentation. But it *was* beautiful and calmed her in this unusual situation.

Before Elias had come to fetch her, a maid had offered Adelaide three choices of dresses to wear. She chose the simplest—a supple red one with gold threading on the sleeves—yet it still felt too luxurious. Em would have loved it, though, and probably would have insisted on trying on all the dresses. And keeping them.

"You look beautiful," Elias had told her when he saw her in the dress. "That color suits you."

"Thank you," Adelaide murmured, avoiding his eyes. Then the prince essentially pulled her down to the great hall. She hadn't complained, because her stomach had been making embarrassing animal sounds by then.

Now, ignoring the curious gazes of those around her, including Elias', Adelaide took a sip of the tart red wine and tried the fish. It melted in her mouth, and the slightly spicy sauce flooded her mouth. She swallowed. "It's delicious."

"I'm glad." He nodded at her then dug into his own meal.

"Where do you hail from, again?" The woman in green—Ermina—asked, and Berold, who sat on the woman's left, glanced over.

"Alesfirth."

"That's quite a distance away," the woman beside Adelaide, whose tight turquoise dress looked like it was eating *her* for dinner, said. "What are you doing here in Dhalion?"

"Elias asked me to come see where he lives."

A few guests gasped and stared at her in horror. It took a moment for Adelaide to realize that her lack of the prince's title had caused their dramatic responses. She smiled inside. Elias winked at her.

"So, what do you think of Dhalion?" A man in a green-buttoned orange tunic asked.

"It's fine." She sipped some wine and attempted to keep her voice and face expressionless. "Of course, the food in this castle, possibly even this meal alone," she glanced at the platters bearing grapes, nuts, baked artichokes, and colorful hard candies, "could feed my entire village for a year."

The guests gaped at her, including Berold, but Adelaide continued eating. These nobles were as frightening as the blooming bushes outside and needed to have their feathers ruffled.

The man in the orange tunic broke the awkward silence. "She sounds much like you, your highness."

Elias nodded, his eyes glowing. At the comparison, something in Adelaide glowed as well.

"And," the man continued, "since I've followed your suggestion to visit my peasants more than just on tax days, there have been fewer complaints and more crops."

"I'm glad it worked, Ruford, because sometimes it doesn't."

After a moment full of the sounds of tinkling forks and goblets, Ermina said, "My compliments, your highness, on your rise to king. Although I was exceptionally sad to hear of your father's death. King Ganelon shall be missed."

Elias nodded to her. "Thank you. He would be glad to know he made an impact on the people in this country."

After the fish course, servants in gold and blue tunics distributed strawberry tarts to the guests. The delicacy was so delicious, Adelaide briefly considered asking for another. It would be amusing to watch the nobles' reactions, but it somehow seemed childish—something that Odo would do, so she resisted the temptation.

When they finished the tarts, a servant stepped up to Elias. "Would you care for some entertainment tonight, sire? The jesters came by earlier when they learned of your arrival."

"Nay. Thank you, Timm." He turned to the others. "All of you are free to stay and listen to them, if you wish. I must rise early and prepare for the difficult task of burying my father, so I'll retire now." He paused by Adelaide's chair, and her heart lurched.

He offered her his arm. "Would you care to take a stroll?"

She stared at his arm. "Um, sure." She pushed her chair back, which scraped loudly in the sudden silence, and took his arm—warm and solid under her tense fingers. The nobles' stares scorched her back as she—a mere peasant—walked away with their almost-king. They would have much to muse on tonight. As would she.

While the pair ambled down a hallway lined on either side with bronze statues of men frozen in different battle poses, she said, "Your guests are going to think you odd for choosing to walk with me rather than staying to discuss the finer points of archery or whatever it is nobles talk about."

Elias pulled open a door at the end of the hall. "They already do. Besides, I care not for such talk. I'm a dragon, after all. We care only for flying and burning things."

Adelaide chuckled at the absurdity of his statement.

"Your company is much more satisfying than theirs," he noted.

"A dragon would probably find any human woman's company pleasing since it's so different from other dragons."

Elias tapped a finger against his lips. When he spoke, his voice was earnest. "Not in the slightest. She would most certainly need to be an exceptional woman."

Adelaide glanced away, her cheeks warm. Lately, her cheeks were as warm as a fevered child's in his company. What was happening to her?

They strolled in-between a grassy training field on their left and a lengthy, low branch of the castle to their right. They had reached the back of the fortress, and the cliff stretched out before them to the splashing sea below.

The sun, half-hidden by blushing clouds, dipped into the sea with orange fingers, turning the water a burning gold—almost the exact shade as Elias' dragon-back.

"Whoa," Adelaide breathed.

Elias strode to the cliff's edge. "Lovely, isn't it? I often come out here to watch the sunset, especially after entertaining guests and council members all day." He gazed at the sky as if ready to leap into it. His eyes shone a deep blue cracked with gold, reflecting the lit sky and sea. His red tunic fluttered behind him in a gust of wind. She had always thought her life as a peasant difficult, but after seeing the vast strength and power Elias possessed as a dragon and how he must always compress it, she couldn't comprehend what he had to sacrifice every day just to appear normal. And he was alone now—the only dragon in Klinhun—and had to hide his true identity from even his closest friends.

Without realizing it, Adelaide had taken a step toward him. She faced the sea. The sun had shrunk to the size of a dandelion seed and floated over the horizon. "What do you think of becoming king?"

"Honestly?"

"Of course."

"I'm terrified." He rubbed his hands through his hair and gazed back out at the rippling water. "Many Klinians still don't trust royalty, and others were just beginning to respect my father. I'm ruler of the dragons now too, but I haven't been to Niclond in a long time." He shook his head, hands lifted. "I was barely older than a hatchling when we left, and I'm afraid many will object to my rule when I return. How can I be a good leader when most of my subjects are older than me, and I've spent more time with humans than dragons?"

He sighed, his shoulders slumping. "I don't know how to unite the two species without my father. He always came up with the ideas. He thought if we could earn the humans' trust, it could be the bridge closing the space between us. But now I'm not sure if it's enough."

Elias' pain and distress yanked on Adelaide. She reached out to him. "You're a wise man. You'll find a way. I mean, you found a way to befriend me." She dropped her hand and shrugged. "What could a dragon be to the trouble I gave you?"

He smiled. "I'm glad I pursued you, Adelaide." He leaned down as if to kiss her, but she turned away, her heart beating harder than the waves on the rocks below. Elias stepped away.

The distance between them felt as far as the distance between her and her family, but fear kept her frozen. Fear that Elias couldn't truly love her, fear that he did, fear of what would happen if she gave in to her slumbering desires. She was a peasant; he was a king and dragon. What future could there be for them?

"Did you know that the dragons have gifts?" Elias asked.

"No."

"They do, given to them at the dawn of time. Music, healing, understanding, light, and truth." He stared out at the sea. "Perhaps they will help unite us somehow."

"What is your gift as a dragon?"

"I was a healer. But I don't think I am anymore. It disappeared when I drank the concoction to become a human."

Before she could ask him more, he wished her good-night. "Enjoy sleeping in the stables." He winked, then strode back to the castle.

Chapter Forty-One

The funeral procession began at first light. It commenced at the castle gate and wound down the stone road to the forest behind Dhalion.

Adelaide rode Suntaria behind the wagon teeming with pungent white lilies, roses, and gardenias. Peeking beneath the snowy flowers lay a golden casket etched with what appeared to be flames. She smiled at the subtle sign of the dead king's true identity.

Berold rode beside the wagon on his gleaming bay, clad in chainmail, his bronze sword swinging at his side. Knights clinked on either side of him, clothed in yellow and blue tunics under their glinting mail.

Elias, arrayed in his velvety red cloak and wearing a slender silver crown engraved with vines, led the procession. Starflare looked as silky as night. Someone, probably Elias, had woven her mane and tail with blue ribbons, and the gold inlaid in her saddle and reins gleamed as brilliantly as Elias' crown.

Adelaide wore a dark blue dress that was as soft and light against her skin as a cloud. No one had forced her to wear this dress; she wore it to honor the man she might have killed, had she not met his son.

When the prince had seen her in it that morning, his eyes had widened, and she'd tingled inside. "You look lovely, Adelaide," he whispered.

For some reason she felt like curtseying, but didn't know how, so she merely nodded her thanks.

A corner of his lips had twitched. "I'm not sure I've ever seen you so bashful. You should dress in fine clothes more often." His eyes meandered to her braid. "Though, you would look more fetching without that piece of straw in your hair... On second thought, leave it in. It shows how different you are from the others."

Once he left her by the gate, Adelaide had removed the solitary piece of straw, her face flaming.

At least twenty nobles rode behind Adelaide, their faces as grave and unfeeling as the jewels weighing down their fingers, necks, and wrists.

Outside the massive castle gates, nobles and peasants stood on either side of the road. Once the sleek horses carrying the knights and nobles rode past, they joined the procession, most on foot.

Adelaide heard nothing but the wagon's creaking, the horses' hooves clacking against the stone, and an occasional cough or hushing of a child as the convoy curved down to the swaying trees behind town.

Elias kept his gaze straight ahead as they promenaded down the path, tears threatening to spill. Last night he had refused to see his father's body laid out in his finest robes. He wanted to remember his father as he'd been alive: strong and kind, wearing his secret identity as easily as he always wore his robes and crown.

He wished he could burn his father's dragon body and toss the ashes out to sea while singing the mourning song as loved ones joined their keening wails to his. But King Ganelon died as a human, and Elias would honor him as such. The people needed to mourn him too, and a human man was the only way they knew him.

Elias had chosen, though, to bury his father outside instead of laying him in the vault beneath the castle with the other kings. It would stir up conversation among the townsfolk, but he couldn't imagine his father trapped in the icy darkness of the fortress, even if he no longer possessed his fire.

The wagon halted below a strongly-scented cedar where Elias and his father had often escaped to chat and listen to the chickadees when life in the castle became stifling. The birds were now silent, as if they too mourned.

Berold nudged Elias, then grabbed an end of the coffin while Elias grasped the other. They rested it in the hole Berold and some of the knights had dug last night at the base of the cedar.

Elias gazed at the shimmering, cold coffin a long moment, then turned to the hundreds of peasants, nobles, and knights waiting with expectant faces. He swallowed. "Here lies my father, King Ganelon," even though that felt far from the truth. How could his father, the golden dragon who could breathe fire longer than any other his age and could soar for three days without growing weary, be stuck in such a little box?

Elias breathed deep to steady himself. "If anyone has final words, let him or her say them now."

A peasant man toward the middle of the crowd said, "He wasn't like the other kings. You could tell he cared about you and would help if he could. No trouble was too small for him to listen to."

A few people nodded, then a woman said, "He was very helpful when my husband died two years ago in the storm. He gave me a job in the castle, and I'll always be grateful to him."

Others explained how King Ganelon had helped them, why they would miss him, or what they remembered most about him. Their words made Elias even prouder of his father, and he had to constantly blink back tears.

When no one spoke for a while, Elias tossed a gardenia into the hole. It landed on top of the glossy coffin. His father once told him this flower smelled as fresh as new beginnings and was layered like scales around a sweet center, much like a dragon's heart.

"My father was a great man and king. I'll always miss him, but his memory will live on in us."

He stepped back, and people came forward to throw a flower into the grave until white blooms completely covered the coffin. Then he, Berold, and two knights shoveled dirt into the grave. In the fresh soil, Elias stuck a bronze sign engraved with the same flame designs as on the coffin. It proclaimed:

"Here lies King Ganelon: father, friend, ruler.
We will remember his goodness and justice forever."

Elias turned back to his people. "King Ganelon!" he shouted, raising his fist in the air.

"King Ganelon!" They shouted as one, hundreds of fists reaching toward the sky.

"I'm sorry again about your father," Adelaide said as she walked beside Elias into town. "I would have liked to meet him." And she would have, now that she knew he wasn't a puffed-up-pastry king.

"He would have liked you."

Adelaide raised an eyebrow in disbelief. She was a serf, after all, and one with a bold tongue.

Elias touched her arm. "It's true. He would have found your stubbornness amusing and your bravery inspiring. He probably would have thought you a good match for me."

"I doubt it, once he realized I was a peasant. And didn't you say he was angry when he found out you were chasing a peasant from Alesfirth?" He had told her about his confrontation with Berold on the way here from Fernohn.

"He wasn't upset that I was beginning to care for a peasant. I don't think Berold told him I was, since I didn't even know it at the time. He was angry because he thought I wasn't taking our deal seriously."

"Very well," Adelaide replied, though not entirely convinced.

On top of the stone dais troubadours in green and black diamond costumes juggled and played flutes. But what drew Adelaide's attention were the tables laden with food, more than even Lord Lambert could have dreamed up.

The tables bowed under fruit-filled cakes in the shape of roses and gardenias dusted with white powder, an entire swan reposing on a platter surrounded by buttery potatoes and honey-glazed carrots, platters crammed with rainbows of whole roasted fish, some kind of smoked meat bordered by opened shells containing a soft pink center, piles of bulbous red, orange, and purple fruit as well as baskets of blackberries, raspberries, and other berries she didn't know the names of.

Interspersed amid the food were tangy red and white wines, teeny cups of nutty mead, and sparkling apple and cherry cider. Barrels of ale and spicy wassail squatted beside the tables.

Elias grabbed a fuzzy, orange-yellow fruit off one of the mounds and tossed it to her. "It's a peach, the fruit I told you about yesterday."

Adelaide took a bite and sweet, sticky juice dribbled down her chin. "It's delicious."

Elias bit into a glossy purple fruit. "We originally traded

peaches and plums, as well as oranges and pomegranates," he pointed to a smooth red-purple fruit, "from Neklosa. Now we're growing peaches and plums here, and they seem to be doing well. All of these are from Neklosa, though, since ours haven't ripened yet."

Adelaide ate until her stomach felt like it would pop open while chatting with Elias and some peasants, wishing her family could be there to sample the excellent food.

Around late afternoon servants cleared and put away the tables to prepare for the coronation that would take place that night. Elias returned to the castle to tidy up, but Adelaide remained, enjoying the cool, salty breeze blowing off the sea and the lazy chatter of peasants as they dawdled on the dais steps.

When nearly everyone had returned home to sleep off their meal, Adelaide strolled down to the seashell-strewn beach near the docks that stretched out into the cobalt sea.

The beach extended from jagged, sharp rocks at the bottom of the cliff where the castle towered over the town to the taller cliff on the far side where she had first glimpsed the sea. It was a lovely sight, but she missed her woods and river. She hoped to return as soon as she spoke to Gunter and the others.

The coronation turned out to be fairly boring. With the other peasants, Adelaide watched Elias kneel in his red cloak and golden breeches atop the dais. An elderly man took the slender silver crown off his head and replaced it with a taller one engraved with what looked like stars and embedded with four triangular indigo gems.

Elias vowed to protect his people and land as long as he lived and to reign with justice, equality, and goodness. Then the man stepped off the dais, and Elias stood.

The crowd kneeled. Adelaide looked up from her spot on the ground and blinked tears away. Elias looked a king in his gleaming cloak and crown, and acted the part as he turned in a circle, inclining his head toward the crowd, as if seeing their allegiance and wishing to honor it.

As Adelaide gazed at him, she knew. There was no one better suited to lead this country than him, dragon or not. His dragon qualities would make him a strong leader and protector, and his human qualities would lend him compassion and gentleness.

After the coronation, the troubadours returned to the dais, playing lively music while servants brought out the leftovers of the feast.

Adelaide still felt full, so she watched groups of people dancing around the musicians, their dresses and robes swirling like flower petals in a current.

Elias came and offered her his arm. "Would you care to dance?"

"No, thank you. I don't dance."

"You don't dance because you choose not to, or because you don't know how?"

"Both."

"I can teach you, and that will solve part of the problem."

"Why would you want to teach me? There are many lovelier maidens to dance with, especially nobles." Adelaide gestured at a cluster of women chatting. They shot envious glances at her and turned away when they noticed her watching them.

Elias sighed. He hadn't even looked at the fluttery girls. "But I want to dance with you. You're the only maiden who holds my attention."

Adelaide sat on a bench. King or not, he couldn't make her dance with him if she wished not to. Part of her did, but mostly she had no desire to make a fool of herself in front of all these people, nor let Elias crush her heart right after it had begun to heal.

The prince shook his head and strode to some older men conversing at the edge of the dais. Adelaide watched him, his words of 'you're the only maiden who holds my attention,' swirling through her mind like a stick in a river, leaving her dizzy.

Chapter Forty-Two

"The king's dead," Gunter said in a breathless voice when he entered Dhalion's tavern and joined his Gyndilian captors.

"You just realized that?" Ligulf asked in-between gulps of his drink. "People here have been talking about it all day."

"There was some kind of coronation last night," Leofric added. "It's too bad we missed it. There was probably lots of good food."

Ligulf glanced at Gunter. "Did you find your friends?"

"Nay, and I searched the whole town." He had been surprised his Gyndilian captors had let him go, but Dunstan had persuaded Baldwin to follow him from a distance, saying how Gunter's friends wouldn't trust him with a stranger nearby and he needed to find them to make plans. Before they'd left, Baldwin had threatened him with a crossbow jammed into his gut. "If you try to lose me or do anything else against me, I'll find your friends and kill them all."

Gunter had believed him.

Dunstan now whispered, "Then it's up to you, Gunter, to kill the new king. We don't have time to wait. The longer we stay here, the more likely it is that someone will recognize us as foreigners."

Gunter gripped the back of a chair. How could he kill anyone? Yes, he had envisioned himself killing the prince, but thoughts weren't the same as actions. The act of murdering someone took more willpower than he possessed.

But this wasn't just anyone, this was the prince—the man who had haunted Gunter's nightmares and plagued the town of Alesfirth with taxes and death. He and his father had allowed Adelaide's sister to be murdered.

Had the man caught up to Adelaide by now? If so, what had he done or said to her? Gunter didn't know the prince well, it was true, but all princes were the same: arrogant and self-absorbed. He couldn't stand the thought of such a man sharing any amount of time or words with Ade.

Again, the image from his dream of the prince demanding everything from his and Adelaide's family came to mind. He wouldn't let that happen. He wouldn't let the prince hurt anyone he cared about again.

He could do this. He would do this. For his family. For Adelaide.

"Give me my dagger," he hissed.

The day after the coronation, Elias was occupied with kingly duties—whatever those happened to be—so Adelaide wandered down to the city. On the way, Berold and some knights passed her. They ignored each other.

Near the beach, under colorful tents, people sold mounds of fruit as well as smaller piles of fresh strawberries, raspberries, and blackberries. Sacks bursting with nuts sat open like large mouths, and wooden boxes filled with bright red, brown, and yellow spices—their sharp scents heavy in the air—made Adelaide sneeze.

Nearing the end of the market, she spotted a familiar face.

Her heart froze, but her legs took her straight to him.

"Conrad." She hugged him.

"Well, good day, Adelaide." He stepped back and looked her up and down. "You don't look much different than the last time I saw you."

Adelaide wore the dress she had traveled the country in, now washed, though it remained stained, and her hair was braided down her back, as usual. But if Conrad had seen her the night before in the silky blue dress, her hair shiny and spotless, he would not have said such a thing.

"You look the same too, except perhaps dirtier."

He grinned. "What do you expect? We've been traveling hard for more than a fortnight, trying to get here in time."

"So the others made it?"

"Most of them, and a few from Pinhurn who said they'd spoken to you. They came up to us at the tavern once they realized we were from Alesfirth."

Adelaide nodded, her stomach churning. This news would have delighted her if her plans hadn't changed, but now it made everything more complicated. "In a few moments bring everyone to the woods behind the tavern. We need to talk."

Conrad dipped his head and walked toward the center of town.

Adelaide made her way to the towering pines behind the alehouse; no one would see them there. She paced while fiddling with her braid, ignoring the chatter and booming laughs from the tavern, wishing this conversation was over.

"It's good to see you again, Adelaide."

She spun around "Good day, Sayer." She shook hands with the pink-cheeked, tan-capped boy.

As the men and Rohesia—the only other girl in the rebellion—gathered round, Adelaide greeted them, surprised so many had come. All but five from Alesfirth had made it, which was more than she expected, considering it was planting season. Even little Hubert had come. This worried more than pleased her, since she didn't know how events would turn out. The twelve-winters-old boy looked so tiny beside his thick-armed sixteen-winters-old brother, Bodin.

"How were you both able to leave Alesfirth?" Adelaide asked Bodin.

The boy tousled Hubert's hair. "My mother's father lives here, and we said we wanted to visit him before he dies, since that'll be anytime now. We have three other brothers to help with the planting, and Sayer," he nodded to the boy several winters older than himself, "said he was going to Dhalion as well, so my Pappa let Hubert and I go with him as long as we're back by the middle of summer."

Adelaide then listened to Aldy, Rohesia's brother, explain how they escaped the farm by pretending he wanted to be a troubadour and had to go to the King's City to learn the trade. Since Rohesia had always been good at playing reeds, she insisted on tagging along. His parents had argued with them, and in the end, the siblings had left in the middle of the night. Rohesia appeared more troubled than her brother during the retelling, and Adelaide's heart squeezed about the rift they'd created in their family for a rebellion that would—hopefully—go nowhere.

Others jumped in, describing their own harrowing escape or brilliant plan. They all had left within a fortnight of each other, though at different times, and met up at the barn to wait for the others. Their journey was much less hazardous than Adelaide's; they didn't meet any robbers. Although, to hear them tell it, it sounded like the most dangerous expedition across Klinhun anyone had ever attempted.

The four men she recognized from Pinhurn didn't speak and gazed around with uneasy glances. There was one face she didn't see that she had expected to. "Where's Gunter?" She asked Conrad.

His eyes widened. "He's not here?"

"Why would he be? Didn't he leave with all of you?"

Conrad shook his head. "He left a few days after you to

find you because he was worried about the prince following you."

"He's the king now," someone whispered.

"He shouldn't have left on his own." Adelaide balled her fists. "He knows I can take care of myself, prince or no prince. And now he's missing." She yanked on her braid, which did nothing to relieve her frustration, and only sent a burst of pain through her scalp.

She massaged her head. Where could Gunter have gone? He should have made it to Dhalion by now. Did robbers kidnap him and take him to Gyndilad like they had wanted to do with her?

"We can't worry about Gunter now," Sayer said. "We must continue our plans before our families miss us or suspect what we're doing."

"What *are* we doing?" One of the men from Pinhurn asked, stepping forward. "Killing the king?" His eyes were as serious as death.

Adelaide lifted her hands in a calming motion as she said, "Nay, we're not going to kill the king. I was able to get to know Eli—King Elias, on my travels. I tried to escape him several times, but he continued following me. In the Kildare Forest, I was kidnapped by robbers who wanted sell me to the Gyndilians."

She ignored the outbursts of alarm. "I escaped from them in the Spearheads, but was wounded and freezing. I would have died if Prince Elias hadn't taken me to a cave and tended my wound." She paused, letting her words sink in and feeling the surge of agony in her back all over again.

"While Prince Elias helped me recover, I realized, to my alarm, that he was a good man. When we were in Fernohn, one of the mines collapsed, and he worked harder than anyone to move the debris and find the trapped men. It became obvious that the people there and here in Dhalion care deeply for him and his late father.

"The prince, now king, isn't perfect, and I understand now, too late, that I wanted perfection from him and revenge for my dead sister. But that can't happen because King Elias is the best king we could hope for at this time. We can't kill Elias, and our rebellion must disband." She stopped pacing, anxious about how they would respond, but relieved as the weight of her secrets dropped off her shoulders.

Stunned silence hung in the air, thick and heavy like smoke.

"What?" The stocky man from Pinhurn burst out. "We just arrived here. You want us to leave after we traveled so long and worked so hard to get here, after all we've risked?" Others from his village murmured their assent.

Adelaide grimaced; he was right. But she didn't know how to assuage his frustration.

"This is what we get from following a woman," the thickset man murmured, shooting glares at Eudo, one of the men Adelaide had talked to at the tavern in Pinhurn.

"You just saw what the prince wanted you to see," another man from Pinhurn said. "Where was he when my baby sister died last spring from lack of food?"

"And don't forget about the attack on Alesfirth," someone else pointed out.

"I asked him about that," Adelaide said. "He and his father didn't come to help because they believed it might have been a diversion to get King Ganelon away from the castle. He sent wagons full of food and supplies, but Lord Lambert and the others must have taken them." This stopped the men's angry voices, but only for a moment.

"He could have come later. Or brought the supplies himself," Sayer said.

"Yeah, that's true," one of the Pinhurn men agreed. "He doesn't care about us and never will. King Elias will be just like King Ganelon and all the other food-hoarding, treasure-loving royalty before them."

The men's rage elevated their voices, and Adelaide tried to hush them. "Be quiet! We're not that far from town."

But fury grabbed the men, turning them into puppets, their faces red and demanding. "For our families! For our people! For our futures!"

The only person not chanting was Conrad, who looked at her in perplexity.

She opened her mouth to tell everyone to be quiet again when some of the men changed the chant. Their voices were softer than before, but still too loud as they said, "Kill the King! Kill the King!"

Adelaide stomped her foot, glared at the men, and opened her mouth to stop them when someone else did first.

"Be quiet!"

The men became as still and silent as the trees around them. Adelaide whipped around to see Berold and five knights marching toward them from the tavern, their swords unsheathed and pointed at them. At the sight of the weapons, a shiver traced the length of her body.

"This looks like a rebellion if I ever saw one, which I have, several times. But even if I hadn't, the chant of 'kill the king,' would have clued me in quickly." Berold turned flaming eyes on Adelaide. "How could you betray Elias? I've never known why, and I'm sure I never will, but he trusts you. Or, he did."

Adelaide flinched at his words. "If you had listened to what I said at the—"

"I've heard enough. I was right to be suspicious of you." Without moving his gaze from Adelaide's, Berold commanded, "Take them to the castle for questioning."

The knights forced their way into the group, grabbing and binding the men's arms. There were a few scuffles, and Hubert attempted to run away, but the peasants were outmatched, and a guard caught Hubert and held the writhing, biting boy tight against him.

"Unhand me." Adelaide jerked away from the knight who

had snatched her arm. "I will come peacefully." He loosened his grip, and she walked over to one of the horses and mounted, hoping the others would calm down once they realized there was no hope of escaping.

It worked for the men from Alesfirth; they let the knights pull them onto their horses. Those from Pinhurn put up more of a fight. One of their noses was bleeding and another had a bruise on his cheek by the time the knights hauled them onto horses.

Soon the peasants' wrists were bound behind them, fear sizzling on their faces as they sat with the knights atop their horses.

Berold mounted in front of Adelaide. "Let us go speak to Elias, shall we?"

Chapter Forty-Three

The ride to the castle was silent and tense. As they drew near the fortress, she noticed expressions of awe on the peasants' faces. It was the largest, most lavish building any of them had seen, and despite their dire situation, they couldn't keep their amazement hidden. Adelaide felt the same way each time she saw the blue-tiled fortress.

The peasants continued to gawk as the knights pushed and pulled them through the castle's entrance hall, but Adelaide was too preoccupied about how Elias would respond to care much about where they were.

But she couldn't help a rush of wonder as she glimpsed the room Berold and the knights deposited them in. A thick wooden throne inlaid with gold and blue gems atop a dais crafted from some kind of sparkling pink rock gleamed down at them. The floor was the same kind of grey stone as the road to Dhalion, but because of its polished, smooth surface, the glints of yellow, blue, and red sparkled like fire.

The knights clinked to position behind the peasants, their faces stoic. Berold stood beside Adelaide with crossed arms.

Elias marched into the room and scowled when he noticed

Adelaide and the others standing there in the clutches of terror. "What is the meaning of this, Berold?"

The knights and peasants bowed. The latter stared at Elias as if he was a wolf about to devour them, but they didn't know how dangerous he could be. For that matter, neither did Adelaide.

"My men and I went to the tavern earlier for some drinks before resuming our duties. I heard some men chanting outside. This group of peasants," he lifted his hand toward the ragged band, "was talking about killing you. They were all grouped around Adelaide, who's apparently their leader."

Elias' mouth hung open as he contemplated the hand pointing at Adelaide. He turned weary, pain-filled eyes on her, which splintered her heart. "Is this true?"

Adelaide swallowed. If only she had had this conversation earlier, when they had been alone.

She curled the end of her braid around a finger. Her fate and that of the others hung from her words. "It's true, Eli—your highness, that when I lived in Alesfirth, I planned a rebellion to overthrow King Ganelon and his son. This was the real reason I was traveling through the country. I needed to find more people to join us so we'd have a better chance of defeating the royalty in the spring, when the men from Alesfirth would meet me here."

She couldn't meet his sword-sharp gaze anymore and looked at the glints of color on the floor. "Then I learned what kind of ruler you are and that Klinhun's problems run deeper than I realized. Overthrowing you and your father would solve nothing and would perhaps even make matters worse." She met Elias' unblinking scrutiny once more, begging him to see the truth in her eyes. "I met with the men today to tell them what I've learned and that we couldn't harm you."

She turned to the knight beside her. "Berold would have known this if he had been listening the entire time instead of rushing to conclusions."

He narrowed his eyes at her. "You're just a filthy peasant." He regarded Elias. "Sire, if we do not do anything about these men and swine," he shot Adelaide a dirty look, "they will just return to kill you."

"That is enough, Berold." Elias' words were soft but burned with menacing rage. The knight bowed his head.

Blazing fury clouded Elias' face as he gazed at his friend, and for the first time since learning his true identity, Adelaide feared him. Right now he appeared powerful enough to split Berold in two with just his hands.

But then Elias sighed, and the fury dissipated, leaving in its wake the man Adelaide knew. "I must think about this." He paced back and forth along the steps of the dais, running his hands through his wavy brown hair. Then he called Berold, and the two conferred quietly together.

Hubert shifted on the other side of Adelaide, and she placed a hand on his shoulder. He looked up at her with wide eyes.

"Everything will be fine," she whispered, she hoped. Surely Elias wouldn't punish the others too much, just fine them. She didn't know what was in store for her, though her thoughts kept swinging to a noose or the mark of a traitor burned into her skin.

Berold strode to the door, and Elias faced the peasants. "I am decided." In the pause that followed Adelaide could almost feel the roughness of a rope being thrust over her head. Her fingers trembled.

"I have been informed that some of you struggled more than others on the way here and seemed ready to kill me this very day." He glanced at the men from Pinhurn. At his penetrating gaze, they dropped theirs to the floor. "These men will be given two lashings each for their crude intentions, then will be accompanied back home by some of my knights.

"The rest of you," he swept his grey eyes over the Alesfirth peasants, "will remain at the castle as my guests in order to see for yourselves what kind of king I aspire to be, as well as to help me see with peasant eyes. You will be compensated for your help, of course, and your families notified."

A few men breathed sighs of relief and exchanged glances of unbelief with one another. Adelaide squeezed Hubert's shoulder. Of course Elias hadn't required more of them; he was a good king. How often and easily she forgot.

He turned to face her, his face aggrieved, and her fear returned.

"Adelaide, please come with me."

She followed him, ignoring the concerned gazes of her friends and Berold's pillared form by the door. She touched Conrad's arm to let him know she would be fine.

"Thank you," she told Elias as they walked out of a hall into the spring sunlight.

He looked at her sharply. "For what?"

"For not punishing the people from my town. All this is my fault, not theirs."

"They didn't seem dangerous, only frightened, and we'll continue to keep our eyes on them while they're here."

"Elias, what are we doing?" Berold asked.

Adelaide flinched; she hadn't realized the man had followed them.

"You shall soon see."

They entered a small stone building that had to be the armory. Hundreds of swords, shields, maces, bows, arrows, and other weapons and armor hung on the walls, lay scattered in haphazard piles on tables and benches, and stood on rickety stands.

A boulder-sized man in a leather apron greeted and bowed to Elias.

"Good day, Ademar. Is the fire hot?" Elias asked.

"Of course, sire. It always is."

"Good." Elias strode between the messy tables, his eyes roving over them. He grasped something from under a pile of loose wood on one of the tables. He lifted it up. It was a long piece of iron with a symbol at the end, like a branding iron for a horse. So, it would be the mark of a traitor then.

Adelaide's hands sweated, and her heart thumped too loud in her ears.

"Ademar, place this in the fire. We have a traitor in our midst." Elias gave the branding iron to the man, who grabbed it, walked to the large fire in the back of the room, and thrust the iron into the pulsating coals. He held it there while Elias, Berold, and Adelaide followed.

The pain wouldn't last long, but the mark would always be on Adelaide's skin, reminding her and everyone else that she didn't belong—that she had turned her back on her country and people, although that was why she had planned the rebellion in the first place.

It hadn't even been her love for Emma or her people that had driven her on to Dhalion, she saw now, remembering Elias' response to his father's death, but anger that her sister was gone. It had been easier to flee the sorrow by blaming someone else, but she'd never been able to escape the grief for long. And in the end, not grief, but hatred, had caught her. She rubbed her face, suddenly disgusted with herself. What had once seemed so noble now appeared rash and hollow.

"It's time." Elias' somber voice stole Adelaide from her thoughts. He took the iron from Ademar and gripped the end in his fist. Glancing at Berold, then Adelaide, he said, "Someone must pay the price for Adelaide's traitorous actions so I'm able to live up to everyone's hopes of being a just king." He rotated the iron bar in the coals.

Adelaide nodded and tried to ignore the frantic pace of her heart. She bared her shoulder, trying to keep her face expressionless since she was certain Berold and the blacksmith were staring at her.

Elias lifted the iron from the fire, the end now glowing an angry orange. Adelaide couldn't keep her eyes off the bright, steaming end, couldn't keep from imagining how it would feel against her naked flesh. She had a sudden urge to flee, but that would only delay the inevitable.

The king raised the orange-white iron in the air, his face inscrutable.

Everyone's eyes fastened on him. He kept his gaze on the iron until he glanced at Adelaide, his eyes overcast.

Then Elias pressed the steaming iron to his shoulder.

Chapter Forty-Four

The stench of burnt cloth and flesh flooded the room.

"Elias!" Berold cried. "What are you doing?"

Adelaide gaped, still expecting to feel the hot metal merging with her skin.

Elias groaned and dropped the brand on the ground. There was a vivid red mark with a vertical straight line and another line lying on top of it on his right arm. Around the wound, his tunic smoked and hung off like dead skin.

Adelaide couldn't comprehend what had just happened. Had he just taken the mark meant for her? Why would he do such a thing?

Berold must have been thinking the same thing, for he asked, "Why in all the forests of Klinhun did you do that?"

"Because I love her," Elias replied through clenched teeth, staring straight at Adelaide. She shivered at the intensity of his gaze and words. "I couldn't see you wounded in such a way, even if you did deserve it. You've changed, so I took the brand instead. And now no one can complain that I'm cruel or unjust."

She reached out to his unhurt arm, touching his tunic. She

knew she had done wrong and was willing to accept the consequences. Punishment she expected; mercy she didn't.

"Wrap it up, please, Berold."

After the knight bound the wound with a piece of cloth Ademar gave him, Elias thanked the blacksmith and grasped Adelaide's hand. "Let's go for a walk, shall we? There is much to discuss."

"Elias," Berold called as they walked out of the armory.

"I'll talk to you this evening, Berold."

As the two walked toward the cliffs, Cyr landed on Adelaide's shoulder.

"Why?" She asked, even though Berold had just asked the same question.

Elias smiled despite the torment he must feel. "I just told you. I care deeply for you, and you've suffered enough. It's partly my fault you wanted to rebel anyway, since my father and I neglected Alesfirth." He shrugged, then winced. "And besides, heat doesn't hurt me nearly as much as it does humans."

Adelaide doubted this; he definitely looked as if he was in pain. But she couldn't move past his confession. "I wanted to kill you though, and probably would have..."

"But you didn't. You stopped fleeing me." He gazed out at the sea, giving her a good view of the bulging burn beneath his bandage. "I suspected what you were doing when you fled with Starflare in Kildare. It wasn't difficult since I saw you steal our daggers in Alesfirth and how much you hated nobility. You're not a very subtle person." He chuckled. "But the more I got to know you, the more I hoped it wasn't true. I told myself you had other reasons for traveling through the country on your own."

"You saw me taking the daggers? Why didn't you arrest me?"

He faced her. "It was what first made me curious about you, and I actually forgot about them after I spoke with you. I wanted to know what you planned on doing with them first."

"How could you l..love," she stumbled over the word, "a person like me?"

Elias sighed and shook his head. "Adelaide, it's not about what you are or what you do. You are Adelaide, unlike any peasant, noble, or dragon I've met, and that's a good thing." His grin warmed her like a fire on a frosty night, and Adelaide wanted to believe him—that he truly loved her—for who she was.

She wondered what it would be like to love and even live with a dragon. A question occurred to her. "Do you have to drink the potion that makes you human every time you change?" She didn't remember him doing that, but she could have missed it.

"Nay. Just the first time."

"What's in it?"

"Just a part of what you're turning into, usually a scale for a dragon, or a hair if you're turning into a human. Clear water from a running stream, and, of course, love."

Adelaide didn't have anything to say about that, so she returned to the topic of dragon gifts from the previous night. "Last evening you said you don't think you have your gift of healing anymore. How come?"

Elias shrugged. "I'm not able to—" He groaned and dropped to his knees.

Adelaide fell beside him. "Elias?" Panic heightened her voice. "What's wrong?"

Blood seeped from his chest, staining his light blue tunic red. Adelaide held him as her eyes darted over his body. A dagger was lodged in the middle of his back. Something about the weapon shook her out of her fright-misted mind. She had seen it before—in Alesfirth, when she had taken it from Elias' wagon and given it to Gunter.

She moaned and glanced up.

Gunter stood several paces away, astonishment on his

face. Adelaide mirrored his expression.

"Adelaide..." Elias murmured, then coughed gurgly.

She turned to him, and to her horror, the blood now stained a large portion of the front of his tunic. "What? What is it?" She supported his head and tore a piece of her cloak to try to stanch the blood.

"Dragons." He focused intense blue eyes on hers. "Don't forget the dragons. Unite them and the hum..." his eyes closed briefly, and he took a shuddering breath.

Adelaide pushed harder on the cloth, not caring if she was hurting him. "Stay with me, Elias. Please, stay with me."

"Humans."

Adelaide nodded. "I will, I promise. But your people, both the humans and dragons, need you. I need you. I.." She gazed at his face, the only face that now knew her, even the traitorous parts, and loved her for it. The only person who had pursued her to the end. "I love you," she said weakly, too late. Tears stung her eyes.

"I know." He smiled, and Adelaide forced herself to smile back.

"You're still a healer, Elias. It didn't disappear when you became a human. You healed me of my grief and anger at Emma's death." She blinked and swallowed. "You freed me." She squeezed his hand. It was too cold. "Please don't leave me, Elias. Not now."

"I don't want to." He squeezed her hand back feebly.

He struggled up, and Adelaide helped him. "What do you want?"

"My pocket. There's a vial..."

Adelaide reached over and brought out a small glass vial filled with a glistening pink liquid.

He nodded. "Drink it after... It will help you and the Klinians."

"What is it?" Although she thought she knew.

He coughed and shut his eyes. "A gift...a gift from the

dragons. Drink...drink it." He shuddered, and she held him close to her, as he had done when her nightmares came.

"I love you...Adelaide. Never...forget...to...smile," he said with an easy grin, staring at her as if he had just won the most precious thing in Klinhun.

"I love you too, Elias. I won't. I promise." She leaned in to kiss him, and when she looked back at his face, his eyes—once mirrors of the sky—now mirrored only emptiness. He flew in skies she could not reach. She closed them.

Tears rained down her face, and unlike when Emma had died, she let them. Elias had seen past her filth and iced-over heart and loved her anyway. He had taught her how to smile again. How could such a beautiful, strong man be gone?

The tears flowed and flowed as Adelaide memorized the sun's glimmer in Elias's hair, the strength of his jaw, the curve of his eyelashes, wishing she had told him sooner, so much sooner that she cared for him too. Pain came anyway, whether you chose to love or not.

"Ade? Are you—" A familiar voice—Gunter's, she realized through her ripping agony—drifted from somewhere nearby.

"Get away from me!" She screamed. "I never want to see you again!" She looked up just in time to see, through a blur of tears, a shape dart away. A sob rose in her chest, and she turned back to Elias.

In the end, she *had* killed him. If she hadn't given that dagger to Gunter so long ago, Elias might still be alive. This thought brought on a fresh round of tears, making it hard to breathe.

After forever, when her tears no longer watered Elias' face, Adelaide kissed him, his lips surprisingly still warm. "I'm sorry, Elias," she whispered.

Cyr landed on the ground beside him. The hawk turned to Adelaide and gave a shrill cry, then another, and another. The sound reminded her of his cries when he found wounded animals in the forest.

“Stop, Cyr. He’s gone.”

The hawk whistled a few more times, then quieted and ruffled his feathers.

Adelaide turned back to her king. “I’ll make up the way I treated you, Elias, I promise. I won’t forget you or what you taught me. Sleep well.” She kissed his forehead and placed his wavy locks behind his ears.

Gripping the vial, Adelaide turned toward the sea pounding the rocks with unrelenting ferocity. She uncorked the vial and drunk all the pink liquid. It had no taste, but was cool running down her throat.

A fire of pure torture ripped down Adelaide’s body, and she fell, immersed in a writhing storm of searing, biting, clawing, scraping. Everything was light and scorching heat—heat from the tips of her toes to the roots of her hair, hotter than a branding iron seared into her flesh.

Then, it was gone. The heat and pain evaporated, leaving nothing but blackness and a pulsing, glowing heat deep within.

Adelaide stood, relishing the absence of physical torment and a new strength filling her sinews. She opened her eyes and breathed deep. The sea, sky, grass, *everything*, appeared washed clean and clear. Scents of salt, pine, manure, and a hundred others overwhelmed her.

Cyr shrieked and soared into a sky holding a sun as red as the blood on Elias’ cloak and clouds as gold as his scales.

Adelaide opened her new silvery-white wings wide and watched Cyr with yearning and joy. For once, she was free to follow him.

For you, Emma and Elias, she thought and soared into the darkening light.

Acknowledgements

What began as an idea in college has, after many tears of frustration, a move around the world, a marriage, and another move around the world, blossomed into a published book. Throughout it all, my Lord and Savior has sustained me. Without him, I'd have no stories to share, especially stories of love, sacrifice, and mercy.

My deepest appreciation goes to my parents who taught my siblings and I the love of reading from an early age. Thank you, Mom, for not telling me any of the first drafts of my novels were awful (though they were).

Thank you, Brad, for reading everything I throw at you and for your honest feedback. I'm so grateful God gave me a husband with a servant heart who's willing to clean up after dinner so I can rush off to write. You're more than I deserve.

All my fantastic, dedicated beta readers—Amy, Christy, Jordan, and Emily—you're worth more than a pile of the best tea and chocolates, and all of your edits made Adelaide and Elias' story the best it could be. Thank you for reading all the various versions of the first chapter. If anyone doesn't like it, you're to blame (just kidding! I take all the blame).

I'm so thankful for Dr. Petrie who read and edited *The Gift of Dragons* for my senior thesis and helped me throw out some horrible titles. Your son's feedback was also invaluable, and I hope he enjoys the final copy if he reads it.

Emma, thanks for being a great writer friend, helping me so much to narrow down the sneaky little synopsis (I'm not sure I ever got it right), and answering all my other questions. I can't wait to read your next book!

I'm amazed by the staff of Atmosphere Press' patience with me, especially Kyle's, as I sent him question after question for months. You have all been so kind, dedicated, and great to work with. I'm grateful, Alexis, that you pushed me to rewrite the first chapter (yet again), so the story could truly shine. What a privilege it was to be one of your last authors.

And of course, thank you, dear reader, for joining the rebellion and following along on Adelaide and Elias' journey of healing and hope. Look for more dragons in the final installment of their story soon!

If you don't want to wait for the next book to come out for more of Adelaide and Elias' world, you can read a deleted scene of Adelaide and her rebellion at: www.rachelagreco.com/gift-deleted-scene.

About Atmosphere Press

Atmosphere Press is an independent, full-service publisher for excellent books in all genres and for all audiences. Learn more about what we do at atmospherepress.com.

We encourage you to check out some of Atmosphere's latest releases, which are available at Amazon.com and via order from your local bookstore:

Yellow on Blonde, a novel by Stephen M. King

A Gathering of Broken Mirrors: Memories of New York Survivors, a novel by Anthony E. Shaw

Ghosts of the Abbey, a novel by Ashley Wellman and Patrick KinKade

And Still We Rise: A Novel about the Genocide in Bosnia, by Jordan Steven Sher

The Prisoner and The Executioner, a novel by Catee Ryan

The Special Case of Hazel Louisa, a novel by Amanda Culaccino

Still Waters, a novel by Anita Othman

The Suffragette and the Soldier, a novel by Katharine O'Flynn

About the Author

Rachel A. Greco dreams of being a dragon but has settled instead for being an author, which is almost as fun. Her short story, *Fairy Light*, won an honorable mention in the Writer's Digest Annual Writing Competition and her story, *Rustle*, was published by White Cat Publications. When not writing, she can be found reading, kayaking, or dancing with elves in the forests of her North Carolina home.

Visit her website for book news and book talk at **www.rachelagreco.com**. You can also find her on Instagram and TikTok as **@rachelagrecoauthor**. Come say hi and chat about magic and dragons!

Made in the USA
Las Vegas, NV
22 August 2022